Caribbean Lives

Brian Lara

James Fuller

Dedicated to the memory of my wonderful father;
I hope I'm half the dad you were to me

Macmillan Education
Between Towns Road, Oxford OX4 3PP
A division of Macmillan Publishers Limited
Companies and representatives throughout the world

www.macmillan-caribbean.com

ISBN 978-0-230-71559-2

First published 2013
First published in the UK in 2013 by
Signal Books Limited,
26 Minster Road,
Oxford OX4 1LY
ISBN: 978-1-908493-62-0

Designed by Mike Brain Graphic Design Ltd
Typeset by EXPO Holdings, Malaysia
Cover design by Macmillan Education/Andy Esson at Baseline
Cover photograph by Corbis /Toby Melville/Reuters
Picture Research by Thomas Bonsu-Dartnall

The author and publishers would like to thank the following for permission to reproduce their photographs:
Associated Press p125;
Brooks la Touche pp36, 46;
Getty Images pp1, 8, 19, 27, 41, 56, 62, 64, 67, 84, 106, 115, 135, 149, 171, 194, 211, 223, 233, Getty Images/Allsport/Hulton Archive p17, Getty Images/Hamish Blair p179, Getty Images/Mike Hewitt p192, Getty Images/Popperfoto pp138, 158, Getty Images/Ben Radford p77, Getty Images/Clive Rose p188;
Graham Morris pp78, 79, 96, 98;
Press Association Images/Rebecca Naden p186;
Rex Features/David Crichlow p209, Rex Features/Ted Blackbrow / *Daily Mail* p107;
Roger Wootton p87.

The author and publishers are grateful for permission to reprint the following copyright material:

David Martin Alexander Loewenthal and Sara Antonia Loewenthal for the lyrics 'Lash Dem Lara' by David Martin Alexander Loewenthal (Alexander D. Great) and Sara Antonia Loewenthal, 1994. Now available on the album *Finest Cuts*, Lion Valley Records. Reproduced with kind permission of David Martin Alexander Loewenthal and Sara Antonia Loewenthal;

The Random House Group Ltd for extracts from *Beating the Field: My Own Story* by Brian Lara, published by Corgi Books, 1995. Reprinted by permission of The Random House Group Ltd;

ABC News Program for a quotation by Brian Lara from his speech on receiving Order of Australia medal, 29 November 2009, ABC News. Reproduced by permission of ABC News Program;

Sky Sports for quotes by Brian Lara, from Sky Sports interviews 18/19 April 1994 and 21 April 2007 with Mike Atherton; and Ian Bishop commentary on Lara's

400, Sky Sports, 2004. Reproduced by permission of Sky Sports;

Sylvester Langdon for lyrics from 'Lara Promenade', composed by Sylvester Langdon;

Wayne Hayde (Watchman) for lyrics from 'Prince of Plunder' composed by Wayne Hayde;

Paul Keens-Douglas for the poem 'Lara Fans' from the CD *Crick…. Crack…. Cricket*, copyright © Keensdee Productions Ltd, 21 Old Paddock Rd, Blue Range, Diego Martin, Trinidad. Originally published in *Role Call*, copyright © 1997 Paul Keens-Douglas. Publisher Keensdee Productions Ltd;

Guardian Media Limited for an extract from 'Lara raises youth development funds' by Peter English, 13 July 2008, http://legacy.guardian.co.tt/archives/2008-07-13/sports2.html, Used with permission of the *Trinidad Guardian*.

Printed and bound in Malaysia
2017 2016 2015 2014 2013
10 9 8 7 6 5 4 3 2 1

Contents

Lash dem Lara

1   I have a tale to relate, it concerns the pride of this lan'
Events we should celebrate in the whole of the Caribbean.
This thing is no mystery
Something to excite we
Re-writing of history by one special man.
In Cantaro watching old film of Sobers winning the Test,
One young boy in front of the TV standing out from the rest.
He practise with broomstick, hitting marble and lime
Dem speculate he could emulate Sir Garfield in time.

Chorus   Everyone in Trinidad know that he could lick them bad
Lash dem Lara – go on and lash dem Lara.
Everyone in T and T say from way back what will be
Lash dem Lara – go on and lash dem.
Although his stature is small
He have no fear of the ball
However they play the game
He hit left and right just the same and
Lash dem. Lash dem, lash dem Lara (100)
Lash dem, lash dem, lash dem Lara (150)
Lash dem. Well the score now reach to 175.
Brian Lara, the finest batsman alive.

2   All you now hush up and listen while I continue my theme.
At Fatima College they played a new young boy on the team.
Opposition tease he
They say he look funny
But he score a century and play like a dream.
When he reach 18 the big time selectors asked him to play
To represent T and T and to do his best on the day.
Then when he reach 20, dem open dey eyes
The captaincy they give to he, to no one's surprise.

Chorus   Everyone in Trinidad know that he could lick them bad
Lash dem Lara – go on and lash dem Lara.
Everyone in T and T say from way back what will be
Lash dem Lara – go on and lash dem.
Although his stature is small
He have no fear of the ball
However they play the game
He hit left and right just the same and
Lash dem. Lash dem, lash dem Lara (200)
Lash dem, lash dem, lash dem Lara (250)
Lash dem. Well the score now reach to 275.
Brian Lara, the finest batsman alive.

3   England and West Indies playing the 5th Test, 1994.
The crowd sensing something big in the air and they start to roar.
The tension is mounting
Everybody counting
They feel that he bound to break the world record score.
He now equal Sobers' best and he face the critical ball.
They start to invade the pitch as it hit the boundary wall.
Then when he play 'County' he make 501.
The ball is smashed, the record's crashed, he's second to none.

Chorus   Everyone in Trinidad know that he could lick them bad
Lash dem Lara – go on and lash dem Lara.
Everyone in T and T say from way back what will be
Lash dem Lara – go on and lash dem.
Although his stature is small
He have no fear of the ball
However they play the game
He hit left and right just the same and
Lash dem. Lash dem, lash dem Lara (320)
Lash dem, lash dem, lash dem Lara (350)
Lash dem. Well the score now reach to 375.

Brian Lara, the finest batsman alive.
Lash dem. Lash dem, lash dem Lara (400)
Lash dem, lash dem, lash dem Lara (450)
Lash dem. Well the score now reach 501.
Brian Lara, the man is second to none.

'Lash dem Lara' by Alexander D. Great, single Lion Valley Records SAR001 (1995); album, *Finest Cuts*, Lion Valley Records SAR010 (2009)

Acknowledgements

It is difficult to know where to begin in acknowledging all the people who have given so generously and willingly of their time during the research and writing of this book; I apologise up front for any who have been omitted from what follows.

Firstly I must recognise the input of former West Indies players Jimmy Adams, Deryck Murray, Tony Gray, Daren Ganga, Bryan Davis and Dinanath Ramnarine; thank you for your insights. There is nothing like talking to people who have walked the walk and, in the case of Jimmy and Daren, men who have spent many hours out in the middle batting with Brian. In a similar vein, England and Warwickshire's Nick Knight and Gladstone Small for their memories of the 1994 and 1998 county campaigns. And to Keith Cook, Cricket Operations Manager at Warwickshire County Cricket Club, for his valued assistance in the research of those two seasons.

Numerous Queen's Park Cricket Club members have assisted with information, introductions or anecdotes but special mention must be made of Trinidad and Tobago team manager Colin Borde, racing connections Roger and Joe Hadeed and former national batsman Tony Dharson.

Sincere thanks are also extended to one Lara family member for taking the time to help straighten facts, dispel many of the myths and half-truths which have perpetuated about Brian's life and career and for adding some personal memories. They did not want to be named and out of respect for that wish I have not done so here or within the text; appreciation is due all the same.

For cheerfully accommodating me and for providing colourful recollections of Brian's formative years, I am grateful to everyone at the Harvard Coaching Clinic but most especially Ken Franco, Dwight Day and Indar Ramgoolam. Theirs is a truly fantastic environment for the fostering of cricket talent and long may it continue producing the next generation of Laras. Gratitude of a similar nature must also go to Harry Ramdass and Barbara Jenkins, at that other august Trinidadian institution, Fatima College.

In a project such as this it is the opening of doors which is key to the ultimate outcome and a number of people proved invaluable in this regard, including Tony Harford, Joannah Bharose and Mark Wilson. Of these, particular mention must be made of Trinidadian cricket writer Vaneisa Baksh who gave generously of both her contacts book and knowledge.

For their personal stories, sincere gratitude is extended to Trinidad and Tobago's ultimate calypsonian David Rudder and, for her more painful recollections, to Leeba LaRoche.

I am grateful to Ray Funk and Alexander D Great for guidance through the world of cricket calypso; to Andrew Hignell, Secretary of the Association of Cricket Statisticians, for generously providing the statistics section; to Ray Goble for other valued assistance with cricketing records; and to Bryan Dhoray at Government Information Services Limited (GISL) of Trinidad and Tobago for his facilitation of Lara footage. To Arlene Jute, Cedric Connor and the staff at the UTT (University of Trinidad and Tobago) Round House, where many hours were spent, thank you for always accommodating me and for your wonderful cake and ice cream. And to Jill McCulloch, heartfelt thanks for starting this journey.

More generally, I would like to extend my gratitude and appreciation to Haffiz Yathali, David Mays, Jennifer Waters, Garry Steckles, Rohit Balkissoon, Paul Cherrie, Robert Frische, Jackie Basdeo, Michelle Omar, Terrance Gopaul, Everard Gordon, Andy Ganteaume, Tony Cozier, Dan Stannard, the National Library and Information System Authority of Trinidad (NALIS), Trinidad and Tobago Museum and all those that have helped or tried to help with introductions; the effort is the same whether successful or not.

A big thank you must also go to Paul Simmons for help with editing and ideas that went above and beyond the call of friendship. I would say I will make it up to you but we both know that's not true.

Thanks also to Macmillan Caribbean's Linda Staniford, Nick Gillard, James Ferguson, Louisa Browne and Holly Edgar, especially for your patience and understanding when my dear dad passed away during the writing of this book, and to copy editor Nicole Foster whose professionalism made her a joy to work with.

Finally, and most importantly of all, to my wife Farah because, without getting too Princess Di about it, I'm aware there have been three people in this marriage for far too long now.

James Fuller, Trinidad and Tobago, West Indies

1 'Lara playin!'

'Trinidad is an island of contrasts and of character. The people are positive in expressing an opinion, in criticising a fault and in encouraging a friend. The latter two attitudes are more often compatible than exclusive. And so it is with their cricket.' Thus wrote Clayton Goodwin in 1986 in *West Indians at the Wicket*. Two decades later, as I sit in a crowded and boisterous wooden stand at Trinidad's Guaracara Park, forthright expression of cricketing opinion is being as robustly extolled as ever and Brian Charles Lara is at the centre of discussion.

'Lara finish, he too old, what he doin takin ah young man spot?'

'Hush yuh arse nuh, Lara still the best batsman in de whole West Indies.'

'Don't talk to me bout Lara, dat man not even de best in Trinidad.'

'Oh gosh why you so, man? Ah movin seat to leave yuh alone with yuh ignorance.'

In the Trinidadian way, this discourse is carried out at high volume and with seemingly increasing levels of frustration. The uninitiated might wonder where it will end; the initiated know where it will end: in the clinking of glasses as two friends spend the day joyously dismembering each other's cricketing standpoints.

There is history to the comments though, as the thirty-six-year-old Lara has represented his country only once in the last three seasons. In 2002/03, when Lara failed to respond to correspondence relating to preparations for the season's campaign, Trinidad and Tobago Cricket Board President Alloy Lequay said he had turned his back on the nation that nurtured him. Injuries and international duty both played a part in an inconsistent appearance record but for some it revealed an uncommitted attitude to the national side.

It is just one of the issues which ensure the softly spoken Lara excites a lot of vocal opinion and, while he is a hero to millions, there is a significant minority that is less convinced about the multiple-world-record holder. Be that as it may, there is still nobody that draws a crowd like him in his homeland.

So it was, in January 2006 and a month after moving to the Caribbean, that I was invited to watch a regional game between Trinidad and Tobago and Guyana. 'Lara playin!' had been the excitable adjunct to the offer. It proved to be two days that provided an unforgettable first-hand introduction not only to Lara's batsmanship but also to West Indian cricket, the capricious nature of Caribbean fans and the sheer unadulterated joy of being involved – and it is involvement – in a regional match.

But if this was a new experience for me, it was like coming full circle for Lara, who, eighteen years and half a lifetime before, virtually to the day, made his first-class debut on this very ground against the Leeward Islands. Scores of 14 and 22 did not herald his arrival as he would have liked but by then his prodigious talent had been amply displayed at youth level and it was a matter of when, not if, the big runs would come. Little must he have realised in 1988, as a teenager dreaming of breaking into an all-conquering West Indian side, the terrific highs and lows that lay ahead in a career which would prove to be both spectacular and controversial.

Guaracara is, like much of Trinidad, an unpretentious place. The sports ground of the national oil and gas company, Petrotrin, it sits in the shadow of the Pointe-à-Pierre refinery's flare-off towers and the cloying scents of industry drift across a ground which is more English non-league football than international cricketing venue. Entering through a ratchety turnstile a handwritten cardboard notice, hastily taped to a wall, announces: 'Admission TT$15'.

It is an open but intimate ground. There is a members' Sports Club; an antiquated media tower resembling a prison sentry box; a central wooden grandstand; five floodlight pylons that put me in mind of my old Subbuteo set; several low-level enclosures with roofs of corrugated sheeting and wire-mesh walls; and a vast two-storey scoreboard with more holes than a machine-gunned blackboard and behind which people scurry about on precarious platforms. You sense very little has changed here in the last fifty years: inside the Sports Club, members, oblivious to the cricket, engage in private snooker battles in a venue that holds weekly ballroom dance classes.

Of course advertising has changed and where once Caribbean regional cricket was the preserve of Red Stripe now it's Carib, as evidenced by a huge inflatable blue and yellow Carib bottle lolling around in front of the Sports Club like, well, like someone who's had too many Caribs.

On my way to the main stand I pass the multicoloured tents of food vendors setting up for the day – chopping vegetables, seasoning meat and mixing salads. It's predominantly local fare: oil-down (breadfruit with coconut milk and flavoured with pigtail); saltfish and tomato; bake and shark (a type of fish burger); roti (a thick curry stew of meat, vegetables and potato wrapped inside a dhalpourie roti skin); stew beef; fried fish; and the ubiquitous doubles (curried chickpeas between two pieces of fried bara).

Since the decline of the unparalleled West Indian team of the 1980s, attendances at regional games have fallen away but Lara's presence on the team sheet has had an energising effect.

The prudence of Lara's inclusion is still being hammered out in the bleachers behind me as I settle down. Looking out onto the ground past the wooden boundary stakes, the scars of recent rain and December's football matches are evident as large deposits of sand cover bare patches in the broad-leaf savannah grass. Four groundsmen, in the sponsor's yellow shirts, attend the wicket: two flick at it lethargically with cocoyea brooms, one shunts a roller labouredly up and down, while the fourth contemplates life and offers instruction as he rests his chin on a broom handle.

Today is the second of a four-day match, with Guyana having notched up 257 for 4 on the first. The conclusion of Guyana's first innings and the start of Trinidad and Tobago's seem incidentals to the much-anticipated main event. That moment arrives when the compact, dapper figure of Trinidad and Tobago's favourite son, the Prince of Port of Spain, Brian Charles Lara, makes his way to the crease and the crowd rises in unison to greet him.

Less than two years on from regaining his world Test match record with a monumental 400 against England, this game and innings, while not ranking alongside his more celebrated feats, would nevertheless distil many themes of his career.

The match situation is one familiar to Lara; arriving at the crease at 15 for 2, his side needs a big innings at a vital stage of the game. Positions of adversity, both on and off the field, provide the backdrop to many of Lara's most memorable performances.

It is not initially the all-out flowing mastery for which he has become famous, though contrary to popular belief his innings rarely begin in this manner. Lara prefers to build from a base, and he does so today playing with minimal risk, not forcing the pace. He has accepted the responsibility of chief run-scorer for any number of teams down the years and it is no different here. Early on he receives a delivery which looks like a half-volley but is content to stroke it into the covers for a leisurely single. Mindful of the damp pitch conditions, and the importance of his role, this will be an innings of measured solidity and class but none the less impressive for that.

He plays with an economy of effort, getting himself into line, flicking, guiding and angling the ball away for runs. More than any other batsman, a silhouette of Lara at the crease is instantly recognisable: the coiled stance with threatening backlift; the leaping leg-side pull; or the flourishing finish to a regal cover drive.

Lara's stance at the crease doesn't look out of the ordinary but, as the bowler hits his delivery stride, there's one last rhythmic tap of bat on ground before it rises high and brimming with intent, then falls, in one fluid and continuous motion into the selected shot. At thirty-six, that backlift is not as high as it once was but it still generates the characteristic power and precision, the hands and blade accelerating through the ball at the point of impact and the follow-through soaring high in front of the face.

He collects five boundaries, each one met with a roar, on his way to 50. On reaching 54, he registers 21,000 runs in first-class cricket and, more importantly in the context of the game, is helping edge his team out of trouble alongside Trinidad and Tobago captain Daren Ganga.

Behind me, someone proffers the assertion that Ganga is a better player than Lara, based on the premise that he has a better set-up at the crease. The remark brings swift and merciless condemnation from those who are sitting with him, and many who are not. It's a mauling as Lara's records are trotted out along with his maiden Test century, a flawless 277 against the Australians in Sydney.

'Best innings ah ever see. If Hooper dint run him out he'd ah break Sobers' record that day.'

'Wha? If Hooper dint run him out, Lara woulda still be battin today!'

Overnight Trinidad and Tobago are 126 for 2, with Lara on 60 and Ganga unbeaten on 45.

That night Lara, a noted bon viveur, plays host at a charitable function and as we settle back into our seats the next morning it is images of this event which greet us in the Sunday newspapers. The crowd has swelled on the prospect of a Lara century and his entrance is greeted by raucous and adulatory cheers. He continues with the same effortless efficiency of the previous afternoon and moves towards his hundred.

An ice cream seller, wearing a Real Madrid shirt and New York Knicks baseball cap, circumnavigates the boundary ringing a bicycle bell for custom and brings his cart to a halt in front of the main stand. He's obscuring the view of the lower tiers and is left in no doubt about it.

'Is you Lara!? You feel is you we come tuh see!?'

The vendors circle continuously, whether bringing ice cream, cold beer in a bucket or fresh cashew nuts and peanuts; the nuts sellers lobbing brown-paper nut bricks into the stands with unerring accuracy and accompanying commentary.

One of them, *Nuts Landing*, is holding an impromptu stand-up show in front of one section of supporters. Dressed as an umpire he is bouncing his lean frame around energetically in front of them, bawling and gesticulating violently with his arms. He bounds from side to side like a West Indian John Cleese, pauses, singling out a spectator for ridicule, makes a wisecrack and then continues with his performance.

From where I'm sitting, what he's saying is indistinct but the reaction is not. Regular wholehearted whoops of infectious laughter peal across the ground before, just as suddenly as he started, *Nuts* waves a dismissive hand at his audience and trudges off in mock disgust, appearing to be the world's least likely sufferer of work-related stress.

Soon after, the smell of fast-approaching rain interrupts that of the refinery. Water begins falling with increasing rapidity, leading to a furious crescendo, but it doesn't have a correlating effect on the ground staff.

'Rain cyah save Guyana from Lara,' shouts one fan as the covers are dragged tortuously into position.

It has been an inclement start to the dry season and threatening rain clouds skirt the ground most of the day. It is still warm though, and once the sun re-emerges patrons bring their white plastic chairs, groundsheets and multicoloured umbrellas back out and reposition them around the boundary edge. The game is a side show for many, this is Sunday at the cricket and they've come for the 'lime' (social) with their coolers packed high with bulging tubs of chicken pelau, bags of ice, bottles of Johnnie Walker and fresh coconut water.

On resumption, and with lunchtime smells still drifting across the ground, Lara nears his hundred. There's a slow handclap as the bowler approaches, followed by an eruption as his delivery is turned down to fine-leg for the required single. Everybody rises and applauds. The watchful nature of Lara's effort is evidenced by it taking him four and a half hours and 196 balls, a run every two deliveries instead of his natural rate of closer to a run a ball. The bat is raised in routine acknowledgement; he still has a job to do and knows it. In any event he is not a hundred and out man.

He continues serenely, playing each ball on its merits. He advances down the wicket to one delivery but it's not there to hit so contents himself with defence. Lara still manoeuvres his body, which in common with most thirtysomethings is somewhat fleshier than in his youth, on nimble feet. There are no false shots and seemingly no huge effort; just the concentration of a man supremely confident in what he was born to do. He watches each delivery hard and plays it late, using the pace of the ball, opening and closing the face of the bat in the course of conducting the shot, manipulating it into the gaps. It's hard to think of it as anything other than artistry. C. L. R. James made the case for cricket as art in his seminal work *Beyond A Boundary* in 1963 and the great man would have found the basis for a strong argument in a Lara innings.

The Guyanese bowlers have no answer. One of them loses his run-up halfway to the wicket, stops and turns to head back to the top of his mark. Any perceived sign of weakness is seized upon.

'He fraid ah Lara! Don't know where to put de ball!'

And so the bacchanal, as they call it here, goes on all afternoon to a backbeat of soca music. There are more rain delays, four in all throughout the day, and after each one a Trinidadian wicket falls, but not Lara's, whose concentration never wavers.

Finally, after nearly six and a half hours of batting, a tired-looking drive brings an edge and he is caught at slip for a masterful 153. The mournful wail of conch shells, ear-piercing airhorns, flourishing flags and wholehearted cheers accompany Lara's stroll back to the pavilion in the late afternoon sun.

In the Caribbean, if a game is heading for a draw, as this one inevitably was after the time lost to rain, the majority of the points go to the side with the higher first innings score. An innings of patience and responsibility, and one that wins him the Man of the Match award, has put Lara's team on the brink of securing those first innings points.

Moments later, when they are secured, the ground erupts and home fans charge onto the field jumping, shouting and dancing with red, white and black flags brandished high and proud. The half-dozen security staff lining the boundary don't bat an eyelid.

It's been an enlightening two days – this is Trinidad and this is Lara.

2 The Cantaro kid

Tipping the scales at precisely 7 lb, Brian Charles Lara was born to Bunty and Pearl Lara at the Port of Spain General Hospital on Friday, 2 May 1969; the seventh boy and second-last child in a family of eleven siblings (Rudolph, Mary, Agnes, Winston, Robert, Mervyn, Richard, Kathleen, Lyndon, Brian and Karen).

It was an unassuming entrance into what was a turbulent time in Trinidad and Tobago, the trailing two islands in the tail of the Caribbean chain, which lie just seven miles off the South American coast of Venezuela.

Trinidad and Tobago had achieved independence from the United Kingdom seven years before, in August 1962, and would become a fully fledged republic in 1976. The years surrounding Lara's birth were marked by increasing industrial, social and racial politicisation and, feeding off the pervading public discontent, Geddes Granger's National Joint Action Committee (NJAC) and the Black Power movement rose to threatening prominence. Allied to the strength and growing militancy of the local trade unions, a combustible atmosphere erupted into revolution in early 1970. The uprising, supported by sections of the nation's armed forces, lasted five days before being quelled.

Around the world, 1969 was the year of Woodstock; of Neil Armstrong and Edwin 'Buzz' Aldrin's moon landing; the beginning of US troop withdrawals from Vietnam; of Colonel Muammar al-Qaddafi's seizure of power in Libya; Concorde's first test flight; the release of Paul Newman and Robert Redford's classic *Butch Cassidy and the Sundance Kid*; and of tennis's first open-era grand slam, by Australia's Rod Laver.

Politics was to the fore in the cricketing world with the South African government's apartheid policy, whereby only white players were selected and only white nations played, forcing the International Cricket Council's (ICC) hand. South Africa was banned from the global game in 1970 and would remain in isolation for over two decades.

For the West Indies, the greatest all-round cricketer the game has ever known, Garfield (Garry) St Aubrun Sobers, was entering the autumn of his playing days. Sobers, who made his Test debut as a seventeen-year-old against England in 1954, is widely regarded as cricket's ultimate athlete – a superb batsman, fast bowler, spin bowler and fielder, earning him the title 'four-cricketers-in-one'.

Sobers had been the leading light in a world-beating side led by the West Indies first black series captain, Frank Worrell. He succeeded Worrell as skipper in 1964/65 and enjoyed early success, but a surprising home defeat to England was the beginning of a decline in the region's fortunes. Further losses to Australia, England and India followed before, in 1971/72, a disappointing home draw with New Zealand heralded the end. Replaced as captain by Rohan Kanhai, Sobers played his last Test in March 1974 against England in Trinidad.

The years that bridged the late 1960s and the early 1970s were a period of flux, uncertainty and change, a time of racial, social and sporting upheaval, but you have to wonder how much of this really impacted upon Lara's childhood in somnolent Mitchell Street, Cantaro; a place which, even today, seems cut-off from the rest of the world.

Trinidad is roughly rectangular in shape, around thirty-five miles wide by fifty miles long, with Cantaro situated in the north-eastern tip of the island, a twenty-minute drive from the nation's capital, Port of Spain.

Originally named El Cantaro ('The Jar'), it is one of several small villages, including Gasparillo, Sam Boucaud, La Pastora and Pipiol, that form Upper Santa Cruz. They lie in the Northern Range's verdant Santa

Cruz Valley, and were initially a collection of scattered settlements which took their names from, and owed their origins to, the agricultural estates that preceded them. The valley was once a rich citrus, coffee and cocoa producer and evidence of this agrarian past remains, as the cocoa trees of abandoned estates still punctuate the verges of the main arterial bisecting the valley, Saddle Road.

Approaching from San Juan, there remains no sign from Saddle Road to the village itself. Only notice boards directing you to Cantaro Geriatric Home and a number of local businesses alert you to its probable presence. Turning off, you meander along a narrow snaking road, flanked by bamboo patches and scrubland, for half a mile to the village edge. Looking up as you drive, montane rainforest-covered peaks pierce the sky on all sides and it is not hard to imagine how remote Cantaro must have felt when Lara was born; in a time when car ownership in rural locales was far from commonplace. Even now that the proliferation of motor vehicles, and a rising local population fuelled by new housing developments, has transformed Cantaro High Street into something more bustling, one street back, and running parallel, Mitchell Street still has a drowsy air. Men tinker under the bonnets of cars, neighbours pass the time of day shielded from the midday sun beneath umbrellas, and pensioners sit on their porches trying to catch a little breeze, as ribby, panting dogs amble across the road.

'There is always a fresh breeze and a lot of greenery,' said Lara of Cantaro in his 1995 autobiography, *Beating the Field*. 'Neighbours walk in and out of each other's houses and everyone knows everyone else.' Rising crime rates over the last ten years may have tempered some of that liberalism but the area retains a community feel.

There are fifteen houses, mostly of modest bungalow-style, and two vacant plots in Mitchell Street, and the Lara family home was, and is, No. 17. Brian's widowed sister Kathleen and her three children, along with his brother Mervyn Eustache and Mervyn's four children, still reside at the house and Lara's raft of junior trophies remain the first things you see on entering.

Lara was born into a passionately sporting family; his father, Bunty, and grandfather, Herbert St Louis, were keen cricketers, and Bunty, an all-rounder, regularly represented Cantaro in what was known as 'The Village Olympics', where villages in the area came together in an annual sporting contest. Lara's brothers were all gifted sportsmen, with Mervyn, Winston and Robert, in particular, proving exceptional footballers.

Even in such a sports-oriented environment, Lara's natural hand–eye coordination and flair for all ball games stood out from an early age. By age four he was already playing cricket on his own in the backyard, hitting limes, small oranges, marbles or tennis balls back and forth against the garage wall, practising shots, often for hours at a time and causing neighbours to stop and watch, marvelling at the little boy's skill.

'He would play about hitting marbles and fruit, and he soon learned all the strokes,' said his sister Agnes Cyrus.

It wasn't long before the young left-hander's enthusiasm saw him taking part in the rowdy, and near continuous, games of cricket played in the streets around his family home. Mitchell Street is part of a tight-knit network of quiet residential back roads and side streets and the layout provided a natural source of players and locations for impromptu clashes.

'Brian would be all over the village playing cricket from dawn till dusk,' says Paul Cherrie, a sixty-seven-year-old neighbour who has lived in Mitchell Street all his life. 'You would always see him with a bat and ball, or sometimes oranges, because back then all around here was orange trees.' Before adding, for my enlightenment, 'If you get the young green ones they're harder and last longer.'

The youngster's bouncing, confident gait became a familiar sight to locals, as I learn from the patrons of Valley Bar, a cricket ball's throw from the Lara home on Stollmeyer Road. Many of the regulars, who appear to have invested the requisite hours to be deemed expert Cantaro observers, have memories of Brian. Some talk of his ability in all sports, others of his confident manner, but the commonly enduring one is that of the youngster's impish figure striding up and down the road outside the bar, bat and ball in hand, perpetually casting about for a willing bowler. He was an undeniable character, with his diminutive frame, cheeky looks and winning smile. He was also an old soul, with many saying his mannerisms, speech patterns and topics of conversation gave the impression of an old head on young shoulders.

Lara offered his view of those early days in interviews with the UK's *Independent* in 2007.

'It was tough just to get a game on the street with my bigger brothers and their friends, so if I did get a hit, as an eight-year-old playing with sixteen-year-olds, I had to be good. I was very competitive right from when I was very small, and there came a time when I was ten years old and they couldn't get me out all afternoon.'

It soon took longer than that, as he explained in a later interview.

'My drive has always been to bat. When I played in my backyard I would bat for a week sometimes. We would play between four and six o'clock every evening, before I got called in for tea and to do my homework, and if my mates did not get me out on one day I would carry on batting the next. That was the rule and sometimes I would bat for a week.'

Lara's neighbour Cherrie remembers two of the Lara boys' cricketing exploits well.

'My front door had a glass window and Brian and Richard would be playing in the street, one batting the other bowling, and now and again you would hear the ball hitting the glass, bap, bap,' he says clapping his hands smartly. 'I would run out there threatening if they break my glass I was going to call the police … They never broke my glass.'

Cherrie was lucky, as Lara's father had to dip into his pocket regularly to pay for panes of glass that thoughtlessly intercepted winning sixes.

Invariably the game played was pass-out, a form of cricket where literally the batsman is 'out' if he allows the ball to 'pass'. The game is less widely played in Trinidad and Tobago today but in Lara's time it was what children were brought up on and inculcated an already natural desire to play shots.

'During the heyday, when you heard about Gordon Greenidge, Desmond Haynes and all these guys, it was part of growing up to play pass-out pretending to be them,' says former Trinidad and Tobago and West Indies fast bowler Tony Gray.

But the game also taught the fine balance between playing aggressively and putting a value on your wicket.

'If you're playing with ten or eleven other guys there's no guarantee you'll bat again once you're out,' says Gray, whose life and cricket career ran parallel to Lara's for many years. 'That focuses the mind.'

Something else focussed the mind in Mitchell Street – the presence of a neighbour known locally only as 'Tants'. Tants was an old spinster and fanatical gardener, doting on her plants as if they were her own babies, a sentiment she regularly relayed to the children of the neighbourhood. With Tants living directly opposite the Laras, her serried floral ranks represented an early lesson in shot selection for the budding batsman.

'If the ball went in her yard you got it back in her time, if at all,' says Cherrie matter-of-factly.

Genius is a word frequently attached to Lara and it is clear he possessed formidable natural talent, but it is also clear that as a youngster his devotion to cricket bordered on fanaticism, often playing for hours alone when others were not available.

'I used to play my own Test matches on the porch of our house using a broom handle or a stick as the bat and a marble as a ball,' said Lara. 'I would arrange the pot plants to represent fielders and try to find the gaps as I played my shots.' These Test matches would, just like the real thing, last days.

The 'plant pots' story echoes tales of other sporting greats and their obsessive devotion to practice at a young age. As a boy, the peerless Australian batsman Sir Donald Bradman honed his hand–eye coordination by repeatedly hitting a golf ball with a cricket stump against the curved brick stand of a water tank behind his home. Similarly, Manchester United footballer George Best practised by striking a tennis ball against the lock of a door, seeing how many times he could hit it, or rebounding it off the kerb in the road outside his home, trapping and returning it continuously.

It is tempting, and perhaps easier, to believe such sporting superstars are born with the natural gifts that will guarantee success, but nothing of worth comes without dedication and hard work. It is a mantra that was instilled in Lara by his father, Bunty, and one which would see him work as hard on his game as any professional cricketer.

Santa Cruz character

'Usually, a fast bowler relates directly to the tensions and traumas of his society. The nature of his skill makes it inevitable that this should be so. Similarly the temperament of a batsman can often be directly the result of the environment in which he was bred,' wrote Dr Gordon Roehler, Professor of West Indian Literature at the University of the West Indies, in a publication celebrating the careers of Lance Gibbs and Rohan Kanhai in 1974.

Someone's surroundings in their formative years, be they familial or geographic, have a powerful impact in shaping and developing character but this was especially true of Lara's batting, says Tony Gray, who also lives in Santa Cruz. Gray sees the area's imprint on Lara: a steely, proud character, with enormous reserves of self-belief.

'In every part of Trinidad there are different mentalities. In Penal for example you will find people are quieter, more subdued; in Port of Spain they're pretty sure of themselves; in Santa Cruz you will find great ego and positivity. It doesn't matter if you're a cook, groundsman, teacher, anything, you will want to be the best around,' says the 6 ft 6 in quick bowler.

'With that attitude comes great pressure too; if you're saying you're the best you had better back it up. They used to play a lot of windball cricket in Santa Cruz, it was very popular. For a final you would get over a thousand people watching and the atmosphere was like Test cricket, it was intense. That exposes you to real pressure from a very early age and builds mental strength; that is the environment Brian Lara grew up in.'

The number of nationally and internationally successful people who hail from what is a small rural district supports Gray's assertion.

Cricketers Dwayne and Darren Bravo, who grew up within two streets of Lara on Sam Boucaud Road, are both West Indian internationals. Dwayne has been playing for the West Indies since 2004 and is the side's premier all-rounder. His half-brother Darren, five years Dwayne's junior, is a fabulously talented left-handed batsman uncannily in the Lara mould, both physically and technically. He made his one-day international debut in 2009, aged twenty, and great things are predicted for him.

Another famous Santa Cruzian is athlete Ato Boldon, the former world 200-metre champion and four-time Olympic sprint medallist, who was also the first double sprint champion in World Junior Championships history.

In the local music scene, the pioneering parang band the Lara Brothers (the original members of which were related to Brian) is a Trinbagonian institution. The group was founded in 1945 and is still performing six decades later.

Poet, actress, activist, artist and globe-trotting speaker Eintou Pearl Springer (Poet Laureate of Port of Spain from 2002 to 2009) also hails from Santa Cruz, as does soca singer Sanell Dempster and international netball umpire Anne Marie Dickson (the first Caribbean umpire to officiate at a world netball final). Add a number of high-profile national politicians and business leaders into the mix and it's clear this is a fertile area not just agriculturally but also for the production of high achievers.

Santa Cruz (meaning 'Holy Cross') is a religious area and religion was central to Lara family life. At one end of Mitchell Street sit both the Kingdom Hall of Jehovah's Witnesses and the local Seventh Day Adventist church. Lara's mother, Pearl, was a committed Seventh Day Adventist and rose to become a deaconess in the church.

'Religion played a big part in our lives,' said Lara. 'If we showed any reluctance to attend church on a Sunday our mother would take us by the ear.'

Brian's neighbour Paul Cherrie, formerly a teacher at Newtown Boys RC school, produced a magazine celebrating the 150th anniversary of the Santa Cruz Holy Cross Roman Catholic church parish in 1995. In it he wrote a profile of 'the parish hero', ending with the words: 'May God continue to do great things for Brian because of his humility.' Adjoining the piece is an image of the font in which Lara was baptised by Father Cyril Ross; it is indicative of the village that Lara's story gets one page, the same billing and column inches as Sister Mary Thomas, O.P. (Order of Preachers), the first person from the region to enter a convent.

Batting hero

As a youngster in Cantaro's streets, Lara's appetite for the game may have been insatiable but access to international cricketing action in Trinidad in the early 1970s more often than not meant radio not television. Far from being a problem, many of the older generation feel that this led to a deeper understanding of the game, the action having to be recreated and visualized in the mind using only the commentator's words. In such a way fielding positions, techniques, tactics and cricket lore became ingrained.

While the format may not have represented a problem, international time zones did. With major Test nations such as India, Pakistan and Australia being variously ten to fourteen hours ahead of Trinidad and Tobago, a 10 am Test match start put the opening salvoes at between 8 pm and midnight Cantaro time, with play going on through the night and deep into the next morning.

The cricket-loving Lara boys weren't going to let the small matter of sleep deter them though and four of them, who shared a bunk bed, spent many nights with ears pressed close to the low-volume, crackling commentary on an old transistor radio.

The sleeping arrangements give an insight into what one family member recalls as being a boisterous and busy household. Of Bunty and Pearl's eleven children, two had already left home when Brian was growing up, big sister Agnes had her own room and Robert and Winston occupied one near the garage. The remaining four boys and two girls shared another, with the bunk bed for the boys (Richard and Mervyn on the top and Brian and Lyndon on the bottom) and a large bed for the girls.

On those night-time vigils, a bleary-eyed Brian listened intently to the exploits of his West Indian heroes and one in particular, the flamboyant Guyanese left-handed opening bat Roy Fredericks, fired his imagination.

The footwork and flair are strikingly familiar. Lara's idol Roy Fredericks opens up against England with wicketkeeper Alan Knott looking on.

Fredericks was a diminutive left-hander, standing at 5 ft 4 in and weighing just 10 st 3 lb, who possessed a high backlift, flourishing follow-through and an indomitable refusal to be cowed by the fastest bowling. He never wore a helmet, or any upper-body protection, and in the Caribbean tradition he met 'pace like fire' head on, sometimes literally. With such a chin-jutting approach Fredericks was occasionally felled but would always return to the fray, earning him the prosaically respectful moniker of 'cement head' from the Australians.

A Fredericks innings was full of character and on 13 December 1975, when Lara was an impressionable six-year-old, he played one of the most extraordinary in Test match history. Facing the menacing might of arguably cricket's greatest fast bowling partnership, Dennis Lillee and Jeff Thomson, on a quick, bouncy track in Perth, Fredericks refused to take a backward step.

Lillee thundered in with the wind at his back, supported by the viciously slingy Thomson, but the bullies became the bullied as the pugnacious Fredericks counterattacked in remarkable fashion. In a whirlwind of cutting and hooking, Lillee's opening five overs disappeared for 35 and Thomson's first three went for 33. By lunch on the second day the West Indies were 130 for 1 from fourteen overs. Thomson unleashed the fastest delivery recorded in Test match history at Fredericks that day, 99.7 mph (160.45 kph), but the Guyanese opener, named Wisden Cricketer of the Year in 1974, took it all in his stride.

In an era where scoring rates were well below present-day norms, Fredericks's first 50 took only thirty-three balls and he reached his century in just seventy-one. With long sleeves characteristically buttoned at the wrists and West Indies cap cocked back on his head, Fredericks hammered the Australian attack for a little over three and a half hours. By the time his 145-ball innings ended, just after tea, he had pillaged 169 out of the 258 West Indies had on the board. It was a match-winning knock, setting up an innings victory which levelled the series.

Lara would become enthralled by the four-pronged pace-attack of Michael Holding, Andy Roberts, Colin Croft and Joel Garner which ushered in the West Indian era of dominance in the mid-70s; also by the belligerent flair of Viv Richards and the technical excellence of Gordon Greenidge – but it was Fredericks who first captured his youthful mind. A close fit in stature and approach, he was a charismatic character on which the youngster could model himself and play out his cricketing fantasies. In the streets of Cantaro, with long sleeves buttoned to impersonate his hero, Lara was given and rejoiced in the nickname 'Fredericks'. Indeed, so influenced did he become by the legend of Fredericks that when he first met him in the flesh years later, Lara, by then a confident young man, was star-struck.

3 The perfect nursery

Just a few weeks after Roy Fredericks's barnstorming effort in Perth, the six-year-old Lara was to have his overwhelming enthusiasm for the game channelled formally for the first time. It was his good fortune that that channel would be Harvard Cricket Coaching Clinic, where his sister Agnes, having spotted a newspaper advertisement, enrolled her baby brother in free weekly coaching sessions.

Harvard sits on Port of Spain's Serpentine Road, barely a 400-yard walk across the open grassland of King George V Park to the nation's hallowed Test match venue, the Queen's Park Oval. What impact training in the shadow of such a stadium has on the fertile imaginations of young cricketers can only be speculated, but it would be hard to think it was lost on Lara who was already obsessed with the game.

After enrolment, Agnes, who became like a second mum to Brian and took a loving interest in his development, bought him a cap, a bat and some whites and drove him down to the clinic for the first two Sundays.

'It was then my father took over, and for the rest of his life, never missed anything Brian did at cricket,' she said. 'Matches, even practices, he would always be there, because he knew that Brian was destined for great things.'

So began an association that would last the best part of a decade. On every Sunday (bar Carnival and Easter Sunday) throughout the January–

June cricket season, from 9 am to12 noon, Brian's batting was tweaked and fine-tuned but never altered fundamentally.

'Nobody tried to mess with his game too much, it was natural, he had it, from his strokeplay right through; all he needed essentially was guidance,' explains Dwight Day, a long-serving Harvard coach and son of one of the clinic's founders, Hugo 'Piv' Day.

If his talent was obvious, so was the young boy's swaggering self-belief.

'He came in with a self-confidence that was unusual to see in a six-year-old,' says the white-haired Day, a smile broadening out across his expressive face. 'It soon got around that he was convinced he would play for the West Indies and was telling people so!'

By age seven, according to his sister Agnes, Lara had already upped his goals from merely playing for the West Indies.

'Within a year of starting at the clinic, Brian told me that he wanted to be the world's greatest cricketer, and already the game was his whole life,' she said. 'When he wasn't playing, he would sit down with a piece of paper and work out fielding positions.'

Thirty-five years after Lara first walked through Harvard's solid dark green metal gates little has changed at the clinic. Training is an animated affair with twenty-five coaches in vivid red polo shirts, all unpaid volunteers, overseeing around 150 excitable children (when Lara reclaimed the Test record score in 2004 numbers briefly topped 300).

The youngsters, both boys and girls, are split into five groups, selected by a combination of age and ability. There are hard courts on which the youngest children are divided into manageable groups, either for games of short cricket or to undertake drills at skill stations. Across from the hard courts three nets are filled with eight-, nine- and ten-year-olds.

As I watch, the coaches playfully admonish their charges or throw their hands to the heavens in mock celebration as a youngster finally takes a lesson on board.

'Balance, don't lean your head over.'

'Your pad have tuh reach first, your bat will come after.'

'Don't jam de bat.'

'Good, yes, I can live with that.'

'OK, getting there, we will work on that next time.'

The children love it and it's easy to see why Lara thrived in such an atmosphere of nurture and encouragement.

It was Brian's father, Bunty, who brought him to Harvard each Sunday and it was he who became the dominant presence in the young boy's life.

Bunty was a traditional West Indian father, a man who believed in discipline, and all the Lara children had chores to carry out. He was unflinching on his values, such as respect for others and working hard to attain your goals. You disregarded these at your peril because Bunty, in common with most Caribbean parents of his generation, wasn't averse to reprimanding his children with a 'lash' (smack) for stepping out of line. One family member recalls Bunty's routine statement before delivering the punishment: 'I'm givin you three, if you run you get six.'

Bunty was the manager of a Ministry of Agriculture propagation station (producing mainly cacao plants) at La Pastora, just outside Cantaro. It was the largest employer in the village and a prestigious job. Bunty's early retirement from this position on health grounds brought a change in the family dynamic, the principal beneficiaries of which were his three youngest children, Lyndon, Brian and Karen. He had more time to spend with his offspring and his main focus became Brian, who he clearly recognised as being gifted. A close bond was forged between father and son, one which Brian readily admits led to him being somewhat spoiled.

As well as being emotionally close, Brian and Bunty were similar characters: generally easygoing in manner and nature but headstrong and determined when they believed in something, and both could flare up when angered.

One occasion Brian saw this side of his father was on a Harvard trip to north-eastern Trinidad. The Harvard team was playing Rampanalgas, near Toco, a two-and-a-half-hour journey from Santa Cruz. Having been driven all the way there, nine-year-old Brian temporarily jettisoned his coaching, played a rash shot to his first delivery and was dismissed. Bunty was livid, so much so that he jumped in his car and drove off. Before leaving he gave instructions that nobody should give Brian a lift back, he was to make his own way home, and if that meant walking then it would give him time for reflection on the foolish shot he'd played. Bunty recognised his son's talent and did not want him wasting it.

Such a reaction was born out of Bunty's emotional involvement in his son's development, and for Brian the importance of having his father take such a demonstrable interest was something which would have a profound influence.

Harvard coach Ken Franco, whose father Anthony Franco was a work colleague of Bunty's, echoes the sentiments of everyone you speak to about his character: humble, generous, resolute and respectful, a man dedicated to his son and the fulfilment of his dreams.

'Bunty was a quiet man, he wasn't pushy the way some parents can be with a talented child. Wherever you were, whether it was practising at Harvard or playing a game somewhere, Bunty would bring Brian, drop him and then go in a corner and watch. He would say "good morning, good afternoon", always very polite, but other than that there wouldn't be much interaction. Bunty's approach was, "I bring Brian to you for coaching, you're the coach, you coach him." He must've been proud but you would never see that or hear him speak of it.

'Bunty really lent a lot of support to Brian and I always feel that parental support is so important. It's important for the child to know that the family is there, and Brian had that.'

Brian enjoyed a happy childhood and an annual highlight was a family trip to the Queen's Park Oval to watch the West Indies take on, and frequently obliterate, touring nations. These outings, organised by Bunty, were much-anticipated events and in the days of a dominant regional side were also routinely and rapidly sold out. This necessitated an early start, and clan Lara would leave Cantaro on the short scenic drive to Port of Spain at 4 am to ensure their seats.

While Bunty, a short but physically strong man, was in the foreground, there was an equally remarkable person in the background, Lara's mother, Pearl.

Pearl was down-to-earth, generous of spirit and nature, a woman devoted to her family and faith and one who was noted for her warmth and hospitality. Indeed, so concerned about the well-being of others was she that Pearl seldom sat down to eat with her own family, being too busy dashing around making sure everyone else was taken care of.

'My mother was less enthusiastic about cricket, she was more into caring,' said Lara. 'She was known as one of the mothers of the village I grew up in. She would invite any young kid into our house for food or anything she could offer.'

As Brian began moving through the ranks and making a name for himself, Pearl did attend some matches but she was happier to remain the backbone of the family unit, to add strength and support from home. Lara always referred to her as a 'stabiliser' in his life.

'Not one who was overly concerned at how my cricket is going, but one who's more worried about her son's safety, his psyche, how he is as an individual,' he said.

Even when Lara shot to international fame in 1994, Pearl remained the unwavering personality she had always been, not accepting that she might have helped her son achieve his goals.

'To God be the glory,' she said. 'I am not happy for myself. I'm happy for Brian. He always wanted to be a cricketer, to do all the things he is doing, and I thank God he is doing it. I am not responsible for what he is doing. God is. I was used as the instrument to bring him into the world.'

Lara has always been fulsome in praising his parents and the tremendous job they did in raising such a large family, saying that, though sacrifices had to be made, as children they never wanted for anything. At high-profile times in his career, such as his Test record 375 and retirement speech, he took time out to pay tribute to them and the strength they instilled in all their children.

Sunday morning ritual

As I sit watching the youngsters being put through their Sunday morning paces on Harvard's hard courts I am reminded, though Bunty's dedication was unquestionably absolute, that the enjoyment of these mornings was not necessarily one-sided. This is not all parental servitude. Trinidad is a place which lends itself readily to relaxation, and these weekend cricket clinics foster a convivial atmosphere. There's plenty of laughter in the air as gaggles of parents sit around tables, shaded from the sun. Food and drink is on sale and it seems very much a social occasion which has taken on a life of its own for the mums and dads. It was no different in Lara's time, says Day.

'Bunty would come with his cooler, sit in the club and spend a little time with some of the others and take a couple of drinks. He was a sociable man, so he would be there for the whole morning … and sometimes a little after.'

It was on these hard courts that Lara, under Hugo Day's tutelage, practised with tennis balls on first arrival before being rapidly promoted to proper cricket balls (known locally as corkballs) and on upwards through the ranks. He progressed through the age groups early at each level: when he was eleven he was grouped with the thirteen- to fourteen-year-olds, and by the time he was twelve he was in Net 1 with the fifteen- and sixteen-year-olds.

'There were three or four other boys who were just as talented at the time but the difference was Brian made the step up all the time,' says Franco, who was the coach of Net 1 the year Brian advanced to that level. 'Whenever there was a next level to reach, Brian reached it, whereas the others fell away.'

The young Lara demonstrated talent in every facet of the game but his principal focus was always batting.

'He wouldn't shirk his responsibilities, he would do his fielding and bowling, he would bowl little leg-breaks, but the batting was his focus, and batting for a very long time. He just loved to bat.

'Brian was actually a very good wicketkeeper and also a very good catcher of the ball. I remember one game down at Iere High School and he was fielding at slip. At that age he was no more than about 5 ft and the guy edged and Brian went like a goalkeeper diving full length to catch the ball. We looked at each other just amazed; there's this short little guy pulling off a catch like that.'

A cricket and football coach for over twenty-eight years, Franco spent time with Lara conducting technical work, called 'short wicket'.

'We worked a lot on his drive. Driving is so important, because the on-drive round to the square drive is a big scoring arc and to become proficient in the shot opens up your scoring options. But one thing Brian used to do is what we call genuflecting. If you're Catholic, when you go to church you will kneel down with one leg in front of the other,' says the sixty-four-year-old, demonstrating with his left leg leading and his right leg behind bending at the knee.

'He would collapse his back knee, getting too low and often not reaching the pitch, meaning he was more likely to hit the ball in the air. So I would tell him, no, bend here (front leg), straighten here (back leg), and we spent a lot of time doing it over and over again so it became ingrained and natural.'

Franco is self-effacing about his involvement with Lara – as are all the Harvard coaches – unwilling to take credit for any impact he may have had on the nascent batsman. But exquisite cover driving became a hallmark of Lara's game, and it's easy to forget that even with his innate brilliance such shots still had to be honed before becoming 'natural'.

In May 2005, the *Trinidad Guardian* ran an article on the best cover driver in the world. Perhaps unsurprisingly, Lara emerged top but that assessment was not as myopic as it might first appear. The article was actually taken from the Cricinfo website and was based on research using a ball-by-ball data recording system which recorded each delivery in sixteen different ways; the type of system which gets cricketing anoraks drooling the world over. It showed that between September 2001 and April 2005 Lara scored 1.82 runs every time he played the shot and was only dismissed once. He clearly hadn't forgotten his 'genuflecting' guidance.

By twelve years old, though, it wasn't batting talent alone that was marking Lara out from his contemporaries.

'In Net 1 you started to see one very ambitious young man,' says Franco, a retired Social Sciences and Physical Education teacher. 'He always liked bigger men to bowl to him, he was never afraid of the older guys. A fifteen-year-old bowling at you when you're twelve can be quite daunting but there was never that fear with Brian. He was a good player but it was his ambition that set him apart.'

Dwight Day also recalls an incident with the twelve-year-old Lara that seemed to underscore the youngster's towering belief in his own ability and judgement.

'I found he was crouching a little too much over the bat so I just tried to get him to straighten up a bit. Well, he didn't say anything, talk back or anything like that, but from his body language and the way he looked at me it was obvious that as far as he was concerned, he didn't have a problem, he knew exactly what he was doing and everything was going pretty well, thank you very much.'

Lara left Harvard at the age of fourteen but maintains contact with the clinic and its coaches, recalling his time there and its impact on him with fondness. Much of this is due to the fact that Harvard's approach was never just a cricketing one, it was holistic, promoting life lessons as well as sporting ones.

'This clinic is not only about producing players, our aim is to help the child in every level of life, by instilling discipline and values,' says Head Coach Indar Ramgoolam, one of the clinic's founders in 1965.

A moral aspect of Lara's batting for which he would become noted, 'walking' without waiting for the umpire's decision when he knew he was out, came directly from his time at Harvard.

'When you're out we make sure that, if you know that, then you walk,' adds Ramgoolam. 'Brian learned that the same as the rest of the boys here. We are instilling in these boys a discipline that will help them throughout their future lives and careers and "walking" is about honesty at the end of the day.'

4 Fatima, Carew and Sobers

Fatima College

The year Lara was promoted to Harvard's Net 1, the twelve-year-old was also accepted into Fatima College, one of the longest-standing and most highly regarded educational institutions in Trinidad and Tobago.

Lara's entrance examination results had not initially been sufficient to gain him a place at the all-boys secondary school, situated on Port of Spain's Mucurapo Road, but Bunty, not a man easily dissuaded in matters of his son's progression, arranged a meeting with the Principal, Clive Pantin.

Pantin, himself a football and hockey international, was swayed by Bunty's sincerity and his desire to secure the best education for his son, calling him 'a very impressive and humble man'. Brian was in.

Lara had played little cricket at his first two schools, St Joseph's RC Primary School and San Juan Government Secondary, sating his cricketing thirst predominantly through the weekly sessions at Harvard and the friendly matches organised by the clinic. From the time he was introduced to structured competitive cricket at Fatima his enthusiasm for the game catapulted to a new level. Yet the youngster, so feted at Harvard, did not immediately catch the eye at his new school, says teacher and sports coach Harry Ramdass.

'Ordinary, very ordinary,' is Ramdass's assessment of the first time he saw Lara play. 'He was very short at that age, not much higher than the stumps, and that was highlighted by the fact that he had a big afro,' smiles the teacher who would be an ever-present during Lara's time at Fatima, coaching or umpiring him right through to U19 level.

'At one time, he got a little worried about his lack of size, worrying he wouldn't grow. But what was different about Brian was the determination. He would go away after the games and practice, all the time practising. Most boys are content simply to hit the ball but he would use cones, constantly driving balls between them, to get the accuracy so that he could hit the gaps in games.

'In the first few games he didn't do that well, which was to be expected really as it was a big step and he was up against boys bigger and better than him. But he learned quickly,' says Ramdass, who retired in 2010 after thirty-eight years at Fatima.

The young Lara's wicketkeeping ability is something that Ramdass, in common with his Harvard coaches, eulogises about.

'We played a national U14 final, which was forty overs a side, at Mount St Benedict and we were bowled out for about 80. They went into bat and Brian was keeping. When they came off for the break after twenty overs the opposition were about 50 for 3, coasting really.

'Well I brought the boys round and told them they hadn't played any cricket as yet and that they'd better give 150 per cent now because, if not, they may as well pack up their bags and say the game is yours.

'We had a spinner, Michael Ruiz, bowling and I said to Brian that any time the batsman misses take the bails, let the umpire decide. So Michael together with another spinner and Brian did the rest, caught behind, bowled or stumped. Any time the batsman missed, quick as a flash the bails were off. We won by eight runs in the end, amazing.'

Size remained an issue though, at least initially, according to former West Indies opening batsman Bryan Davis, who was coaching the Fatima 1st XI at the time.

'He played with the 1st team at thirteen but I had to move him from opening the batting, which he had liked, down the order because he couldn't run with the bigger boys. He was playing with sixteen- and seventeen-year-olds and was tiny for his age as well. I put him down at No. 5 and he made a hundred in the next match without reaching the boundary once.'

The precocious teenager was dreaming big, says Davis, remembering a conversation with him one day after practice.

'He said to me, "Mr Davis, Garry Sobers's world record 365 not out, how come it's lasted so long?" I said, "Because, Brian, you don't bat and play cricket for records, it's not like running races and trying to beat the fastest time. If the circumstances warrant that you can bat in the context of the game and you have the opportunity then you can go for it, but that doesn't happen every day and on top of that the person has to have a tremendous amount of skill, concentration and stamina." He just looked at me in kind of wonderment and said: "I'll break that."'

Lara took this confidence onto his first overseas tour, when he visited Barbados with the Harvard Coaching Clinic. There he crossed paths with future West Indian Test player Carlisle Best. It was an important moment for Lara, says Harvard Head Coach Indar Ramgoolam.

'During the tour we played several two-day games against schools, ending in a match with Ellerslie College. Brian was thirteen and Best was at Ellerslie, working with a group in the school. He saw Brian practising and was shocked by the way this little fella played. Best said, "Well I want to see him play a game" and in that game he scored 76. He was really impressed and was the first high-profile player to single Brian out and say he could really bat, that he was something special. That was really important for Brian.'

Best was so impressed with the teenage Lara that he gifted the youngster a bat.

'From there he came back and just scored runs and runs and the rest is history really,' adds Ramgoolam.

Around this time the adolescent Lara had some choices to make and the first was a sporting one.

Growing up, the year had always been divided neatly between cricket in the dry season (January–June) and football in the wet season (June–December). Lara was brilliant at both. As a footballer he played in midfield or attack but found most success as a skilful and fluent front man – playing as a striker or on either flank. His speed and agility made up for a lack of size, allowing him to ghost past much bigger players, and some standout schoolboy performances saw him recognised with a call-up to the Trinidad and Tobago U14s. Here he played alongside Dwight Yorke and Russell Latapy, two future international stars and lifelong friends who found most club success with Manchester United and Porto respectively. By this time, Lara was already playing in the Santa Cruz men's team and, even at this age, was a pivotal player.

For Brian the looming choice between football and cricket could have been a difficult one, for Bunty it was not.

'Like every youngster, Brian was a lover of football,' said Bunty in a 1987 interview, recalling the inevitable showdown. 'He was also good at it and, although I was not a football lover myself, I always loved to see Brian play it. One Sunday, Brian and his nephew, Marvin Guerra, wanted to go to St Augustine Senior Comprehensive School, where there was a trial to select a national youth football squad to tour Puerto Rico.

'The same day, Harvard's clinic had double-wicket and single-wicket competitions and I told Brian that if he was going to football, count me out, but if he was going to play cricket, count me in. Brian told Marvin to go ahead to the football as he was coming with me to play cricket.'

Harvard coach Ken Franco knows the story well but adds some telling extra detail.

'I seem to remember the only way Brian was going to get anywhere was a lift from Bunty so it narrowed the options a bit,' he smiles. 'But at that time Bunty's thoughts would've been no different to anyone else's, my father was the same. If you had a talented child it would be cricket, only cricket. The attitude was, football, where you going in football? In cricket there was the West Indies team and contracts to be had in England; you knew you could have a career.'

The teenaged, and now cricket-focussed, Lara was also about to be introduced to the most venerable cricket establishment in the country. For Bryan Davis, as well as coaching at Fatima, had a long and ongoing association with Queen's Park Cricket Club (QPCC). He had played for the club, alongside his brother Charlie, for many years and was now chairman of its junior selectors. He liked what he saw in Brian and although his initial approach to Lara's father was politely turned down, a year later the situation was different.

By this time, Brian had made a number of good friends at Fatima College, including Davis's sons Barry and Gregory and David and Michael Carew, the sons of former West Indies batsman Michael 'Joey' Carew. Indeed, the proximity of the Carews' home, in Warren Street, Woodbrook, to Fatima – it was just a short walk away and convenient for study breaks or just socialising – meant Brian had become a regular and warmly welcomed visitor. These friendships contributed to a change of heart.

'I was coming from a match in the country and I drove in and saw Bunty standing underneath the Jeffrey Stollmeyer Stand,' says Davis. 'And he just said, "Mr Davis I spoke to Lara" – he always referred to his son as "Lara" never "Brian" – "about that thing we discussed and he wants to join Queen's Park." I said: "OK, why the change?" He said, "Well he has the Carew brothers here, he has your two sons, and he would really like to play with his friends."'

Joining Queen's Park, though, would not mean any special favours from Davis, who was also a selector for the Trinidad and Tobago U19s. He recalls an incident which suggested it was a team both Bunty and his son felt the fourteen-year-old should already have been a part of.

'I was an U19s selector, I was actually the manager in 1985 and I was picking a team to go to Guyana. This was the first time Brian was going for selection and it was just felt that maybe we should give him another year, let him get a bit bigger. He was fourteen and don't forget he would be playing against the best eighteen- and nineteen-year-olds in the region, it's a big step and he had plenty of time. So we picked the fourteen and then three reserves and he was one of the reserves.

'Well I didn't see him for a while until one day at the Oval with Bunty. I said, "I'm not seeing you here at practice, young man," and he just turned his head away from me. I got the vibes that because he wasn't picked he was annoyed. He didn't say anything to me at all and Bunty now looked a little embarrassed, not really knowing what to say, and just said, "Don't mind he lookin small and that, Lara can play pace." Brian was obviously disappointed but I don't think it was a bad decision.'

Carew and the Queen's Park Cricket Club

The volume of cricket Lara was now playing had dramatically increased. Turning out for Fatima U14s, U16s and U19s, as well as games at QPCC, meant he was often playing six days a week. The continual travelling back and forth between Port of Spain and Cantaro was becoming a strain, but another, more pressing, concern finally led to a major turning point in the young man's life.

Bunty had become worried about the people Brian was socialising with in Santa Cruz, feeling some were questionable characters who might lead his son down the wrong path. That one of these young men was subsequently killed in a shootout with police would tend to validate these concerns. There were numerous family discussions on the matter and, over the course of time, the option of Brian moving to Woodbrook to stay with the Carews on a more permanent basis presented itself. The arrangement was one of natural progression, as the Carews, with whom Brian had regularly stayed and become very close, already viewed him as one of their family.

'He was really friendly with my children, and he stayed at home by us and became part of the family for many many years,' explains Joey Carew.

As well as Lara's friendship with the Carew boys, Joey had begun to take a keen interest in the prodigious young batsman's development. Carew, a left-handed opener who played nineteen Test matches for the West Indies, was renowned as being an ardent student of the game – so much so that he was nicknamed 'Knowledge' by other QPCC members. Beguiled by Brian's talent, Carew took him under his wing.

'I saw the progress he was making; he was very talented, much helped by Harvard Cricket Club,' he said. 'What I liked about Brian was that he loved to look at these [cricket] videos, loved to discuss cricket, and ours was a cricketing family. And then, with his cricket mind and acumen, he could gather so much information so quickly. I recognised that he was going to go places.'

The priceless opportunity of picking the brains of a former Test player was one which Lara relished, adds Tony Gray.

'Brian went to Joey Carew at about fourteen years old and that really helped develop the thinking side of his game. He had had the physical and technical development from one of the best nurseries in the Caribbean, Harvard, and then the explosion of tactical and cricketing knowledge from Joey.'

The atmosphere in Port of Spain was more relaxed than Lara's previous home environment and the youngster began to spread his wings. An interest he developed early on was one for which the Carews held a deep affection – horse racing. At that time racing in Trinidad was rotated among three tracks: the Queen's Park Savannah, Union Park and Arima. The Savannah was closest of these to the Carews' house and the most frequented by the family. Brian soon began to enjoy participating in horse racing's corollary, betting, and not without success it seems. One family member recalls being asked by a teenaged Brian to temporarily look after TT$1,000 he had won at the races.

The biggest influence, though, remained cricketing. The game was the topic of discussion morning, noon and night and visitors to the Carew home would invariably be other cricketers. Being a former international batsman, Carew rubbed shoulders with the region's greats and many passed through his doors; on top of which his boys Michael and David were as enthusiastic about the sport as Brian. At one stage, Michael was even deemed a better prospect than Brian, possessing as he did tremendous footwork and a wonderful eye. QPCC members relate how, the season after Andy Roberts retired from international cricket, the fearsome paceman was bowling at a group of young players at the Queen's Park Oval that included Michael. Showing supreme confidence, Michael stepped out and hit him over long-on for six.

Though this talent ultimately failed to flourish to the degree many predicted, growing up, the game was all-consuming for the three boys. So much so that even if their beloved Oval was closed it didn't stop them. The ground is only locked up completely for three days of the year: Christmas Day, Boxing Day and New Year's Day but, on these occasions, the trio resolved not to be deterred and began their own tradition of scaling the gates, lobbing their kit over and getting inside to practise regardless.

The impact of this fertile cricketing environment was clearly helping Lara's game. As a fourteen-year-old he scored 745 runs for Fatima in the Trinidad and Tobago North Zone Secondary Schools Competition at an average of 126. It wasn't just the volume of runs, but the manner in which he was approaching his cricket, that showed Lara had taken his game to new heights.

'At U16 level we were playing against St Anthony's College and they had a very good side; all we had was Brian really,' says Harry Ramdass. 'I recall the St Anthony's coach saying before the game that the league was theirs. Well, he was reckoning without Brian. What Brian did was amazing. He knew each bowler, each fielder, all their strengths and weaknesses, and used that knowledge to farm the bowling and won the match that way.

'He would hit the ball towards the fielder's left hand knowing he would have to pick it up and turn to throw it back and that would allow time for a single. He thought way ahead. I've never coached another boy like it.'

With a population of just 1.3 million, national news in Trinidad and Tobago can give time to more localised issues, including junior sport. Footage of Secondary Schools cricket is aired on the nightly newscasts alongside the exploits of world sportsmen and reports of it are carried in the national newspapers and on radio broadcasts. Such coverage ensured Lara's name was already becoming known to a broader audience by the time, as a fifteen-year-old, he forced himself into the national U19 team.

The mainstay of competition for the regional U19s is the annual inter-island competition, the Northern Telecom Youth Tournament. In a fortnight of fiercely contested three-day games, Trinidad and Tobago, Jamaica, the Windward Islands, Leeward Islands, Barbados and Guyana vie for regional supremacy. Trinidad and Tobago had finished a disappointing fourth in 1985 but the 1986 competition, also held in Guyana, proved a breakthrough for both Lara and his country.

On 14 March 1986, Lara made his U19 debut playing alongside his fellow Fatima pupil and friend David Carew against Barbados. Footage of him in this match is notable for a number of reasons, most striking of which is the size difference between Lara and his adversaries. He is a boy among men, with the slightness of his shoulders and arms as pronounced as his dearth of inches. This physique affected his boundary count but his natural poise and confidence at the crease, and the grace and fluency of his strokes, are clear for all to see.

Equally evident is his utter despondency when dismissed, drawn out by the spinner and stumped. A huge swipe of the bat as he begins his journey to the pavilion is not petulance but sheer frustration at his error. You can see the mind ticking as he walks back, processing what went wrong and what to do differently next time. There was no similar mistake in the second innings, as an undefeated 23 saw his team home in a drawn game.

Even during the course of a competition of such short duration, Lara visibly matured as a performer, with 61 against bitter rivals Jamaica and a crucial 80 in the final nine-wicket victory against the Windward Islands which clinched the title.

The Jamaica match was one in which another future West Indies player and friend, Jimmy Adams, got his first look at Lara.

'Some of us had been involved in youth cricket for a couple of years and we didn't think much of this kid coming to the wicket. He was only about 4 ft and the pads were literally under his chin. Then he carved us for 60-odd in a very short time. It was a quick introduction to the kind've talent he had.

'As Brian was going back to the pavilion our off-spinner Nehemiah Perry said if this kid was only fifteen, and he just did what he did to us there, that he was going to be around for a long time.'

The following year Lara's influence was even more pronounced when the Northern Telecom was staged in Jamaica. After sixteen days of near continuous cricket, he finished with a tournament record 498

An early taste of leadership as Lara captains the Trinidad and Tobago U19s in the 1988 Northern Telecom Youth Championships.

runs, averaging 62, and Trinidad and Tobago took the title for a second successive year.

Throughout these formative years Lara had been benefiting not only from the environment at the Carews' but also that of the Queen's Park Cricket Club. The club's home, the Queen's Park Oval, has a culture and aura of tradition – more pronounced when Lara first arrived, in the days before the 2007 redevelopment altered the atmosphere of the ground.

'Growing up in the Queen's Park environment Brian was very conscious of the history of cricket in Trinidad and Tobago,' says former West Indies wicketkeeper Deryck Murray. 'You would find most of the Test players came from Queen's Park, or played for them at some time, so he would be very aware that you had the Stollmeyers, Gerry Gomez, Joey Carew, Willie Rodriguez, Charlie and Bryan Davis, myself, etc.'

And these older players were frequently around to give counsel, as Tony Dharson, a former Trinidad and Tobago batsman who played for QPCC 1st team for ten years, recalls.

'Joey Carew, Bryan Davis and Charlie Davis were always around giving advice or telling people about former players and so on. The experience of these men, there was nothing they hadn't seen in a cricket match and any one of us youngsters could sit down and talk to them, they were very open. It was like being in a history lesson being in that dressing room, there was so much to learn for those who wanted to learn. Brian was definitely one that took full advantage of that.'

In any cricketing discussion, Murray says, the young Lara had purpose to his questions.

'He would want to find out: "How old were you when you first played for Trinidad and Tobago?" In hindsight it was then obviously something he set himself to do. "When was the first time Charlie Davis made a hundred?" Right, OK. "Charlie Davis made a hundred at Lord's", OK. And you just felt that, whereas with the average person they would be making conversation, with Brian it was more that he was storing everything up almost as benchmarks for himself.'

This motivation to emulate heroes and set new standards was something many saw in the young Lara.

'At that age he already had records on his mind,' says Dharson. 'I played with a team called Silvermen and hit 213 in the PYM (Progressive Youth Movement) Under 21 League on a ground in Malick, which was a record. A few years later I went back to watch a game and Brian, who was fifteen then, was playing. He was already too good for that league, he was so far ahead of the other players on the field, so I said to him, "Hey, Brian, what you doing down here?" He just said: "I come here to break your record."'

By now Brian had become literally like a son to Joey Carew and could often do little wrong in his eyes. The boys weren't beyond using this to their advantage though, as one story of teenage high-jinks, well known at QPCC, reveals.

'One night, not long after getting their driving licences, Michael and Brian waited for Joey to go to bed and then went out in his car without asking,' says a QPCC member. 'They were hanging out in the bars and nightclubs and then at some stage during the night they crashed the car. So they go home now and it's said that Michael was driving the car but they decide it might be better if Brian owns up to it. So they park up the car, go inside to wake up Joey and face the music. "Hey, Joey, ah bounce [crash] de car nah, ah mash it up and ting, ah sorry bout that," says Brian and they stand there waiting for the storm to burst. But Joey just says, "No, no problem. You don't worry, Brian, I will fix that, anything wrong with you, you hurt?"'

Sobers

In 1987, the seventeen-year-old Lara first met a man who would become a guiding force throughout his career, Sir Garfield Sobers.

Charlie Davis, Bryan Davis's brother and another former West Indies Test player, had followed Lara's career since childhood. When he travelled to watch him participate in the inaugural Sir Garfield Sobers International Schools Competition, at Bridgetown's Kensington Oval, he contacted the great Barbadian all-rounder.

'I recall back in 1987 when he first came to Barbados to play for Fatima and I was at home sitting in my house, about 250 yards from the ground,' says Sobers, '… and this youngster came to my house and he said, "Sir Garry, Mr Davis wants to see you, he has a youngster that he wants you to meet."

'When I got there I was introduced to this young man and he was so excited, he put out his hand, he shook my hand and he said: "You Sir Sobers, you Sir Sobers?" And I said yes and he was introduced to me.'

Watching the match, Sobers quickly appreciated why Davis had been so enthusiastic.

'I saw this young man when he went into bat and believe me you can see all the qualities of greatness … by the way he walked, his approach to the game, you knew that coordination that he had that that was ability, a tremendous amount of ability. That sort of coordination you will only see in geniuses.'

To anyone watching on from the outside world, Lara's progress to this point had been seamless and gave rise to the popular view that it was all down to natural ability alone.

'A lot of people think he was just born a great batsman, I don't think so,' says Tony Gray, who hosts a weekly cricket show on Trinidadian radio. 'His progression followed a logical sequence of positive influences, added to that he played a range of sports which allows you to become athletically gifted and diverse.

'His cricket was varied too: he played pass-out and windball cricket; went to Trinidad's first indoor cricket centre where they used compound balls; played corkball cricket against bigger men on both turf and matting wickets. You talk about all-round cricket education.'

The continuation of that education was ensured when, in September 1987, Lara and Richard Sieuchan were selected for a four-week, TT$21,000, coaching programme at the acclaimed Alf Gover Cricket School, in Wandsworth, London.

Lara's friend and countryman, Belmont-born pace bowler Gray, had by now earned himself a county contract with Surrey and was in England when the two youngsters arrived.

'They were about seventeen at the time and we would hang out a bit,' says Gray before recalling a less happy incident for the new boys abroad.

'During one lunch break from the cricket school Brian and Richard went into Wandsworth to McDonalds. Brian had on a gold chain and was approached by a young man, who asked him if what he had on was gold. Brian said yes and quick as anything the guy swiped the chain and took off. When they told me about it that night I laughed so hard. Coming from Trinidad in those days, the crime situation wasn't as bad as it is now, so he was maybe a little naive.'

Things might not have been going smoothly in the streets of London but Lara was enjoying his time at the Alf Gover Cricket School. Gover, a fast bowler for Surrey and England in the 1930s and 40s, was very much old-school and when he died in 2001, aged ninety-three, the *Guardian's* obituary gave a flavour of the man and his beloved establishment.

'There were four nets, low-beamed and, at one time, gas-lit. Gover was a patrician figure – upright, immaculate, with swept-back silver hair, England sweater pulled down long and usually a silk cravat knotted at his throat. His technical expertise was immense.'

However alien the environment must have been to a teenager from rural Trinidad, it was one in which Lara thrived, as had Gray and other West Indians such as Viv Richards, Andy Roberts and Ian Bishop before him.

'He had plenty of natural ability,' Gover, who presided over the school for nearly half a century, wrote of Lara in the *Cricketer*, 'and we concentrated on enlarging his range of strokeplay.'

By the time he returned to Trinidad and Tobago, Lara was on the cusp of attaining one of his first major ambitions – breaking into the senior Trinidad and Tobago team. It was a goal that would soon be realised.

5 Destiny delayed

In Trinidad and Tobago, a series of trial matches are held between teams of players deemed most likely to form the senior national squad for the upcoming regional season. In the fourth such match leading up to the 1988 campaign, Lara was playing in a team led by former West Indies batsman Larry Gomes, and his path once more crossed that of fast bowler Tony Gray. Gray was in the midst of a successful stint with English county side Surrey, where on a bouncy Kennington Oval wicket he had snared forty-eight wickets at an average of 15.58 in 1987.

'It was my third season with Surrey and by 1987 I was second behind only Richard Hadlee in the county averages,' says Gray. 'So things were going well and I came back with a bit of a reputation. We had a trial game here, at the Queen's Park Oval, that year and I was playing against Brian.'

We sit chatting in the lower tier of the Oval's Carib Stand, overlooking the scene of the duel. Gray, who is an imposing figure even without a ball in his hands, points and gestures regularly as he relives the match.

'I had my fire up, running in from the Gerry Gomez Media Centre End. I was going to show him something. But there he was, this little short-arse eighteen-year-old boy with his left-handed batting, just playing me with ease.' Judging by Gray's facial expressions two decades on, it was a frustrating afternoon's work.

'Let me tell you something, I was running in with everything, boy. I tried yorkers, I tried beamers, I tried everything and this kid was just batting me no problem, angling the ball away, through the gaps. I thought to myself, what the hell is this? I can't remember how many he made and I don't want to know either.'

For the record, not Gray, Lara made 159, including seventeen fours and a six. It was his first century of the trials and he was hailed by the newspapers, not for the first or last time, as 'the country's newest batting sensation'.

'I badly wanted to get a century after missing it in the last trial,' said Lara afterwards. 'I worked hard for it but was a little nervous in the 80s. My mind went back to Gilbert Park [where he made 91] and I was thinking whether I will make it this time. I fought off the feelings and dug in until I reached the target. It was a wonderful feeling and I started looking for the big one, a double century.'

The thirteen-member squad was announced the following day and to nobody's surprise the Fatima schoolboy was in.

Lara made his first-class bow at Guaracara Park on 22 January 1988, against a Leeward Islands side that contained a man with whom he would share a West Indies dressing room for the best part of a decade, fast bowler Curtly Ambrose.

A first innings score of 14 would not seem to suggest major success but Lara had come in when his side was wobbling, at 34 for 3. The youngster showed a calmness which belied his years, contenting himself in occupying the crease for his team and restraining his attacking instincts. That was until one injudicious stroke, against the experienced left-arm spin of former West Indies bowler Elquemedo Willett, proved his undoing.

Mike Gibbes, of Trinidad's *Sunday Guardian*, gives a sense of the clamouring anticipation that had bubbled and built throughout a glittering youth career when he used his match report to issue a cry for sobriety in future Lara assessments.

'Let us be judicious in our praise: if he bats well, let us say so sincerely but if he is guilty of a rash stroke as he was to Willett at Guaracara on

Friday, let us record the fact objectively with the same fidelity as we do his thrilling pyrotechnics on his way to another century … And while we are about it, let us remember that Trinidad and Tobago are not a one-man team.'

It was a game effort by Gibbes but never one which had a realistic chance of success. Indeed, just one week later you could hear the adulatory floodgates creaking ajar as Trinidad and Tobago and Lara squared up to Barbados, a nation famed for its fast bowlers and whose 1988 vintage included Joel Garner and Malcolm Marshall.

Marshall, a friendly and approachable character off the field, was anything but on it. With his bustling, open-chested approach to the wicket, he allied a mastery of both in and away-swing with an unyielding work ethic. His whippy arm-action ensured venomous bouncers at will and though by 1988 he was nearing the end of a glorious career he remained a fearsome adversary. Just a year after this Red Stripe Cup encounter, and at the same venue, he would bowl West Indies to victory over India with 11 for 89.

At the other end, the threat was scarcely less formidable with the 6 ft 8 in Garner, nicknamed Big Bird, renowned for steepling bounce and a toe-crunching yorker.

'It was incredible to see Joel Garner and Malcolm Marshall throw everything at Brian,' says Tony Gray, who also played for Trinidad and Tobago that day. 'Garner and Marshall, two of the great West Indian bowlers, tried their hearts out, it was like a David and Goliath contest and he took everything they had.

'What amazed me was the way he used the face of the bat; he just had the ability to put the ball in the gaps. It's a synchronisation of mind, body and bat and no matter what field Barbados would try to put he found a gap.'

Lara had come to the wicket at 14 for 2, with the ball still new and in the hands of Garner and Marshall. With his side in trouble, he began to rebuild the innings alongside his skipper, Larry Gomes, with a fourth-wicket partnership of 75.

Watchful at first against both opening bowlers, particularly Garner, who was getting the ball to lift and cut away from the left-handers, he later opened up to attack the spinners Hendy Springer and Winston Reid. A pull for four brought up Lara's maiden first-class 50, shortly after Gomes had fallen, and he finished the second day's play on 82 not out.

A century in his second first-class match was not to be, though, and he fell LBW to Garner on the third morning for 92, having been at the wicket for five and three-quarter hours.

'Even though this was the first time Brian was coming up against bowlers of that quality, he was not afraid to play his shots,' says Rohit Balkissoon who, as Trinidad and Tobago's scorer for over twenty-seven years, has enjoyed a privileged view of Lara's rise through the ranks. 'A lot of youngsters coming into a side are reluctant to express themselves but not Brian. And he wasn't out either,' adds the scorer unequivocally. 'People at the ground, and from my vantage point in the scorebox, could see the ball was clearly going down leg-side yet he was still given out LBW.'

It had been a strikingly mature innings, played out in front of dozens of his Fatima College schoolmates in the stands. The knock would prove to be Lara's last contribution to the 1988 senior regional cause, though, as he had been selected to captain the West Indies U19s at the inaugural Youth World Cup in Australia.

Staged mostly at rural venues throughout South Australia and north-western Victoria, the Lara-led West Indians made it to the semi-finals at the Adelaide Oval before falling to a narrow two-wicket defeat to Pakistan. The competition was conspicuous for the number of future Test cricketers who participated. There were fifteen, including future captains in Lara and Jimmy Adams of the West Indies, England's Mike Atherton and Nasser Hussain, Pakistan's Inzamam-ul-Haq, Chris Cairns from New Zealand and Sri Lanka's Sanath Jayasuriya.

As 1988 dawned it is easy to forget that Lara was still a schoolboy, but the demands of his burgeoning cricket career were affecting the youngster's studies.

'In Form 6 he had to leave school early to go to Australia for the U19 World Cup and, with the other cricket demands, it became an extended period of absence which meant he missed virtually all of his last year,' says former teacher and sports coach Harry Ramdass.

'Because he was on national duty, the Ministry of Education offered him the opportunity to repeat that year and complete his studies. But, by that time, he was in the Trinidad and Tobago team and it was obvious he was destined for great things, so cricket took over somewhat. He has told me though he wishes he had come back, just to finish his studies and get his passes.'

The fact that Lara did not see out his time at Fatima College was used as evidence to substantiate one early rumour about him – that he was a poor student. Ramdass refutes this.

'He was average mostly but better than average in Form 5, as he did very well there to get into Form 6. But in Form 6 he never really had the chance to settle down. If you take into account all the time cricket consumed, he was actually a better student than many.

'He had his normal problems as a boy growing up; he missed his work a couple of times and got detention but nothing out of the ordinary. I don't remember any disciplining for rudeness or anything like that.'

Though a newcomer to top-level cricket Lara had been long-touted as not just a future international player but as a future West Indies captain.

'From the age of sixteen or seventeen you could see he had the potential to develop into a really good captain,' says Bryan Davis. 'He also had the desire. I remember saying to him one day that I had a book I would like him to read called *The Art of Captaincy* by Mike Brearley and he said, "I've already read it, Mr Davis."

'He was so good and bright and his cricketing brain was developing. He captained the Trinidad and Tobago U19s marvellously well when he was seventeen and eighteen, then West Indies U19s at the Youth World Cup.'

Captaincy at the Youth World Cup was followed in April 1988 by Lara, still just eighteen, being chosen to lead the West Indies U23s against the touring Pakistanis – a side containing two legendary bowlers in Wasim Akram and Abdul Qadir. In July of that year, as Davis says, he led the Trinidad and Tobago U19s for the last time in the Northern Telecom Tournament. Despite topping the tournament batting with 416 runs, over a hundred more than the next batsman, his team could not

I won't make that mistake again. A teenage Lara ruefully contemplates his dismissal after making 22 against Barbados U19s in July 1988.

repeat the successes of 1986 and 1987 and Barbados deposed the two-time reigning champions.

He continued his development in his first full senior regional season in 1989 by topping the national batting averages and registering his maiden first-class century, 127 in the season opener against Guyana.

Leadership was once more conferred in March 1989, when he captained the West Indies U23s against the touring Indians, and Lara led from the front, scoring 182 (half of which came in boundaries) in a drawn game. The timing of such a big century, against high-profile visitors, could not have been better and supporters clamoured for the youngster, now nineteen, to be given his chance at Test level.

A month later, with West Indies 1-0 up in the three-Test series, he was duly called into the twelve-man squad for the third and final Test at Trinidad's Queen's Park Oval. But, in what would become a familiar pattern, the youngster could not force his way into an established line-up and was given the twelfth-man duties instead. Even so, it was the first time he had been in the Test frame, confirmation that he had caught the selectors' attention and his time was nearing.

Bunty's death

Lara's Test call-up had been met with great jubilation by the Lara family and in particular his father, Bunty. Sadly, that joy was fleeting as, on the evening of the first day of the Test, 15 April 1989, the sixty-two-year-old suffered a heart attack and passed away. A diabetes sufferer, Bunty had had two previous heart attacks, and retired early due to ill health seven years before, but his death was still a massive shock to Brian.

The man who had devoted himself to the pursuit of his son's dreams in such a determined but dignified manner was no longer there to guide him. As a mark of respect the entire West Indies team attended Bunty's funeral, a gesture which touched Brian.

'It was the saddest time of my life,' he said.

The depth of that sadness, on the cusp of achieving what father and son had strived so long and hard to attain, would become apparent in future years as Lara repeatedly evoked Bunty's memory and praised his influence. In 2012, Lara dedicated his ICC Hall of Fame induction to his father, saying he had been moulded by him and given everything he needed to succeed in cricket and in life, even in trying times.

The entire West Indies team attended Bunty's funeral, a gesture that touched Lara deeply. He called it a special tribute to the man who ensured that Brian himself could make such a lasting contribution to cricket.

Returning to cricket a few months later, in October 1989, Lara was once more given the captain's armband, chosen ahead of more experienced players such as Carl Hooper, Clayton Lambert and Tony Gray to lead the Young West Indies, effectively a West Indies 'A' team, on a month-long tour of Zimbabwe. It was a successful trip, in which the tourists were defeated in just one of their ten matches, with Lara notching a century in the first four-day game.

His next appointment was more of a surprise, for on return from Zimbabwe, and in just his third year of regional cricket, Lara was installed as national captain for the 1990 season. At twenty he became Trinidad and Tobago's youngest-ever skipper, and many felt the move had come too soon.

'He was thrown in early because he was a very good batsman and also because he was tactically sound,' says Gray, who played under Lara in that side. 'There was no resentment from the older players, we gave him a chance, but he just wasn't ready. Gus Logie was in the team, Phil Simmons was in the team, there were options.'

Even one of the men who installed Lara is of a similar mind.

'I have to put my hand up here because I was part of the selection committee,' says Bryan Davis. 'Lance Murray [Deryck Murray's father], Vice President of the TTCB, came and objected to it strenuously, saying he was too young. We argued that he was the best choice but in hindsight it was a mistake. It was too much too soon and I think that spoiled his development as a captain to a degree.'

Lara's batting form fell away; he failed to score a fifty all season and finished with an average of 22. His first stint as skipper had ended winless and saw Trinidad and Tobago finish bottom of the regional standings but he bristled at the suggestion that the captaincy was to blame.

'I was captain of several teams before that and always got runs, and no one ever said it was too much for me then. It was just a matter of having a bad trot like all batsmen have.'

Trinidad and Tobago did regroup sufficiently to give the youngster some taste of success in an otherwise desperate campaign, when they triumphed in the Geddes Grant Shield one-day competition.

Just six weeks later, Lara was reminded of sport's fickle nature when playing for a West Indies Board President's XI against the visiting England team. England had just taken a surprise 1-0 lead in the Test series and brought a full-strength side to Guaracara Park for the clash. Lara says he dreamt beforehand he would score a century and, having not passed 45 against inter-island opposition in eight attempts that year, proceeded to rattle up 134 against the tourists.

'It was a brilliant innings,' says Trinidad and Tobago scorer Balkisson, who recorded Lara's knock that day. 'As I sat there next to the English scorer, Malcolm Ashton, I asked him: "What do you think about that little boy there?" He told me: "That little boy will be one of the greatest Test players in the world." I'll never forget it. He hadn't seen him before but that was how impressed he was by that innings.'

The performance saw Lara back in the West Indies squad for the 3rd Test but once again he lost out in the final cut as the selectors stuck with what they knew and chose his compatriot Gus Logie in the starting XI. Logie would also be the man to replace him as Trinidad and Tobago skipper in 1991, but before that regional season could get under way, another opportunity to break into the West Indian side presented itself on the Pakistan tour.

A top-order spot had become available when Viv Richards opted to stay home in Antigua to recuperate from surgery. Lara was at the head of the queue and got his long-desired first taste of full international cricket when he made his debut in the opening one-day contest.

As baptisms go it could hardly have been more intimidating. In front of a partisan 25,000-capacity crowd at Karachi's National Stadium, Lara emerged to a cauldron of noise to face one of the fastest bowlers in the world, Waqar Younis. With firecrackers exploding and the home fans roaring him in on a wave of sound, Younis – famed for his vicious late-swinging yorkers – was in the midst of a match-winning spell. Lara made 11 before falling LBW to the irrepressible paceman, who bagged five wickets and the Man of the Match award in Pakistan's victory. The youngster was summarily dropped for the next two ODIs and likewise overlooked for the first two Test matches; in favour of Carlisle Best and Gus Logie.

He did his best to advance a case for selection by hitting 139 against a Pakistan XI in a warm-up game before the 3rd Test. However, even with Richards's absence and Best having a miserable time with the bat (he averaged 9.7 in the one-day series and a meagre 5.5 in the first two Tests), it would require a stroke of fortune, or misfortune depending on how you view it, to see Lara make his Test debut. Had Best not sustained a fielding-practice injury prior to the match, splitting the webbing of his right hand, Lara still would not have played.

In the event he did and, batting at No. 5, came in for his first Test match innings at Lahore's Gaddafi Stadium on 6 December 1990. The West Indies were 37 for 3 and with the three-match series tied at 1-1 it was a decisive period of play. In such a position, with the Pakistanis' tails up, strength of character was needed and that was precisely what was provided by Lara and his fourth-wicket partner Carl Hooper. The two combined for a two-and-a-half hour, ninety-five-run stand, resolutely defying a Pakistani bowling line-up featuring four celebrated names in Imran Khan, Wasim Akram, Waqar Younis and Abdul Qadir. Lara finally fell to Qadir for 44 and even though it would take Hooper's magnificent 134 to make the game safe, the young Trinidadian had proved himself capable at the highest level.

Returning from Pakistan, Lara went on to enjoy a stellar season in the Red Stripe Cup, breaking the competition record for most runs with 627 at an average of nearly 70. Unfortunately the record would last barely a week as Desmond Haynes scored over 200 runs in Barbados's last game against Jamaica to usurp it and establish a new mark of 654 runs.

All the same, the richness of Lara's form shone bright, and a century and six half-centuries in ten regional innings demonstrated remarkable consistency; added to which he had handsomely outscored all his challengers for the West Indies middle-order batting positions. It appeared that the selectors had heeded this evidence when he was called into the West Indies squad for the 1st Test against the touring Australians in Jamaica. But he again failed to make the starting XI and was overlooked for the remainder of the series as well.

'To my dismay, I was named as twelfth man,' said Lara. 'That killed my spirits. I didn't know what I had to do to impress the selectors.'

That the West Indies triumphed 2-1 in an ill-tempered series could be said to vindicate the selectors' judgement, but it did little to appease Lara's mounting frustration or the disquiet growing amongst a Trinidadian public that eyed his continued exclusion with suspicion.

Accusations of inter-island and selectorial bias loiter close to the surface of Caribbean cricket and pop their heads above water at any given opportunity. It was now perceived that an ageing Richards, the only captain under whom West Indies never lost a series, was keeping Lara out of the team until he retired.

Veteran Trinidadian sports journalist Everard Gordon explains why he feels this was the case.

'Once Viv Richards was around, Lara wasn't getting a run in the Test team because Richards recognised Lara's Achilles heel, he wasn't a team man, he was selfish. There was only one thing Brian Lara was concentrating on and that was Brian Lara. If this worked for the team, well cheers, if it didn't, then it didn't. He was a selfish player; he wanted to do well for himself first and foremost, that was Brian's attitude and Richards didn't want that.'

Jimmy Adams, who played fifty-four Test matches for the West Indies, is less sure.

'I've never seen anything to suggest that [Richards was keeping Lara out]; I think it was more to do with the fact that the team was winning. Statistically some of the batsmen might not have kept their places in a losing team but that wasn't the case.

'It was frustrating for Brian. I think he did something like twenty-seven or twenty-eight Test matches as twelfth man carrying the towel. I don't think there was any doubt he was good enough but the team was winning and the selectors were happy to keep things as they were.'

Whatever the truth of the situation, it would come to a head on the West Indies 1991 tour of England. The tour would witness Lara's growing dissatisfaction – especially given the assurances he had been given over his selection pre-tour – escalate to confrontation. The flashpoint came in an innocuous net session at Warwickshire's Edgbaston nets, prior to the 4th Test of the five-match series, when Richards struck a ball firmly back to Lara. He jumped out of the way but landed awkwardly on his ankle. The incident came late in a long tour and one on which the twenty-two-year-old left-hander had once more been passed over for Test selection. He had had enough.

While his twisted ankle was being attended to he told tour manager Lance Gibbs – the greatest West Indian off-spinner of all time – that he wanted to go home. The statement was less about injury and more about frustrated ambition. Two years on from being named in his first squad, he had played just the lone Test match against Pakistan. Lara's overriding life goal had been to play for the West Indies and he was eager to progress to what he, and many others, believed to be his destiny. His level of self-belief was such that, by this point, he felt he deserved to be in the side or at the very least given the opportunity to stake a claim. But for a number of selectors and established players this self-confidence manifested as arrogance and they felt he should accept his place in the pecking order.

One of Trinidad and Tobago's other favourite sons, famed calypsonian and ardent cricket fan David Rudder, has a view on this aspect of Lara's character.

'People say he's arrogant. What I say is that you have to be, otherwise you cannot become what you can become. It's like describing Lara as arrogant because he can change his mind in mid-shot and play another stroke before the ball comes, or Viv Richards, walking out and hitting the first ball for four. Arrogance or supreme confidence in your own ability?

'Having that sort of confidence always sets you apart from others because other people are normally insecure. So when people criticise you a lot of the time what you're facing is them feeling challenged by you. It's a reflection of them,' says the man who penned the cricketing anthem and crowd favourite 'Rally Round the West Indies', which is played before each West Indies international.

Lara was now enduring what he described as 'the most miserable period of my life', a situation not helped by his interactions with the team manager and some senior teammates. The relationship with Gibbs had been strained almost from the start of the trip, after a confrontation in an Indian restaurant in which Lara felt he had been belittled for his batting style and saying he would like to emulate Garry Sobers. The youngster largely steered clear of Gibbs thereafter and his dealings with some of the West Indians' star names were not much better.

'I felt I tried to have as much respect as I could for the senior players but didn't think some of them showed the younger ones much respect back,' said Lara. 'One of them had made a remark at practice which implied I got into the side because Joey Carew was a selector.'

Lara left the tour and the series, which West Indies and England shared 2-2, with his strained ankle ligaments in plaster and his bruised ego smouldering.

Around this time, there was a growing perception that Lara's attacking style meant he would become a star more suited to the one-day game than the longer format. Lara himself has always cherished Test cricket as the ultimate challenge but he wasn't going to eschew any opportunity to impress in West Indies colours and did just that at the 1992 World Cup in Australia and New Zealand.

He was almost alone in impressing in a disappointing West Indian campaign, as they finished sixth out of nine teams in the first round and were eliminated – despite Lara having scored 333 runs, at an average of 48. But he had finally done enough to secure his long-sought elevation to the Test team – helped by the fact that amongst others Richards had retired and Logie and Hooper were injured. It meant that Lara and Richards had appeared in just one West Indies international together, the 3rd ODI in England in 1991.

His return to the Test team, for what would now become an extended stay, came in April 1992 when the West Indies hosted South Africa for their historic first Test following two decades of cricketing isolation. The choice of opponent, after the abandonment of apartheid, was no mere coincidence of course, and the 'one-off' game in Barbados was loaded with political and racial undercurrents.

'We did not like the implication of losing to them, of all nations, as we had always felt supported by many black Africans,' said Lara, who also revealed the impact of Nelson Mandela on his childhood.

'I was aware of Nelson Mandela through my parents in the 70s when I was a kid. He was a revered figure. I had a very good understanding of what he stood for as a child. The rebel tours by West Indian sides in the late 70s and 80s were also a significant part of my understanding of what was happening in South Africa.'

The first issue facing the match though was one born of more parochial antipathies. The Barbadian public, upset that their own Anderson Cummins had not been selected for the West Indian side, elected to boycott the match in protest. It made for a peculiar Kensington Oval atmosphere but one which led to the foundation of the West Indies' most popular and enduring supporters' group, the Trini Posse.

'We were virtually the only people in the ground,' recalls Trini Posse founding member Nigel Camacho, who was in attendance with around forty friends. 'We had gone with all our regalia and our flags and were determined to have fun, so we were making plenty of noise and playing our music. The following day a newspaper came out and underneath a picture of us the caption read something like: "The boycotted Test match … except for the Trini Posse". That's where the name came from, we liked it and so it stuck; the Trini Posse was born,' adds Camacho, who is also a QPCC management committee member and staunch Lara fan.

Despite the unusual situation in the stands, the match itself turned into an epic, with South Africa dominating the first four days and finishing the fourth on 122 for 2, needing just another 79 for victory. If they succeeded it would be the West Indians' first defeat at the Kensington Oval since 1935, a proud fifty-seven-year record.

That night Lara was out having a quiet drink in Bridgetown when he ran into some South African players doing the same. He warned them not to drink too much as they would all be batting in the morning, an idea which was laughed off. The routinely superb Curtly Ambrose and Courtney Walsh combined to make a reality of Lara's taunt, though, instigating a South African collapse of spectacular proportions.

From the start of play on the fifth and final day, the tourists lost their last eight wickets for just twenty-six runs. They were bowled out twenty minutes before lunch for 148, handing victory to the West Indies by the improbably comfortable margin of fifty-two runs.

For Lara the victory was especially sweet as it marked the successful end of an agonisingly long seventeen-month wait between his first and second Test matches. Many had shared his exasperation during that hiatus but Jimmy Adams says the situation had actually laid the foundations for what was to come.

'I think that without the West Indies selectors planning this, they inadvertently created a genius. Because he began his career believing he had time to make up. Make up he did.'

6 Arriving in style

The West Indies arrived in Australia in 1992 almost unrecognisable from the team which had contested the series between the traditional foes less than two years before in the Caribbean, and the changes were not lightweight tinkering. Gone were four of the giants of the West Indian game whose careers had run as a constant throughout the previous two decades: the incomparable 'Master Blaster' Viv Richards; one of cricket's finest openers in Gordon Greenidge; the premier fast bowler of the 1980s and arguably of all time, Malcolm Marshall; and the best wicketkeeper-batsman ever produced in the Caribbean, Jeffrey Dujon.

Finding substitutes for such great and established players would not be easy, and a poor showing under new captain Richie Richardson at the 1992 World Cup did not augur well. The cracks in the West Indians' previously unquestionable supremacy were beginning to splinter and deepen and – to paraphrase Winston 'Gypsy' Peters's classic calypso – while the ship was not yet sinking it was certainly beginning to reel and groan.

If this was the end of an era, a changing of the guard, then at least some of the youngsters being asked to step up showed substantial promise: players like Brian Lara, Curtly Ambrose and Jimmy Adams. All the same, the Aussies scented blood and a chance for retribution after the punishment meted out to them at the hands of the West Indian quicks in recent years. In the event, it would turn out to be one of the great series – not that the first two Tests were indicative of that.

The West Indies escaped from the first, in Brisbane, with a draw. Set 231 for victory, nearing lunch on the final day, they slumped to 9 for 4 and eventually clawed their way to 133 for 8 at the close. Fast bowlers Ian Bishop and Courtney Walsh were the unlikely batting heroes at the end but, in all probability, the fifty-five minutes' play lost to a freak hailstorm on the third day had been the true saviour.

Clashes between Australia and West Indies have produced some of cricket's classic moments but they have also witnessed a number of fractious exchanges down the years and Lara found himself at the centre of one such controversy during this 1st Test.

'Healy fumbled a leg side stumping off Matthews but then knocked the wayward ball back towards the stumps, Lara was still short of his ground and umpire Prue ruled him out,' reported Wisden. 'Television replays showed the wicketkeeper's glove, not the ball, had dislodged the bails, and Healy later said he had told the umpire as much.'

West Indians everywhere scented Antipodean subterfuge and the incident sparked a long-running assertion that Lara was on the wrong end of too many borderline and outright incorrect umpiring decisions, particularly in Australia.

Everard Gordon, who coached Lara as a young boy at Harvard Cricket Coaching Clinic, was so taken by the impassioned and continued espousal of the theory that, nearing the end of Lara's career, he conducted an analysis of all the perceived injustices.

'I have a lot of records and accounts of cricket and there was so much agitation about this that I started doing research into it,' says the journalist, who has been writing for the *Trinidad Guardian* for nearly twenty-five years and who once played professional cricket in England's Lancashire leagues for Todmorden. 'I got up to nineteen occasions that I could testify that he was unfairly given out but, so what, Bradman must've got a lot of them, so must Len Hutton or Sachin Tendulkar, any one of those, that's just the way the game is. My feeling is that Lara just got his share but since he was a West Indian we saw it more as a thing against us as a region. If it had happened to Tendulkar, for instance, we wouldn't make a big fuss about it but because it was Lara it was a big deal.'

Injustice or not, any hope the West Indies might have gained from their 1st Test escape evaporated in the second where Australia secured a 139-run victory, seizing the lead and the initiative in the five-match series. The game at the Melbourne Cricket Ground had been won by Shane Warne, just one year on from his Test debut, who ripped through the tourists' second innings, taking 7 for 52.

Five days later the teams rejoined battle in the 3rd Test at the historic and atmospheric Sydney Cricket Ground, where the West Indians held a miserable record; eight defeats in eleven Tests and a solitary win some sixty-two years before in 1930/31, in the sepia-tinted days of Don Bradman, George Headley and Learie Constantine.

Australia began in Sydney where they had left off in Melbourne – on top. Posting a formidable 503 for 9 declared in their first innings the West Indian reply was soon faltering and, when ageing opener Desmond Haynes was bowled by off-spinner Greg Matthews early on the third morning, they were 32 for 2. At the midway point of the match and series West Indies were 1-0 down and 471 runs adrift. Losing at Sydney would mean going two behind and, with just two matches remaining, no chance of winning the series. This was exactly the type of situation in which Lara revelled.

In the second over of the third day, Lara's boyishly slight figure walked across an outfield made lush by unseasonably persistent rain to join his captain Richie Richardson at the crease. His team was still 271 runs from avoiding the follow-on.

If he was nervous he didn't show it. Batting in an open-faced maroon helmet and facing a bowling attack spearheaded by the pace and aggression of Craig McDermott and Merv Hughes and supported by the spinners Warne and Matthews, Lara was soon into his stride.

'I had just watched two days of batting and to me the Australians seemed pretty comfortable with the pitch,' he said. 'I didn't want to put myself under any undue pressure, and I decided to go out and bat as confidently as I could regardless of the position we were in.'

He did just that. Displaying the composure of a seasoned master rather than a batsman feeling his way into a Test career, Lara executed a series of fluently timed strokes: back-foot drives and cuts; sweeps and paddles to leg off the spinners; slashing square cuts and pulls off the fast men; and exquisite front-foot cover drives off both. The Lara confidence, noted since childhood, was being transferred to the international stage for all to see.

When he had reached 35, the slate-grey skies which shrouded the ground throughout the match broke and rain forced the players from the field. In the dressing room, he took a phone call from Sir Garfield Sobers, who had recognised the potential for something special to develop. Sobers told him simply: 'This is your day, son. Just keep on batting.'

Lara too had sensed his form was something out of the ordinary, saying, '… there was hardly a false shot. I was amazed at my timing and stroke-play from the very start.'

As he passed 50, Lara had a look of intent already well known to bowlers on the Caribbean regional circuit.

'He has a level of concentration that I have not seen in anyone else,' says former West Indies leg-spinner Dinanath Ramnarine. 'You play against Brian in table tennis, football or anything and there is an intensity there; he doesn't want to lose at anything. Mentally he gets into a zone and you're in trouble when he does.'

McDermott bounded in brandishing the war paint, a thick stripe of zinc cream daubed across nose and upper cheeks, de rigueur for 1990s fast bowlers. Any width was punished but some deliveries, not discernibly errant, were crunched away with similar disdain. Different angles of attack were tried, with the quickies coming round the wicket attempting to angle deliveries into Lara's body and tuck him up for room; it didn't work.

The spinners were having no more luck. Sydney is a traditional spinners' wicket, but the expected turn had been negated by damp conditions and Lara would say later that the track amounted to a 'batsman's paradise'.

The young Trinidadian's scoring rate was outstripping that of his captain and, as he turned Warne down behind square-leg for the single that registered his first Test match hundred, Richardson was on 82. Batting in his trademark broad-brimmed maroon sunhat, Richardson warned Lara not to lose his concentration, telling the youngster to take the opportunity to score heavily to make up for the inevitable dry spells in the future.

Lara heeded the advice and the partnership grew, building to record-breaking and, in terms of the series, momentum-shifting proportions. As the stand passed 217, it became the best for the West Indies for any wicket in Australia. Frequent rain delays, as squally showers swept in and forced the players from the field, failed to disturb Lara's concentration and at the end of the day's play he was 121 not out, with Richardson unbeaten on 94.

The fourth day brought no respite for the Australians as Lara moved up a gear. Playing with renewed determination he put the pressure firmly back onto the Australian bowlers. If anything his timing had got better and everything fractionally short, from fast or slow bowler, was pulled away with aplomb. His shots seemed gloriously carefree but they were not careless.

Australian captain Allan Border, who, on the game's second day, had become the second player in history, after Sunil Gavaskar, to pass 10,000 Test match runs, cast a bemused figure. He frequently stood with hands on hips, as the boundaries flowed, seemingly at a loss as to how to combat the young West Indian.

'It was just a phenomenal knock, for a bloke who's so young to show that maturity,' he said later. 'He was just relentless in that he never hit the ball over the top. You feel that when you get well into the hundreds you start looking to hit over the top. He never did. Just for sheer crisp hitting of the ball into the gaps, it was as good as you'd ever want to see.'

The placement noted by Border was evidenced in a number of back-foot drives from straight deliveries. Instead of playing them back from whence they came, through the 'V' either side of the bowler in the conventional manner, Lara angled them through the covers, piercing the gaps and picking up fours.

With Richardson playing a supporting role, Lara brought up his 150 with a crunching square drive off Matthews. Off the field Matthews was friendly with Lara and was the man who, according to West Indian cricket commentator and writer Tony Cozier, gave Lara the moniker of 'The Prince of Port of Spain' following a night out in the Trinidad and Tobago capital during the Australians' 1991 Caribbean tour.

By the time Richardson departed, having made 109, the score had reached 324 for 3 and the partnership had contributed a match-saving 293 runs. The West Indies skipper said later that it had been hard concentrating on his own batting whilst admiring Lara's.

The only disappointment at the SCG was the crowd: registering 83,115 over the course of the match this meant the grand old stadium was barely a third full each day. The inclement conditions were blamed but one who *was* present was Sir Garfield Sobers, and this was a compliment in itself, according to one former Australian captain. Ian Chappell revealed that while Sobers may have been one of cricket's great all-rounders he was not one of its great watchers and yet, so captivating was Lara's innings, he remained transfixed, watching every ball.

After the fall of Richardson, Lara's progress continued unabated and at 185 not out he passed his highest score in first-class cricket. Shortly afterwards he recorded his first-ever double century when he deflected a Warne leg-break fine. He completed his third run to register the landmark, raising his bat and helmet high in triumph in what would become a familiar celebration in years to come.

'I felt elated being out there defying the Australians and coming up with my best ever performance at such a much-needed time,' he said.

The full repertoire had come out: a dismissive slog sweep off Warne for four and two back-foot smacks over midwicket for further boundaries were allied to fine sweeps and imperious cover drives.

The lights of the scoreboard burned brightly in the overcast conditions and flashed up records, both approaching and passed, as Lara batted on. At 227 he claimed the highest score for the West Indies against Australia, surpassing Gordon Greenidge's 226; at 257 he registered the highest first-class score by a West Indian in Australia. Still over a hundred runs short

Turning a series on its head. The twenty-three-year-old displays class and determination to score 277, his first Test century, against Australia at Sydney in 1993.

of Sir Garfield Sobers's Test match record, that was precisely the target now on his mind.

'I had never felt so much in control of an innings, and when I passed 250 I started counting down to Sir Garry's record of 365,' said Lara.

Nor was Lara looking tired, as he continued to display terrific footwork, getting into position to time shots perfectly. He advanced down the track to Matthews, turning one delivery into a half-volley, whipping into it against the spin and thumping the ball through wide mid-on for another boundary.

The twenty-three-year-old had been batting with calmness and authority for nearly eight hours when suddenly, and surprisingly, it was all over. In retrospect it ended in the only way which seemed possible, run out.

The young Trinidadian rocked back as he had dozens of times throughout his innings and played Matthews effortlessly into the covers, setting off as he struck the ball with a nonchalant 'yeah' to his partner

Carl Hooper. He was a third of the way down the wicket, accelerating for the single, when he got a hollow sensation in the pit of his stomach. Hooper, who hadn't been backing up, wasn't running either. Lara skittered to a halt across the dark brown wicket, turned to sprint back and dived despairingly for the crease, but Damien Martyn's accurate whipped throw from cover to wicketkeeper Healy found him short of his ground. Prostrate, he looked forlornly to the square-leg umpire and saw him slowly raise his finger.

In Trinidad at least, the unfortunate Hooper would become as well known for this incident as for anything he did with a bat or ball. But such was the alacrity of the pick-up and release by Martyn it would have been a tight run even if Hooper had been committed to it.

Regardless, Lara, who had fallen just twenty-three runs short of a triple hundred, walked off to a standing ovation. His 277 was the highest score ever between Australia and the West Indies (beating Doug Walters's 242 in 1968/69) and the fourth highest maiden century in Test match history.

The manner in which he accelerated on the fourth day was shown by the fact that he outscored his three batting partners by more than two to one; while he rattled up 156 runs they mustered just 74 between them.

The appreciation for Lara's innings was immediate and universal. Tony Cozier said it was of 'such all-round brilliance that it is inconceivable anyone could ever have batted better for so long'. The great Guyanese batsman, and former West Indies skipper, Rohan Kanhai, called it 'one of the greatest innings I've ever seen. Back foot, front foot, timing, placement, against spin bowlers and fast bowlers alike, he was marvellous.'

The knock was greeted with equal delight from the Australian press, with the *Adelaide Advertiser*'s Rod Nicholson calling it 'one which, in this modern era, may never be seen again'.

Kirk Perreira, writing in Trinidad's *Daily Express*, took a slightly different approach though in a column entitled: 'Brian Who? Now They Know', where he lambasted Trinbagonians in particular for displaying apparent surprise at the innings.

'He always had it and followers of the game know that. There is no doubt in my mind that in a matter of time the world will be hailing the boy

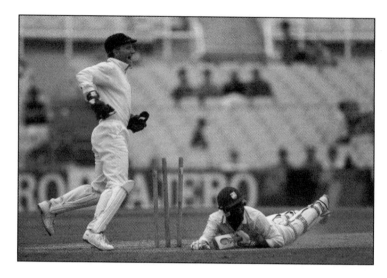

The end of a 'gem'. Run out just twenty-three short of a triple hundred, by Australian wicketkeeper Ian Healy, in what Lara still regards as his finest innings – so good he named his daughter Sydney after it.

from Santa Cruz as one of the best ever, maybe of all time,' said Perreira, and finished by urging people to '… stop lauding his achievements as if it was the least expected thing from him. Bat on "Bri Bri".'

The Trinidad and Tobago Cricket Board of Control (TTCBC) even established a fund for Lara, through which grateful citizens could demonstrate their admiration for the young batsman by monetary donations. The account number to which people could donate: 728-277-5.

Lara himself called the innings 'a gem'. Much to his chagrin he later mislaid his Sydney bat but when asked, in June 2007, by former England bowler Angus Fraser, whether he had a memento of his epic innings he replied: 'Yes, my daughter.' So special was the innings to Lara that he named the daughter he has with Trinidadian model Leasel Rovedas in memory of it.

'I scored my first century in Sydney and persuaded a young lady by the name of Leasel Rovedas to name our first daughter Sydney,' said Lara in 2009. 'She fought for a little bit but I think she understood the importance of that century.'

However it was viewed, it led to a total of 606 and ensured the 3rd Test would be drawn, halting the Australian impetus and reinvigorating a West Indian side that had been flagging.

'The team spirit and our performance sky-rocketed after the Sydney Test,' said Lara. 'Everyone seemed very focussed and was not just looking forward to levelling the series but winning it.'

The West Indies took this renewed self-belief into the one-day arena and claimed the Benson & Hedges World Series 2-0, in the best of three final, against hosts Australia. Lara scored 67 and 60, opening the innings in both games, which were sandwiched between the 3rd and 4th Tests. The victories helped reinforce the tourists' momentum as the teams headed to the Adelaide Oval.

Confidence soaring and swagger returned, the West Indies won a compelling and unusually low-scoring contest at one of the world's most picturesque grounds. When Craig McDermott gloved a Courtney Walsh lifter through to wicketkeeper Junior Murray, in a scene that is beloved of television rain delay shows, the West Indies had won by one run. It remains the narrowest victory since Test cricket began in 1877.

Ambrose was instrumental in the Adelaide victory, where he took ten wickets, and was even more so in clinching the series at Perth. The pacey, bouncy WACA pitch was ideally suited to the 6 ft 7in Ambrose, whose miserly, aggressive lines of attack produced the spell of his life. His seven wickets for one run, in thirty-two deliveries, destroyed the Australians' first innings just after lunch on the opening day. The home side never recovered and lost the game by an innings and twenty-five runs and with it the Frank Worrell Trophy 2-1.

The series would go down as one of cricket's classics and there was little doubt in anyone's mind as to where and when the balance of power had shifted.

'It [Lara's 277] drastically altered the course of a series that was slipping away from his team,' said Wisden in 1994.

Lara himself recognised it as a defining innings.

'There are moments in any sportsman's life when he realises he has reached new heights and it happened for me on that overcast day in Sydney.'

7 Seizing Sobers's crown

Lara's 277 in Sydney heralded his arrival as an international batsman of the highest class, and he enhanced that standing on the return journey to the Caribbean. Having left Australia, the West Indies stopped off in South Africa for a triangular one-day series with the Proteas and Pakistan.

The impetus built up Down Under proved unstoppable and the West Indies emerged victorious with Lara, performing predominantly as an opener, named Man of the Series for his 341 runs, including two centuries, at an average of 68.

He arrived home to vastly increased media demands but his superb run of form continued against Pakistan, now touring the Caribbean in what was billed as an unofficial world championship clash. Imran Khan, captain of Pakistan's 1992 World Cup winning team, fanned the flames by proclaiming that his side would depose the West Indians as Test match kings.

The five-match one-day series was drawn 2-2 after the fifth – at Guyana's charmingly old-fashioned and fondly recalled Bourda Ground – was declared a tie following a final-ball pitch invasion by over-exuberant West Indian fans celebrating victory with play still live.

Lara had again shone in the shortened format, hitting 114 in the first match at Kingston's Sabina Park (his third one-day century in five innings) and followed up, three days later, with 95 not out at Trinidad's Queen's Park Oval.

Controversy raged in the lead-up to the 1st Test as four Pakistani players – Wasim Akram, Waqar Younis, Mushtaq Ahmed and Aqib Javed – were arrested for constructive possession of marijuana. Enraged, Pakistan threatened to cancel the tour and the situation was only finally defused by a placatory letter from the West Indies Cricket Board of Control apologising for any embarrassment, but not before the Port of Spain Test had to be postponed for twenty-four hours.

In that match, Lara was closing in on one of his dreams, a Test century on his home ground, when, for once, things did not go his way. He was on 96 and in the last over of the second day with a packed and partisan Oval crowd behind him. Facing the occasional left-arm spin of Asif Mujtaba, Lara was determined to make his hundred before close of play. The bowler floated a delivery wide outside his off stump, which Lara, deciding this was not the ball to attack, attempted to pad away; it bit, turned sharply, ricocheted off the left-hander's back leg and rolled onto the stumps. It would be one of the rare occasions Lara would perish in the nervous 90s.

In the end, the Test series proved far less competitive than anticipated, with the West Indies winning 2-0 and only rain in Antigua preventing a probable whitewash. The West Indies and Pakistan would clash again in the final of the Pepsi Champions Trophy, in Sharjah, in November, and the West Indians triumphed once more, thanks largely to an exhilarating run-a-ball 153 from Lara. He followed this up with another Man of the Series performance in Sri Lanka a month later, rounding off a wonderful twelve months.

The runs continued to flow at the start of 1994 as Lara reclaimed his Red Stripe Cup record with 715 runs, averaging 79.44 and scoring three centuries in the process. A brilliantly compiled 180, against Jamaica at the Queen's Park Oval, stood out above all others.

In a reflective of six of Lara's best innings, conducted by Wisden Asia Cricket in June 2003, Trinidadian journalist Fazeer Mohammed selected this knock as his favourite, saying, 'his virtuoso performance in front of a couple of hundred diehards will live long in the memory of those who had the privilege of seeing it … One stroke – where he advanced down the pitch and hoisted [Courtney] Walsh over extra-cover for six – typified his dominance.'

Lara, restored to the national captaincy, had come to the wicket at 38 for 2 on the first day and so intelligently did he rotate the strike, and so well did he bat, that only nineteen runs were scored by his partners while he struck twenty-four fours and two sixes in his 180. It came out of a Trinidad and Tobago total of 257; 70 per cent of the team's runs had come off Lara's blade.

The first international series of the year was the visit of Mike Atherton's England and Lara was eyeing it eagerly. Keen to build on his 1993 performances, a weak English team seemed likely to provide him with an opportunity to record his first Test century in the Caribbean, and perhaps more.

In a pre-series interview, Lara acknowledged his performances against Australia and to a lesser extent Pakistan but announced, ominously for the tourists, that it was time for real runs to flow including a minimum of two centuries.

Those runs did not flow in the one-day series, won by the West Indies 3-2, with only 112 in five games but it was always the Tests upon which Lara had been focussed. In the first, at Jamaica's Sabina Park, he hit 83 in a comfortable eight-wicket West Indian victory. The second, at Guyana's Bourda, went to the home side as well, by the even more emphatic margin of an innings and forty-four runs. Lara starred, top-scoring with an innings of 167, during which he passed 1,000 runs in Test cricket and notched the first of his predicted two centuries.

In the 3rd Test, at Port of Spain's Queen's Park Oval, a second innings blitzkrieg from Curtly Ambrose and Courtney Walsh routed the English for just 46 (the second lowest total in their history and worst for over a hundred years). Ambrose and Walsh bowled unchanged, returning the extraordinary figures of 6 for 24 and 3 for 16 respectively, to set up the win; 3-0 and the series was gone.

'In that hour the series was lost and our dream was shattered by an astonishing spell of fast bowling by Curtly Ambrose,' wrote Atherton in his autobiography *Opening Up*.

Bowling full on a wearing pitch, Ambrose struck with the first delivery of the England second innings, pinning Atherton LBW with a ball nipping back. The England skipper, who watched his side go two wickets down shortly after returning to the dressing room, explained the rapidity with which the tourists then folded.

'I retired to the shower and when I emerged we were six wickets down, our innings in tatters and the series effectively over.'

Centuries in both innings from Alec Stewart, and eight first innings wickets for England's tireless workhorse Angus Fraser, gave the tourists a much-needed 208-run victory, albeit a consolation one, in the 4th Test at the Kensington Oval. The West Indies' proud fifty-nine-year unbeaten record at Bridgetown had fallen, and much of the criticism was levelled at Lara for the manner of his second innings dismissal. Many observers felt that, with the West Indies in trouble and needing a responsible innings, he had played a rash shot to be dismissed for 64.

There was little time for England to celebrate as back-to-back Tests meant the fifth and final game was scheduled to start at the Antigua Recreation Ground (ARG) just three days later.

Unbeknown to England, Lara had set out his stall for at least a hundred in the game and the criticism received for his Barbados dismissal only served to steel the youngster's resolve.

'I had one until then, an 80, a couple of 50s, but I never really went on to get another hundred,' he reflected later. 'I thought that this was the match that I had to fulfil that.'

With Desmond Haynes (finger) and Richie Richardson (hamstring) both ruled out through injury, the home side were forced into changes and, having won the toss and opted to bat, their openers Phil Simmons and Stuart Williams were soon back in the pavilion. At 12 for 2, and with the Bridgetown result fresh in the mind, the momentum had seemingly swung back in England's favour. But the premature demise of the West

Indies opening pair, on an easy-paced pitch, merely afforded Lara the opportunity to construct a major innings.

He began watchfully, alongside Jimmy Adams, with the pair intent on eking the home side away from danger. A supine surface and the English attack's lack of hostile pace meant Lara soon dispensed with his open-faced helmet, replacing it with a simple maroon West Indies cap. It took him over two and a half hours to bring up his 50, which he did with a four through midwicket off Graeme Hick's off-breaks. It was pedestrian progress by Lara's standards.

The partnership continued to build, stretching over the 150 mark, and Lara began hitting his stride. He became increasingly dismissive of anything fractionally offline and any optimism the tourists had felt after the two early breakthroughs had long since dissipated. He pulled Tufnell through midwicket for four to bring up his century, his second 50 coming in just fifty-nine deliveries, half the time of the first, and the tempo was building.

'I wanted to build an innings,' he said later. 'I realised I'd given away my innings on numerous occasions and I was not going to do it this time. I mean not before I got a hundred, if I was going to take a chance it would be after 100.'

Lara lost Adams with the score on 191, the pair having added 179 for the third wicket. The impetus they had built had energised the crowd and now, with the series won and the old enemy cowed, they were in the mood to party. Lara's increasing dominance was stoking them up as he pulled Caddick ferociously through midwicket to roars of delight. Soon after, as the shadows began to lengthen in the late evening sun, a routine turn to square-leg off Phil Tufnell brought up his second 150 of the series.

Nearing close of play, Fraser dug one in short and the twenty-four-year-old rocked back to hook. As he often does when playing the hooks and pulls, Lara got deep in his crease and perilously close to the stumps. But he was safe and by the end of Day One his 164 not out had guided the West Indies to 274 for 3.

The young Trinidadian's 277 in Sydney had sown the seed of his record-breaking capabilities and his first-day dominance had many predicting that this time he would be successful.

'It was really in the dressing room on that first night when you thought, well, if he goes at four an over, which is what he was doing at the time, he will get close and he's capable of doing it,' says Adams. 'Once he was not out overnight, worked out his numbers and overs, there was no way he was going to let Garry's record go. In hindsight I believe he had the record in his heart for quite a long time and if he ever got in sight of it he would go for it.'

Trinidad and Tobago and West Indies leg-spinner Dinanath Ramnarine backs up Adams's supposition that the record was already in Lara's mind.

'I remember him saying to us in the Trinidad and Tobago team that year that he would break Sir Garfield Sobers's record.'

There is nothing a West Indian crowd loves more than putting the English team to the sword and by the second morning they were anticipating a bloodbath. An expectant and packed Recreation Ground was awash with noise and colour: horns sounding, trumpets blowing, music blaring, drums and tyre irons being punished.

Two legendary entertainers, singer-songwriter David Rudder and ARG fixture DJ Chickie, were doing their bit to add to the heady atmosphere. Chickie – a man who had once won a Man of the Match award for entertaining fans at the home of Antiguan cricket – was in his element.

'One Test match, it was rain all the way through but people still paid their EC$40 each day to go into the stands and listen and party with Chickie,' says Rudder. 'First time ever a non-player was named Man of the Match. He's brilliant.'

The two combined to augment the party mood with Rudder giving impromptu renditions of 'Rally Round the West Indies'.

'When things really started to hot up I would take a microphone and sing. Everything was spontaneous, and that was the great thing about Antigua, it was just the spirit of what was happening.'

Lara's first boundary of that second day was a whipped pull off his hips from Caddick. It was effortless, all the time in the world, and he was off and running again like he'd never left the field.

A sumptuous back-foot square drive off Chris Lewis for another boundary edged him closer to 200 and moments later, as the noise crescendoed in the stands, he tucked one into the leg-side for the single needed to register his second Test double century. Already there were handwritten signs being waved by spectators urging him on to the 366, though Lara said he wasn't thinking that far ahead.

'What I was thinking was that if I get to 250 I would be quite happy then slowly try to crawl past my best ever, 277. Thinking back to Australia, when I got back to the dressing room and had a bath and I realised I was only 14 runs short of Viv Richards' record, the 291, I thought you know you're going to take it stride by stride and get to 277, then 291, and then hopefully you're going to get to the triple century.'

Almost unnoticed at the other end, Keith Arthurton had been with Lara since the demise of Adams the previous day. With the West Indies score on 374, he was dismissed by Caddick to end a stand of 183 runs, of which Arthurton had added just 47. On and on Lara went, more measured brilliance than the belligerent perfection of Sydney. It was a rhythm that had England captain Atherton saying the innings and where it was heading 'looked all so inevitable at the time'.

Lara, now batting with nineteen-year-old Shivnarine Chanderpaul in his first Test series, pulled Phil Tufnell through midwicket for four to become the eleventh West Indian in history to register a score of 250. Chanderpaul, an unorthodox left-hander with a crabby style, would himself shoulder the burden of responsibility for the West Indian batting after Lara retired, but for now he simply had to support the Trinidadian.

As Lara moved alongside Richards's 291, the Antiguan legend's highest Test score, the English skipper adjusted his field.

'On 291 I took first slip out for the first time and he nicked Andrew Caddick's next ball through the gaping hole,' said Atherton. 'He could quite conceivably have been taking the mickey. I wouldn't know because the scale of his talent was way outside my understanding.'

A straight drive off Caddick for a boundary four took Lara to 298 and within sniffing distance of becoming the thirteenth player in Test history to score a triple century. He steered another Caddick delivery through backward point and set off. Angus Fraser, after a heavy workload, was treading water on the boundary in pursuit of the ball and Lara seized the opportunity to sprint through for his second and the milestone.

Having offered fervent support all day, the crowd erupted and spilled out onto the pitch. Barely had Lara finished raising his bat and punching the air in celebration than an enthusiastic fan grabbed him round the waist and manhandled him into the air. Another sprinted up to hug his hero as the police struggled to retain control but Lara accepted it in the spirit it was intended – he had become only the third West Indian to score a Test triple hundred (following Sobers in 1958 and Lawrence Rowe in 1974).

He was getting into rarefied air and, as Day Two drew to a close, there could be no denial of what the focus was now. He was 320 not out overnight and but for three agonising rain delays, accounting for twenty-three overs of play, would already have reached the record.

The rain interruptions demonstrated the mental fortitude Lara brings to his batting. Breaks – be they drinks, weather or scheduled – are often a time after which wickets fall. The batsman's concentration broken, on resumption he must mentally start again. Hard enough in normal circumstances but for Lara to be withdrawn from the action an additional three times over the course of the day, when the buzz all around would have been of nothing other than *the record*, and to continue undistracted showed supreme willpower. And the Day Two rain had denied him not only the opportunity to break the record but also a good night's sleep.

He later revealed he had been awake from 4 am on the historic third morning mentally rehearsing his innings, wrangling with himself over the best way to reach the landmark. Should he opt for total safety and push forty-six singles or go out hard, hit a few boundaries, and then retreat back into his shell for the last fifteen runs? By the time he walked back out on to the Antigua Recreation Ground he had been up for seven hours contemplating the answer.

Day Three began nervously, and the morning session was to prove more agonising ordeal than majestic jaunt to glory. A back-foot drive for four through the covers off Fraser was encased within panicky singles and nervy prods as fluency deserted Lara for the first time in his innings. The atmosphere in the ground had changed as well, the tension all-pervading. England's go-to bowler Fraser pitched a full delivery in the footmarks, virtually the only bit of rough on the pitch, jagging it tantalisingly past Lara's outside edge to anguished groans from the stands. The Middlesex man, who embodies hangdog in sunny times, peered lugubriously at Lara with hands on hips. A wry smile spread across his face before he made his now-famous comment: 'I don't suppose I can call you a lucky bugger when you are 340.'

The incident served to remind just why records such as Sobers's stand for so long. First everything has to come together to present the chance: match situation, pitch conditions, opposition attack, the batsman's skill, the batsman's form, concentration and stamina; and then there's 'luck', because one mistake, one late deviation of the ball to feather an edge, and it's all over, the chance of a lifetime gone. It's the reason the Test record has been eclipsed only eleven times since the very first Test match in 1877.

Shortly after his play-and-miss to Fraser, Lara tucked a delivery into the leg-side for a single off Lewis to raise his 350, only the third man to reach such a score in Tests. The acknowledgement was routine and perfunctory; nobody cared about 350, only 365.

Each run was now accompanied by raucous cheering as Lara crept towards the magic mark. On 361, a cover drive off Caddick pierced the field and raced to the boundary, skipping over the rope and into the advertising hoardings for four. It took him past Len Hutton's 364, in 1938 at the Oval against Australia, and brought him level with Sobers's 365.

The crowd's early tension had transformed into unadulterated delight and 12,000 supporters danced in the stands in premature celebration. Policemen in their marl grey shirts and black hats ringed the boundary, facing the crowd in readiness. There was a punch of gloves and words of encouragement from Chanderpaul as the great man himself, Sir Garfield Sobers, waited on the boundary edge for his record to fall.

Atherton made them all wait, piling on the pressure. The England skipper was not letting Lara have anything for free. He repositioned his fieldsmen, bringing everyone up except third man and long leg, to stop the single.

In Cantaro, Trinidad, Lara's mum, Pearl, sat focussed on her television screen, with five of her children, eight grandchildren and a phalanx of reporters and cameramen. Earlier she had been unable to watch, nerves forcing her away from the action, but now she waited.

At 11.46 am, the shaven-headed Lewis approached the wicket, and Lara, to a cacophonous din. The delivery was short and pulled savagely into the midwicket fence. As everyone's eyes instinctively traced the ball's path from bat to boundary, Lara, going deep in his crease to execute the stroke, had grazed the off-stump with his right leg. The bail bounced and wobbled but, beneath the batsman's fearful gaze, did not fall.

Lara raised his cap and bat in relief and collapsed into a hug from Chanderpaul as a tidal wave of humanity descended on the wicket. The police may have known what was coming but there's a difference between knowing and being able to do anything about it.

Atherton summed up the confusion.

'Darrell Hair, the Australian umpire, was flapping because the crowd were running all over the pitch. He grabbed the spectator nearest to him by the scruff of the neck and gave him a roasting. It was George the groundsman.'

As Lara was cordoned off from the melee by police, like a rock star being shepherded through a backstage door, a grey-haired stately figure hobbled stiff-legged to the middle. The crowd parted and the man who had scored 365 against Pakistan, on 1 March 1958 in Kingston, Jamaica, hugged Lara in heartfelt congratulation.

In the background, fans were swinging over the edge of the stands. In the middle, Sobers exchanged fatherly words with the new king of batsmen; it was a moment of serenity amidst a sea of chaos. As they spoke,

Lara pulls England's Chris Lewis for four to break the Test record highest score in 1994; in the process his right pad brushes the leg stump rattling a bail which thankfully does not fall.

Dropping to his knees and kissing the Antigua Recreation Ground pitch after breaking the record in an iconic photograph.

a writhing mass of disembodied arms snaked over and round the police for any access point to their hero, patting him, touching him. Breaking from the moment, and the strong arm of the law, Lara sank to his knees and kissed the ARG wicket in an iconic image.

Moments later Sobers, still on the outfield and with the celebrations continuing around him, remarked: 'Records are always going to be broken and I don't think a better person could've broken the record because for me, as far as I'm concerned, he is the only batsman really today that plays the game the way it should be played.'

It took ten minutes to clear the ground and locate the ball, as Fraser later recounted.

'With the playing area devoid of spectators, the umpires looked at each other, then the players, and asked: "Who has got the ball?" The square-leg fielder ran to the boundary and, amazingly, found the ball resting against the boundary rope.

The old and the new. Celebrating his 375 with former record-holder and batting mentor Sir Garfield Sobers.

'At the end of the West Indian innings, I went into the umpires' room and asked if I could have the ball to give to Brian. They said they were going to use it as a spare. I told them it was a piece of cricket history. After signing it myself and then getting Andrew Caddick, Philip Tufnell, Graeme Hick and [Chris] Lewis to sign it, I presented Lara with the ball at the end of the Test.'

At close of play, the new world-record holder said he had just been relieved to get over the mark. He was not the only one.

Of the many personal stories that are interwoven with moments of history, one of Lara's great friends, Sir Hilary Beckles, Principal of the Cave Hill (Barbados) Campus of the University of the West Indies, relates the day a learned professor played hooky.

'I was supposed to fly back to Barbados to teach a class at Cave Hill Campus but at 200 I knew that something incredible was going to happen, and,' he pauses and begins to grin, 'I wasn't feeling very well, so I called the Cave Hill Campus and told my secretary, "Please put a notice on my door telling the students that I won't be teaching today because I'm not feeling very well."

'And Brian did what he had to do but, while he was doing it, the television cameras came in and there Garry [Sobers] and I were sitting together and all of my students saw me at Antigua "not feeling very well". The greatest embarrassment of my life, I believe.'

Calypsonian Rudder tells how he, having been present for the first two days, came even closer to missing Lara's record-breaking shot off Lewis.

'I had my flight out of Antigua that morning so I went down to check-in early to get everything sorted. Then it's back to the Recreation Ground and I'm waiting on Brian breaking the record but he's not going real quick. I'm looking at my watch all the time and then I hear my flight has come in early; first time ever BWIA [British West Indian Airways] arrives early.

'So they're doing all their baggage checks, and they keep making announcements, "Would Mr David Rudder please report to the check-in counter." I'm now holding back the plane from leaving.

'I have one foot out of the gate watching Lara, willing the man to break the record. As he does I'm through the gate and heading for the airport. I was last man on board and as I'm walking down the aisle everybody's looking at me real daggers, you know.'

By the time Rudder's plane was leaving the VC Bird International Airport, Lara had been dismissed. Play had resumed after the ten-minute delay but soon after, on 375, Lara drove loosely at Caddick and nicked behind. Characteristically, he walked before being given out by umpire Steve Bucknor and left the field to congratulatory handshakes from the England players and another ovation from the crowd; life would never be the same again.

In Cantaro, Lara's mum burst into tears when her boy was finally out, not because of the dismissal but because he had achieved a lifelong ambition. Amidst constant well-wishing phone calls she fielded reporters' questions and gave insight into Lara's early days, saying he had always demanded to play cricket with his older brothers in the yard. Dressed in an oversized Laramania T-shirt, Pearl also revealed that Brian had been breastfed as a baby, stating that a breastfed child was a strong child.

'He has been going forward all the time,' she added. 'From what I can see he would just continue going, breaking his own records now.'

At the end of the day's play, an emotional Lara faced the cameras and recalled his moment of history.

'It was the greatest feeling ever; I couldn't imagine it you know. At three o'clock this morning tears came to my eyes. I said look, Brian, if you really break this record what's really going to happen. I couldn't sleep; it was a lot for me. And coming today and producing it, getting to the record and then hearing that Sir Garfield was on the field waiting to congratulate me. I know that the crowd was after me and everything but Sir Garfield Sobers is Sir Garfield Sobers.'

There had even been a moment of quiet vindication for the new world-record holder in the dressing room afterwards.

'As a youngster, a particular West Indies manager gave him [Lara] a very, very hard time on a tour,' says teammate Adams. 'He ended up leaning on him for trying to suggest one day he might be as good as Garry Sobers. Who does he think he is sort of thing.

'Interestingly enough, when Brian broke Sobers's record the same man came into the dressing room congratulating him, shaking his hand, all smiles and all that. Me and Brian just looked across the room at each other and looked at the man. It was a funny moment.'

Lara finished the series with 798 runs at a steepling average of 99.75. He had duly collected the two centuries predicted and added a couple of fifties for good measure. His mother, Pearl, and sister Agnes were given complimentary first-class BWIA tickets and flew over to be with him amidst the delirium. But if Antigua and the wider cricketing world were excited by Lara's achievement, the celebrations in Trinidad and Tobago were on another planet.

'Trinidadians are always looking for an excuse to celebrate,' recalls Rudder. 'If somebody discovers it have an extra roti in the pot that wasn't expected, that's cause for celebration. So now imagine you have a real reason to celebrate, like a son of your soil scoring 375 and breaking Sobers's Test match record. Oh god,' he laughs, 'everyone was on a high, high, high, you know.'

Prime Minister Patrick Manning's government declared a public holiday and swiftly bestowed a plethora of gifts and honours on the twenty-four-year-old. Amongst them was the offer of a plot of land on which to build his dream home. His choice of location was no accident, says former Trinidad and Tobago team manager, and close friend, Colin Borde.

'There is a Ministry of Agriculture facility right next to where he has his house now, near the Kapok Hotel. He used to get dropped off there by his father and picked up every afternoon after school. It reminded him of his days with his dad and that was special to him; he always said when he got older he would buy a house right there. So when he got the opportunity that's where he chose.'

Lara was duly given the land on a hillside overlooking Port of Spain's vast Queen's Park Savannah, as well as being handed a key to the capital at City Hall, receiving the Trinity Cross and Hummingbird Medal Gold (along with Sir Garfield Sobers) and having a city street renamed the Brian Lara Promenade in his honour. A motorcade was also organised, beginning in Arima and with stops around the nation, so that his compatriots could meet and greet their hero, and babies could be touched by the hand of genius. Alongside him that day, as in Antigua, was Shivnarine Chanderpaul. The presence of the two players, one of African and one of Indian descent, was symbolic in a nation where the two largest ethnicities (each with around 40 per cent of the population) are Afro- and Indo-Trinidadian.

'It was felt it would be a great thing to show that it was not just the Nile out there but the Ganges as well,' says Rudder, 'and use it as a metaphor for what could be achieved in this country if everybody got together.'

While being whisked from function to function, former coach Ken Franco remembers Lara somehow found time to take Chanderpaul around Harvard Coaching Clinic, showing his teammate where it had all started. He may have been at Harvard when he was supposed to be in Cantaro, as the residents of Lara's home village had to wait to mark their favourite son's return. Not that this proved an insurmountable problem.

From 7 am on the morning of the motorcade, Cantaro had swung into action with banners and signs proclaiming: 'Welcome to Cantaro, the home of Brian Charles Lara, Cricket Superstar'. By 8 am, Baya's Bar was full, with drinks being sunk to the toast of 'Take one for Brian'; Pan Jammers Steel Orchestra tuned up opposite the Merry Boys Pub and taxis shipped people in from neighbouring areas as Pearl Lara went about her normal routine, attending morning service at the Seventh Day Adventist church.

Initially scheduled for a morning stop, Lara was delayed, sparking rumours that he wasn't coming at all, reported one local newspaper. 'No! They can't do us that! This is the boy hometown and they not bringing him here?'

He arrived at 4.15 pm but was soon gone again, to collect his Trinity Cross at the President's residence. Lara promised to return and his supporters countered with the well-intentioned, if not overwhelmingly altruistic, assurance they would 'hold the fort' until he did.

England skipper Atherton, seemingly powerless to escape his nemesis, also witnessed the scenes of unadulterated revelry in the twin-island republic famed for its Carnival.

'I was holidaying in Trinidad the week after his 375 and Laramania was in full swing,' he said. 'There seemed to be a party, parade or dinner in his honour every minute of the day, and it would take a strong man indeed not to have his head turned by such adulation.'

8 Annus mirabilis

One of the most remarkable aspects of Lara's 375 was the fact that, far from being his singular towering achievement of 1994, it served merely as a precursor to one of the richest veins of form the game has ever witnessed. The beneficiary of this blistering run was English county cricket, and more specifically Warwickshire, but it so nearly didn't happen at all.

South African fast bowler Allan Donald, who had been with Warwickshire since 1987, was the county's long-term and much-loved overseas player but international duty rendered him unavailable in 1994. Warwickshire needed to find a one-season replacement for the man nicknamed 'White Lightning', the first South African to take 300 Test wickets.

A number of candidates were considered, with Lara's name appearing alongside others including Shane Warne, David Boon, Phil Simmons and Manoj Prabhakar, with the Indian all-rounder favoured by first team skipper Dermot Reeve. Prabhakar was an excellent swing bowler, who it was felt might prosper in English conditions, as well as a versatile batsman, and negotiations progressed quickly to the point where, in late 1993, the Indian signed a contract for the following season. And that would have been that had matters not taken an unexpected turn.

In mid-March, with Warwickshire's opening county fixture against Glamorgan only six weeks away, Prabhakar was forced to return home from India's tour of New Zealand with an ankle injury that necessitated an operation in Mumbai. Understandably concerned, Warwickshire asked him to prove his fitness by reporting to the club in person. Behind the scenes, Lara, in the midst of his defining series against England, had been contacted as a potential replacement.

On 6 April, with examination undergone, the county's medical staff ruled that Prabhakar's injured ankle might not withstand the four months continuous sport which is a county season, and a deal relinquishing both parties of their obligations was struck.

Negotiations with Lara now intensified. Warwickshire had enjoyed successful associations with a number of West Indian players in the past and their last county championship winning side, in 1972, had included four, in Rohan Kanhai, Lance Gibbs, Deryck Murray and Alvin Kallicharran.

Warwickshire Vice Chairman Tony Cross flew out to Barbados, while talks with Lara's agent, Jonathan Barnett, continued. These were swiftly concluded on Cross's arrival, with a £40,000 contract being signed at the Kensington Oval.

'I always play to win and I will expect a lot from the other players in the Warwickshire team,' said Lara. 'I hope they expect a lot from me and I'll try to produce for them.

'I see this as part of my cricket education,' he continued. 'The West Indies are touring England in 1995 and I'll try to get as acclimatised to the conditions as I can.'

County coach Bob Woolmer remarked on the opportune timing of the signing from a Warwickshire perspective.

'Fortunately we had signed Lara just two days before this epic innings [the 375]; one can only imagine how the price would have rocketed had it all taken place a week later.'

There had been other interested suitors, including Nottinghamshire, Worcestershire, Middlesex and Lancashire League club Denton, but Lara opted for the Bears to fulfil a long-held ambition of playing county cricket. The fact he had not been the first choice of skipper Reeve, however, would have unforeseen repercussions later in the year.

The twenty-four-year-old was apprehensive about the reception he would receive in England, so tumultuous had the last week and a half been in the Caribbean, and must have felt these fears justified when he was greeted by a swarm of fans and media at Heathrow Airport on 27 April, all baying for a piece of him.

'I was a cricketer here to play cricket but I was being treated like some kind of world-famous celebrity. I found the hype rather frightening,' he said, perhaps a little naively.

It was the first sign of what was to come, as his performances in the coming weeks served only to intensify the glare of the spotlight.

Lara's impact on his new employers had begun even before he landed, with over a thousand new Warwickshire members signing up at £60 a time in the wake of his record-breaking Antigua innings.

'Commercially it made a big difference because he was hot property at that stage,' says Warwickshire CCC's Cricket Operations Manager Keith Cook. 'The interest was quite phenomenal, phones were ringing off the wall, people wanting to become members, box holders, everyone wanted to be part of the club.'

Cook recalls the day life changed at Warwickshire, as Lara was whisked from Heathrow to his unveiling as a Warwickshire player at Edgbaston.

'Normally press conferences here are a chap with a microphone on the boundary edge but we had to set up a room for it quickly in the Pavilion Suite. Dozens of people were there, sponsors, press, TV cameras. They were filming him as he arrived, stepping out of the car, it was almost like the arrival of a film star or royalty.'

Lara, who became the first Warwickshire player to be presented his county cap before even playing a game, sought to temper expectations by saying he would take things 'stride by stride' and hoped not to disappoint. With the preliminaries over, and his debut against Glamorgan looming the very next morning, Lara finally left for his new digs, accompanied by the welcome presence of his friend and compatriot Dwight Yorke, who was in the midst of a hugely successful stint with English Premier League side Aston Villa.

The calm before the storm as Lara receives his county cap from Warwickshire skipper Dermot Reeve. Despite a hugely successful summer, with three domestic trophies secured, the pair would endure an acrimonious relationship.

Although a new world-record holder, a number of pundits were unsure as to how effective Lara would be in transforming Warwickshire's fortunes. The *Independent*'s Glenn Moore was not alone in thinking the best chance of success for the Bears, who had captured the NatWest Trophy in 1993, lay in the limited overs competitions.

'It will take more than the brilliant Trinidadian to lift Warwickshire from 16th to first in the championship but, as the booming membership suggests, cricket is not yet just about winning,' he wrote, adding that, 'the lack of bowling, even with the addition of the slow left-armer Richard Davis, rules out a championship attempt.'

The loss of one of the world's premier fast bowlers makes Moore's assessment of Warwickshire's bowling resources understandable, but what would become apparent was that huge totals in four-day cricket created their own opportunities, buoying bowlers and undermining opposition batsmen. With Lara, not only were larger totals possible but they were attainable in a shorter time frame, opening up options for Reeve and the Warwickshire attack. It was not just weight of runs but rate of runs that would alter the course of games.

One of Lara's teammates in 1994, former England fast bowler Gladstone Small, says the sixteenth placed finish in the 1993 County Championship was something of a false result in any case, as Warwickshire had been building nicely for some time.

'We had been developing for a few seasons, got to a couple of finals, won the NatWest, and narrowly missed out on winning the championship in 1991. We had the best cricket coach I ever played with in Bob Woolmer, a great captain in Dermot Reeve and a great mix of senior players and good youngsters coming through, so Brian really put the gloss on all that.'

Had Lara, exhausted from the accumulated exertions of the preceding weeks and his flight from Trinidad, made a low-key entry into county cricket he could have been forgiven. Overseas players often take time to adjust to English conditions, especially early in the season when wickets are greener and the ball moves around more.

So it worked in Lara's favour when, on the morning of his first county match, Thursday, 28 April, Glamorgan skipper Hugh Morris won the toss and elected to bat. Lara spent the whole day in the field, and part of the next, acclimatising to his new surroundings, an exploratory over of leg-breaks late on Day One the extent of his exertions. If it was favourable for Lara it was frustrating for those, including a swollen media pack, who had come to watch cricket's newest batting superstar.

They would have to wait until after 2 pm on the second day, with the conclusion of Glamorgan's innings and the fall of Warwickshire's opening wicket, to witness Lara's county batting career commence.

He had not faced a delivery since he walked off the ARG eleven days before and his vaunted powers of concentration can never have been more clearly demonstrated than in this innings against the Welsh county. Not only did he score a debut 147, at nearly a run-a-ball, but he did so with no sign of the intense scrutiny he was now under and no hint of the physical toll which the previous month's historic events had taken. The 3,000 watching Warwickshire faithful rose to give him a standing ovation as he left the field.

His hundred had come up in 104 minutes, between lunch and tea, and was part of a 215-run stand with fellow left-hander Roger Twose. Twose, who finished with his highest first-class score of 277 not out (more runs than he had scored in the entire 1993 season), was one of many who would be inspired to raise their standard in 1994.

'We all lifted our games that year, whether playing against him or with him,' says Nick Knight, who would be vice-captain to Lara at Warwickshire in 1998 but was playing for Essex in 1994. 'You get a heroic figure in the dressing room, as Brian was at that time, and you want to show him what you can do. I remember Roger wrote a tongue-in-cheek message on Brian's locker when he arrived: "Welcome, to the second-best left-hander at the club".'

Lara's debut hundred had reinforced a hallmark, clear since his Cantaro youth, when he bisected plant pots with marbles – his ability to hit the gaps hard. Glamorgan captain Morris noted there were no 'green knees' amongst his fielders.

'His placement was great, but he hits the ball so hard that fielders have got no chance if it is slightly wide of them,' he said.

The innings, two days after he stepped off the plane, had set up a Warwickshire innings victory and a remarkable English summer was under way.

Warwickshire's next opponents, Leicestershire, had signed fellow Trinidadian Phil Simmons, and if Lara had made an impressive start

Simmons had made a better one, becoming the first county player to score a double hundred on debut and simultaneously registering a club record score with his 261 against Northamptonshire.

'Lara vs Simmons!' trumpeted the *Trinidad Express* ahead of the clash but it was Lara who would come out on top, and he celebrated his recent twenty-fifth birthday with hundreds in each innings, even though Leicestershire served notice as title challengers by having the best of a match which ultimately ended in a draw. Lara's hundreds had been of contrasting styles, with the second a resolute rearguard 120 not out, shielding his lower-order partners from the strike for close to three hours and saving the game for his side as Leicestershire pressed for victory on Day Four. He had become the first Warwickshire batsman in a decade to register two centuries in a match, the last being fellow West Indian Alvin Kallicharran in 1984.

Now with four consecutive centuries, speculation began to build about the possibility of a new record for successive first-class hundreds and, as Warwickshire descended on Somerset, the best of Lara's already sparkling English summer was yet to come.

In a soggy match, effectively reduced to a single innings game, Lara scored his fifth successive, and most unlikely, century. Somerset posted 355 for 9 in their first innings and then, with rain washing out one and a half days' play, both teams made early final day declarations to set up a run chase and potential result. When rain accounted for the afternoon's play as well, the visitors required 234 runs in just thirty-three overs in the final session after tea. More than seven runs an over is hard enough under normal circumstances but on a damp track, sodden outfield and in murky light it was improbable at best. Lara is a man galvanised by the improbable.

His first 50 came in fifty-one balls – good going, but a bejumpered Lara was just warming up. Paul Smith added valuable assistance in a seventy-four-run stand but when he went for 38 the target remained a daunting 151 from twenty-one overs, still stubbornly above the seven-an-over mark.

Lara made his move and Asif Din, at the non-striker's end, got the best view in the house as he accelerated through the gears. Lara took just twenty-one deliveries to bring up his second 50, for a seventy-two-ball hundred, hitting Graham Rose imperiously over deep square-leg for six on the way.

Warwickshire, or rather Lara, was now rattling along at nine runs an over. Even more extraordinary considering that a heavy outfield and large boundaries square of the wicket had reduced Lara's boundary count, meaning he had to run his runs. Supreme fitness is not something often spoken about in Lara's game but the exertion implicit in his Somerset knock illustrated his physical condition at this time.

'It was an innings measured in every way,' wrote Simon Wilde in *The Times*. 'He always got to the pitch of the ball, always seemingly found the gaps in the field, and played perhaps two hurried strokes in the entire innings. And he ran between the wickets like the wind.'

When he was finally bowled by Pakistani leg-spinner Mushtaq Ahmed, his partnership with Din had realised 126 in fourteen overs, 99 of them to Lara. The away team sauntered home with twenty balls to spare – for Warwickshire it was another victory, for Lara another hundred.

To the outside world, Lara's sensational batting and Warwickshire's winning run must have seemed like so much sweetness and light. It was anything but, according to skipper Reeve who, in his book *Winning Ways*, says tensions between him and Lara had been high from the outset. They first came to a head at Somerset when Reeve, returning from England duty and sitting on the balcony watching proceedings, had played a practical joke. Aware Lara had received a new mobile phone and taken it onto the field, Reeve rang it. Lara, positioned at first slip, answered.

'Brian, I think you're standing a bit close to Keith [Piper],' said Reeve.

Lara looked up to see some teammates on the balcony waving and immediately hung up.

The timing of the phone call is disputed, with Lara saying it was during play, getting him into trouble with the umpires, and Reeve stating it was before a ball had been bowled. What was certain was Lara had not seen the funny side.

With bad blood bubbling, Warwickshire travelled to Lord's to face Middlesex, where Lara was gunning for six successive centuries and a share of the first-class record held jointly by Charles Burgess Fry, Sir Don Bradman and Mike Proctor. Conditions at cricket's headquarters were not encouraging.

There are few sports where weather and pitch conditions play such a vital role in players' performances as cricket and, unfortunately for Lara, Lord's had served up a prodigiously seaming wicket and bitterly cold weather. He never looked comfortable and, after more than an hour of scratchy strokeplay, fell for 26, to nineteen-year-old Richard Johnson. A flick to a leg-side delivery had succeeded only in guiding a faint edge through to wicketkeeper Keith Brown. It was an innocuous way for the run to end, a 'nothing shot' in Lara's words. Even so, few players can have received a standing ovation for an unconvincing 26 such as the one afforded Lara by the Lord's spectators.

Whatever disappointment there may have been was brief, as natural order was restored in the second innings with the twenty-five-year-old making light of the conditions with a quick-fire 140. He had become the eighth player to score six centuries in seven innings and had enabled Warwickshire to declare in time to offer a chance of victory. How they went about trying to secure that victory, though, would provide the second flashpoint in a simmering personal battle.

As Warwickshire pressed for the win, Middlesex began blocking out for a draw. Reeve, in an attempt to reignite the contest, introduced Lara's leg-spin in conjunction with an attacking field. It worked. With gaps aplenty the Middlesex batsmen began going for their shots again, hitting Lara for thirty-one runs in two overs, before he left the field with a shoulder strain.

The chase resumed, Middlesex started losing wickets and were hanging on at the end with Warwickshire falling just one wicket short of victory. But Reeve's decision to unexpectedly throw the ball to Lara had rankled with the Trinidadian, who complained of not being given time to warm up. According to Reeve, Lara had taken exception to being asked to bowl without 'a run-saving field' but it was clear this was about more than cricket.

'It was a clash of two egos basically,' says Gladstone Small. 'Senior guys like myself, Tim Munton and Andy Moles saw things happen but made sure it didn't get into the fabric of the side. We let them have their battles but not let it spread. I mean in a team of eleven players not everyone gets on but as long as when you're out there you're performing for the common good that's the main thing.'

Lara was certainly still performing, and he carried his hot streak of form into the next game against Durham at Edgbaston.

First-class cricket's first quintuple

Durham had become the eighteenth county to be afforded first-class status when they were admitted to the championship in 1991 but, three years later, they were still finding their feet and their bowling attack was deemed one of the weakest on the circuit.

On a batsman-friendly surface, the championship newcomers rattled up their highest-ever total, of 556 for 8 declared, with John Morris notching a superb 204. The stage appeared set for a Lara run-feast on Day Two, but it didn't develop as expected.

Coming to the wicket after the demise of Dominic Ostler, the early stages of Lara's innings were not promising. Facing the Barbadian fast bowler Anderson Cummins, Lara was expecting a short-pitched delivery first up and he got one, but he mistimed his shot and was nearly caught and bowled. A few overs later he was even luckier when Cummins knocked his leg stump back only for umpire Peter Wight to call a no-ball. The West Indian's woes continued after the tea interval, as Jon Culley of the *Independent*, explained.

'First ball after tea, on 18, he escaped again when Chris Scott unaccountably dropped a routine wicketkeeper's chance. Next ball, Lara almost played on and the one after that he nudged dangerously close to first slip.'

Lara, so convinced the edge to Scott would be caught, had already taken a couple of strides towards the pavilion. When it was spilled Scott, hoping the ground would open up and swallow him, exclaimed: 'Jesus Christ! I hope he doesn't get a hundred!'

By the end of Day Two Lara was unbeaten on 111 and became the first man ever to make seven centuries in eight innings.

Rain wiped out any prospect of play on Day Three and, when the captains failed to agree on declarations and targets, with it went the chance of a result. Thus it was that Lara emerged on the final day with free licence to bat as long and expansively as he wanted. On a good batting surface against a game but limited attack, the best batsman in the world could not have asked for more, and Lara is a man who recognises opportunities. In his sights was a thirty-five-year-old record many cricket followers could not envisage being bettered: the highest individual score in the first-class game. It was a standard set by one of the game's early greats.

In January 1959, in the semi-final of the Quaid-e-Azam Trophy between Karachi and Bahawalpur, played on matting at the Karachi Parsi Institute Ground, opener Hanif Mohammad scored 499 for the home side before being run out attempting his 500th run.

The diminutive Pakistani shared Lara's ability to concentrate for long periods, and one year earlier, in January 1958, had demonstrated this in extraordinary fashion when batting for more than sixteen hours (the longest innings in Test history) to score 337 to save a match against the West Indies in Bridgetown, Barbados.

Exceptional player though he was, Mohammad was in a different mould to Lara and he could not have conceived of what Lara was about to unleash on Durham – but then few could.

From the resumption on Day Four Lara was in the groove and plundered the Durham attack for 174 runs in the two-hour session before lunch, a phenomenal strike rate which put him on 285 and in sight of some esteemed records. The first major one was the highest first-class score in England, Archie Maclaren's 424 set in 1895, but Lara was already thinking beyond this.

'He actually predicted what he was going to do,' says the Barbados-born Gladstone Small, who played seventeen Tests for England. 'I remember sitting with him at lunch on that final day with Keith Piper and he just said: "Do you think I can go for the record?" I thought, what record; does he mean his personal record? I said, "What the 375, you'll piss that." He said, "No, Hanif Mohammad's record." I had to think for a second, I didn't know what the hell he was on about. Then it dawned on me, the 499, well he was only on 285 at the time!'

A surprised Dermot Reeve was also approached at lunch by Lara and asked not to declare.

'He told me about the record of 499, that he fancied it, and I thought, this guy's a confident character – he's still got to get another 200-odd before the close,' said the Warwickshire skipper.

Lara galloped on another 133 runs between lunch and tea, a session in which Trevor Penney was dismissed, having contributed 44 to a third-wicket stand of 314. By now, on 418, Lara was one hit away from Maclaren and eighty-two runs short of Mohammad. The crowd had swollen from 300 to 2,000 on the news that Lara was engaged in another thunderous onslaught, and one which might end in first-class cricket's first quintuple century. But if he was to seize the record he had to hit the eighty-two runs required in an hour and a half, as play would be halted at 5.30 pm not 6 pm, given that there was no chance of a result.

As the clock ticked round to 5.28 pm, part-time bowler John Morris stepped up to bowl the last over of the day. Lara was on 497, three runs shy of taking Hanif's record and a seemingly routine task. That was if he had realised it was the last over of the day. Lara believed he still had another thirty minutes, as the last hour had been called at 5 pm. He was reckoning without the 'no result' rule.

Unaware, he blocked the first three deliveries and then, incongruously, was struck on the helmet by a medium-pace bouncer on the fourth. 'I've found his weakness,' quipped Morris.

Piper was concerned, more by his partner's shot selection than his being struck by a looping bouncer, and walked down to see if he was aware of the game situation, as Lara recalled.

'"You've only got two balls left," said Keith. "Are you sure?" I asked him. "I've checked with the umpires," he said ... I knew I had to hit one of those remaining deliveries for a boundary and, as Morris bowled, I came down the pitch and swung through the line towards extra cover. There was no fielder close enough to stop it and I felt relieved, happy and tired all at the same time.'

It had been a nervy time for some journalists as well.

'I can remember the phones ringing as he was clocking up the runs and getting closer to 500,' says Warwickshire's Cricket Operations Manager, Keith Cook. 'The Test match at Trent Bridge had finished early and a lot of the journalists and media were on the phone asking: "Is he still in, is he still in? We're on our way over from Nottingham." They got to Birmingham mid to late afternoon and I recall Patrick Eagar arriving just in time to photograph Brian hitting the record-breaking runs.'

Supporters ran onto the pitch to congratulate Lara, perhaps not with the same unbridled exuberance of Antigua, but the sentiment was there if in a slightly more English way.

The champagne flowed in the dressing room afterwards and amongst the dozens of congratulatory phone calls was one from his mentor Joey

Let the celebrations begin. Champagne and plastic cups all round as Lara breaks Hanif Mohammad's highest first-class score with 501 against Durham in 1994. His joyous Warwickshire teammates include England seam bowler Gladstone Small (front right).

Carew. There was a call also from the deposed record-holder Hanif Mohammed, arranged by his brother, Mushtaq, who lived nearby and had witnessed the innings.

In the pursuit of such a mammoth record, many others are inevitably toppled on the way: at 300 Lara became the first triple-centurion at Edgbaston; 306, Warwickshire record score (beating Frank Foster's 305 in 1914); 323, highest score by a West Indian in England (beating Viv Richards's 322 for Somerset against Warwickshire in 1985); 325, equals Don Bradman's 1938 record of 1,000 runs in seven first-class innings; 406, highest twentieth-century score in England (beating Graeme Hick's 405 not out); 425, highest first-class score in England (beating Archie MacLaren's 424); 457, highest individual score in a day (beating Charlie Macartney's 345 for Australia against Nottinghamshire in 1921, Lara's new mark would eventually be 390 runs); 494, most boundaries in an innings (beating 68 by Percy Perrin for Essex v Derbyshire in 1904).

'I don't think I'm a great cricketer,' said Lara later, having undergone a marathon signing session of commemorative scorecards. 'It's nice to have records and be on top but I've still got a lot of cricket ahead of me and I need to be more consistent.'

Even if Lara didn't think he was a great cricketer as yet, there were plenty about who did and comparisons with the hitherto untouchable Sir Don Bradman had begun. The highest first-class score, along with the Test match record secured in Antigua, had stood for over thirty-five years; Lara had eclipsed them both in forty-nine days. In the history of the game, only Bradman before had held cricket's two most important records simultaneously.

As the press and cricket fans in general descended into states of frenzied hyperbole, a future teammate of Lara's, Nick Knight, playing for Essex at the time, recalled a different reaction amongst fellow professionals.

'I don't think there was an incredible reaction on the county circuit to the 501 to be honest because it had got to the point where everyone was expecting so much from him. He was batting so brilliantly it was almost inevitable he was going to break records and that even the big one could go.'

King of the world. The scoreboard tells the story of top-class cricket's first quintuple centurion.

There was little time to celebrate his latest accomplishment, though, as the very next morning Warwickshire were involved in a Benson and Hedges Cup semi-final against Surrey at the Oval.

'The fanfare that followed the 501 was incredible; he had to do countless interviews and media stuff, then the next morning was up early to do a breakfast TV show, so by the time he turned up at the Oval he was absolutely knackered,' says Small.

'When we were fielding it was obvious the guy was bushed, so we made up an excuse that he tweaked a hamstring and he went off and just fell asleep in the dressing room.

'When we came off [after the Surrey innings] he was still flat out, absolutely dead to the world.'

Surrey had made 267 in fifty-five overs and Lara would not have batted had his side not needed him. At 120 for 4 they did and he somehow summoned the strength to produce another match-winning knock.

'He usually batted at three but ended up batting at six and went and got 70 and won us the game,' adds Small. 'Absolutely incredible in the context of what was happening at the time.'

Lara's 70, with his captain and sparring partner Dermot Reeve making 46 not out in a supporting role, had seen Warwickshire home and progress to a Lord's final.

The game was a perfect example of just what a hamster-on-the-wheel existence the English county scene was at this time. Of the forty-one days from the morning of Lara's first match against Glamorgan, on 28 April, to the Benson and Hedges semi-final on 7 June, Warwickshire had thirty days of scheduled cricket. Granted Lara missed one of these, the friendly at Oxford University, but it still represents an incredible workload with virtually no recovery time, and all of which came on the heels of the West Indies–England series and the celebratory circus following his 375. Not that it was all work, work, work for the party-loving Lara.

'Myself, Brian, Keith Piper and Paul Smith we shared a few nice moments and some good nights out,' says Small. 'He loved the social life and there were a number of pretty Trinidadian girls that rolled through Birmingham that summer. He had a big circle of friends and fans obviously and he enjoyed himself.'

After such nights out, Lara would often try to catch up on sleep in the dressing room whenever possible. It was a habit for which Small himself was already known.

'In the Warwickshire dressing room we had the physio's room and there were three physio's tables. One of these was always known as being my bed basically but when Brian came, because he was out partying quite a bit, he took over one of them. He actually brought a duvet in because, being a Trini, he used to get cold when he was sleeping.'

When he needed other distractions, Lara would most often be found on the golf course or in the company of his good friend Dwight Yorke. Yorke, from Trinidad's sister isle Tobago and a striker who would go on to play for Manchester United, became a regular Edgbaston visitor in 1994.

'Dwight would often be at the ground, pick Brian up and off they would go. They spent a lot of time together. He had just discovered a real passion for golf and of course nearby we have the Belfry, which is also close to the Aston Villa training ground. Most afternoons, as soon as cricket was finished, he'd pop over to the Belfry to practise.'

Lara did not score heavily in Warwickshire's next county game against Kent and by the time the Bears travelled to Northampton, who included West Indies menacing paceman Curtly Ambrose in their ranks, some were predicting the end of Lara's glorious run. The game was billed as a match-up of world's best batsman and bowler, something Lara was not comfortable with.

'It put unnecessary pressure on me and I was not happy about it. Pride would be at stake and it was difficult enough facing a bowler of Curtly's calibre without any extra provocation.'

Whether he felt additional pressure or not, Lara performed superbly, even though Ambrose too played well. The Antiguan had never dismissed Lara before and he was aiming to set the record straight. Ambrose gave his all, working Lara over, having him dropped in the gully and pinging him on the back of the helmet; he scored just twelve runs from forty-five deliveries bowled to him by Ambrose. Still it was Lara who emerged victorious with 197 in a Warwickshire total of 448 for 9. In so doing he had brought up his eighth century in eleven innings, equalling another Bradman record.

But it was also Northampton where Lara's ongoing personal spat with Reeve reached its nadir and where, according to Reeve, the Trinidadian repeatedly told him to 'f*** off'. The seeds of the confrontation were sown when Rob Bailey edged Tim Munton behind and the Warwickshire players went up for a catch. Square-leg umpire Allan Jones ruled the ball had bounced before being taken, so Bailey was not out. Lara made a remark about Jones's eyesight, insinuating the catch had been good, which was overheard. 'There was nothing wrong with my eyesight when I gave you not out first ball yesterday,' retorted Jones.

A few overs later, Bailey edged again and this time the ball clearly carried. As the Warwickshire players came together for the celebratory huddle Reeve sensed Lara was still smouldering from the earlier incident and anticipated further comment.

'I simply said "Brian – don't!" and that led to the torrent of abuse and four-letter words at me, in front of the whole team,' said Reeve.

Lara's version differs amid assertions that Reeve called him a 'prima donna', but it led to what the new world-record holder called 'the low point of the season for me'.

Reeve says that in a subsequent phone call made by him as a placatory measure, Lara referred to the pre-season negotiations, saying the captain hadn't wanted him at the club in the first place.

County coach Bob Woolmer was the man who had to tread the centre ground between skipper and star player carefully. The hugely respected Woolmer, who passed away at the 2007 World Cup while coaching Pakistan, gave his assessment in his book *Woolmer on Cricket*.

'Dermot, who holds the stage well himself, was put out that Brian became too much the focus of attention, and there were a number of occasions when he and I differed as to how Brian should be handled.'

Woolmer does not absolve Lara from responsibility and describes how he trained spasmodically and often turned up moments before a game, missing the pre-match warm-ups and drills. This behaviour was viewed differently by members of the Warwickshire set-up. Some, most vocal of whom was Reeve, felt it represented a double-standard, others, including Woolmer and Club Chairman Dennis Amiss, felt that the extraordinary position Lara was in, and the incumbent pressures it brought, meant he should be given some latitude.

'I thought that pushing Brian over relatively minor issues such as time-keeping would be counter-productive,' said Woolmer. 'After all, he continued to score runs through all this, at the same time being put under outrageous pressure by his agents to make a bit of money (sorry – a lot of money).'

Woolmer engaged 'two allies', Tim Munton and Gladstone Small, in a policy of counselling caution.

'There were times when he [Lara] needed mollycoddling,' says Small. 'Myself and Munty would say to Woolie to let BC sit out the fielding, the warm-ups and pre-match stuff; that it would probably be in our best interests, that sort of thing.

'The commercial stuff took its toll and sometimes he wouldn't be too enthusiastic about playing. He didn't seem to be as motivated by the one-day stuff as he was for championship cricket, when he could bat and bat and bat.

'But these guys live in a different zone, have different pressures, so sometimes you have to give them a bit more leeway. As long as they perform when they need to and Brian certainly did that.'

Two games after the Northampton showdown, Nick Knight lined up for Essex against Warwickshire at Edgbaston. At the time Knight was a young player trying to secure a regular spot in a strong Essex line-up.

'I remember standing at silly point and Brian was batting against Peter Such,' he says. 'It was the over before lunch and he couldn't get a mark on the crease so I offered to do it for him. He just said, "Nah, don't worry about that," and next ball advanced down the track and whacked it for six.

'Last over before lunch and he hit two sixes and a four. Normal human beings playing cricket play for lunch, but he just didn't care; if it was there to be hit he would whack it out of the park last over or not. I remember standing there thinking, this bloke's a bit different.

'The thing is, when Brian was doing this, it was very much pre-Twenty20 and the modern attacking way of thinking. He was a pioneer in the way he played, his attitude to tea breaks, lunch breaks and generally. He just approached the game differently.'

The match, which was won by Warwickshire by 203 runs, was a personally successful one for Knight who registered a half-century and a century in a losing cause. He recalls an incident with Lara that had a significant bearing on his future development.

'After the game Brian made a special effort to come over and tell me how well he thought I had played. For him to put his arm around me and say fantastic, well done, you can really kick on from that, and even indicating areas to work on; as a young player it was incredible and something that lives with you. In a funny way when I look back at my whole career that game was, if not pivotal, then extremely important.'

Warwickshire must also have been impressed by Knight because he signed for them during the close season and remained with them for the next twelve years.

As the season progressed, Woolmer noted that the pressures Lara was under were taking their toll, and niggles, both physical and mental, became more acute: 'He became reclusive and much harder to get hold of.'

Injuries were an increasing problem and Woolmer says he cast a sceptical eye over some of these, such as when Lara missed a match against Lancashire with a sore knee, verified by an unusual source.

'Eventually, he brought me a doctor's note from a gynaecologist in Berkshire,' said the Warwickshire coach.

One close friend says that this malaise which began to take hold of Lara could also be attributed to the fact he had become disillusioned with county cricket.

'He became bored with county cricket, he didn't think the standard was good enough and most importantly he was disappointed,' says former Trinidad and Tobago manager Colin Borde. 'Any young West Indian cricketer growing up really wanted to play cricket in England and Brian had always wanted that.

'But he felt people were making deals to get batting points and bowling points, about how games would pan out, and he thought cricket should be played in the middle not in the dressing room.'

Even if county cricket had not turned out to be quite what Lara had expected, nobody ever questioned his professionalism. Warwickshire coach Woolmer said Lara was fully committed to the team and never let them down, sentiments echoed by Small.

'Brian cared, it may have looked easy on the outside, but he worked at it and it mattered to him that he performed. He never got blasé. He was a winner and he had that winning mentality.'

That mentality shone through in practice as well.

'He used to love netting and I enjoyed bowling at him too. He had a drill where he pulled the leg stump out of its hole and placed it eight inches outside his off stump, so he created a channel. Any ball wide of that stump he left but anything in that channel he absolutely pulverised. His whole essence of batting was to hit the ball first and only defend if it was a really good ball. We had some wonderful tussles.'

Lara saved one more grand innings for the championship-winning match, when his 191 against Hampshire set up an innings victory; it was his ninth hundred for Warwickshire. On the back of 2,066 Lara runs, at an average of 90, the Bears were crowned champions for the first time in twenty-two years. They were 42 points clear of second-placed Leicestershire, the highest winning margin since 1979. The Sunday League was added to the trophy cabinet and in two Lord's Finals, both against Worcestershire, the spoils were shared; with Warwickshire taking the Benson and Hedges Cup and Worcestershire claiming the NatWest Trophy. It represented a unique treble.

'Before that year, when the guys were batting I could usually be found sleeping,' says Small. 'But that summer I gave up on sleep and just watched this incredible guy bat, you couldn't take your eyes off it.

'The extravagance of his strokeplay was amazing. Left-handers are known for playing and missing a bit, wafting, but he hardly missed or edged a ball all summer. It was phenomenal, the guy was really zoned into what he was doing.'

Warwickshire may have seized the silverware but it wasn't only within their camp that Lara's impact had been felt.

'The 1994 county season was remarkable for so many reasons and they all stemmed from Lara's exploits,' explains Nick Knight. 'The focus on cricket was unprecedented, the effect it had on other players, whether you were playing with or against Lara, was tangible. There was a buzz on the county circuit like nothing I've experienced before or since and it was all down to what Brian was doing.'

Lara's tally for the 1994 calendar year, taking all first-class matches into account, was extraordinary. He had scored fourteen centuries, including a double, triple and quintuple, averaging 80 on his way to the mammoth aggregate of 3,828 runs. Quite a year.

9 Lara in popular culture

Cricket, calypso and Carnival

By the end of 1994 Brian Lara was big news and nowhere was he bigger, and more vociferously feted, than in his Caribbean homeland. Indeed, the prolific young batsman from Cantaro was now even becoming a focal point for the creative arts, most particularly music.

Trinidad and Tobago is a land synonymous with colourful and imaginative musical expression and calypso has been at the forefront of that for over 200 years. Traditional calypso has its roots in the storytelling traditions of African slaves and was a medium for spreading news on current affairs, with lyrics which were often political or ribald, or both.

'Calypso is social commentary and therefore necessarily a reflection of the hot topics of the day,' says one of the finest calypsonians of all time, David Rudder. 'It was basically the poor man's newspaper, singing editorials, spreading the word.'

With cricket so intrinsically linked to West Indian identity, it naturally followed that the exploits of the region's greats would be immortalised in song; from Headley and Constantine to Ramadhin and Valentine and on through to more modern-day stars such as Richards and now Lara. So entwined did music and cricket become that the idiosyncratic verve and swagger with which the West Indies played the game became known as 'Calypso Cricket'.

With his beloved mum, Pearl, at the Lara family home in Mitchell Street, Cantaro, Trinidad, in 1994.

The most famous of all cricketing calypsos is the 'Victory Calypso' (composed by Lord Kitchener and popularised by Lord Beginner), which celebrates the West Indies first Test victory in England, at Lord's, in 1950. It was a victory, inspired by spin twins Sonny Ramadhin and Alf Valentine, which led to a series triumph and the emergence of the West

Indies as a major force in world cricket. It also led to the immortal, and fondly recalled, lines: 'With those two little pals of mine, Ramadhin and Valentine'.

In the mid-1990s there was no hotter topic in cricket than the flashing blade of Brian Charles Lara, and the calypsonians went to town.

Alexander D. Great, who was born in Belmont, Port of Spain, but now resides in the UK, was one of those inspired to put pen to paper and 'Lash Dem Lara' was the result.

'The title actually comes from something I saw scrawled on the side of a bar in Port of Spain's Maraval Road in 1993,' he says. 'Lara obviously hadn't broken the records by then but he was already very prominent and someone had scribbled *Lash Dem Lara* on the wall of this bar. And of course you have to have a bit of double meaning in calypso so with *lash*, you not only have the meaning of hitting the ball hard with the bat but also *lashing* the opposition as well.

'My approach is from an historical point of view, telling the story,' says the man nicknamed 'The History Calypsonian'. 'So, with lines like, "He practise with broomstick, Hitting marble and lime", I wanted people to know that's what he did, he practised like that to hone his accuracy. I wanted to build the picture of this young man who rose from these beginnings to become such a huge figure on the global stage.'

The song was written in May 1994 and the singer gave a copy to Lara that summer in London. Twelve months on, Great travelled to Trinidad and Tobago for the 1995 Carnival and was amazed to find the buzz about the young left-hander undiminished.

'The atmosphere was absolutely euphoric, everybody was talking about Lara. It was a year after he broke the record but it was the first Carnival since it happened,' says Great, who has been the BBC's Calypsonian-in-Residence for the last ten years. 'There were about thirty-five calypsos on Lara that year. It was phenomenal, though many of them were just written and never recorded, played at the concerts and in the tents, but a good half a dozen really raised their head above the parapet.'

One performance of 'Lash Dem Lara' really stood out for the performer that year.

'Rhyners Record Shop, in Duke Street, Port of Spain, used to put on a street show in the week leading up to Carnival. The audience used to come with rotten fruit ready to pelt anybody they didn't consider good enough, so it was pressure. I was told by one of my cousins in the crowd when I started to sing he overheard a man saying he was about to pelt me, but then his wife tell him, "No, let me hear what he have tuh say." By the time I got through the first verse the man decided he actually quite liked the song so I escaped.'

In the UK the song became popular with the BBC, who regularly played it when covering pieces on Lara, and it led to Great being asked to perform at the official opening of Lord's Lara Exhibition in May 2007. He says the song went down surprisingly well with an atypical crowd.

'I ended up singing it about eight times!' he exclaims. 'There were all these old English colonel-types who kept saying, "Sing that song about Lara again would you, it was awfully good!"'

With so many songs written about Lara in 1995, the way in which his achievements were being chronicled was diverse. Many lauded his exploits by recalling the 375 itself, with common themes of reference including which England bowlers came in for punishment; Lara's stature and skill; and how the record-breaking runs were scored.

Amongst these are Delamo and Gypsey's 'Up and Away Lara' and Defosto's 'Four Lara Four', which evokes the investment in Lara's early development and the rewards now being enjoyed: 'Is what you sow is what you shall reap, I always hear wise people say, Is harvest time and things getting sweet.'

Becket's 'Laramania' also recounts the 375 before relating that Lara's 501 had caused him more work with the consequent necessity of additional verses, and closes with the line, 'Ah got to hurry out o' the studio, Before he break a next world record tomorrow.'

Others took a different tack. In 'Lara Promenade', Magruff sympathises with the young left-hander's workload: 'Since Lara make the three-seventy-five, Is just by sheer luck that boy still alive, All how he tell them he want a rest, That he under pressure and serious stress.'

All Rounder's 'Laramania' tells the tongue-in-cheek story of a 'pretty, pretty señorita' that has travelled across to Trinidad and Tobago from Venezuela just to be in the land of her hero, because she has the Laramania. The country's many other attractions are extolled to the girl by All Rounder – who, incidentally, is also a cricket umpire in real life – but in vain as all she wants is Lara.

Watchman's 'Prince of Plunder' is a terrific example of the calypsonian's art. In it he charts the problems of the West Indies' two oldest and keenest rivals, Australia and England, in handling the other-worldly talent of Lara. Mocking each mercilessly, he suggests England will soon create a rule limiting batsmen to one four an over (a reference to the law brought in restricting bouncers per over, following the West Indies successful employment of short-pitch bowling).

He rams each verse home with a chorus pillorying a fictional bowler, facing Lara, who keeps begging his captain for a rest because he's tired of getting hit for four and six. The final three lines of this chorus change each time and contain the evocative stanzas: 'Ah rather tackle Bobbit's wife Lorena, She cutting off mih manhood much easier, Than to bowl to Brian Lara', and, 'Ah rather cross in front a Maxi driver, Or carry O. J. Simpson wife to dinner, Than to bowl to Brian Lara.'

For sheer unabashed joy in celebrating Lara's achievements, though, it's hard to get better than Austin 'Superblue' Lyon's 'Signal to Lara'.

Each year at Carnival a coveted title, Road March, is awarded to that season's most popular song, the winner being the tune played most often at the band judging points over the course of Carnival Tuesday. In 1995, the clear winner was Superblue's infectiously catchy, high tempo 'Signal to Lara'. It is full of the upbeat energy that is Carnival season in Trinidad and Tobago and, in a nation that needs no second invitation, the call to 'Jump for joy and party' in the wake of Lara's achievements was heeded.

'"Signal" is a very good song and it connected to the feeling at the time,' says Rudder. 'Superblue has the rhythm of the people and Lara had just broken the record so there was no way it could be stopped.'

Even if not explicitly about Lara, many other calypsos in 1995, as well as a parang titled 'Lara' by the Lara Brothers, made reference to him or his influence. After 1995, and with the demise of West Indian cricketing superiority, references to Lara in calypso would shift emphasis from record-breaker to saviour.

Bally's 'We Coming Back', in 1997, emphasised the fact that nothing unites the Caribbean like cricket and urged the region's people to take the spirit of the historic feats of yesteryear and move forward with the new champion, Lara: 'Let us go ahead with strength and with pride, With Walsh at the helm, Lara at he side, Three seventy five, five hundred and one, That is what we call a phenomenon.'

After the West Indies relinquished their status as world's best side, the call for Lara to be installed as captain and to lead the revival gathered pace.

Contender's 'Ah Ready' related the falling cricketing standards which had caused the region to relinquish its hegemony after fifteen years, and how Lara must now be the man to take the reins and move the team forward. Making reference to some well-publicised misdemeanours – 'Is true I abuse the physio, Mr Dennis Waight, Is true I reach St Vincent, Twenty-four hours late' – Contender contends that that is all in the past and 'It's plain to see ah ready, To take on the captaincy.'

It is a song which echoes many of the themes reverberating around Caribbean cricket at the time. Lines such as 'Time to stop being paranoid' and 'This ain't no coup or no overthrow, I just ready to run the show', allude to Caribbean insularity and particularly the mistrust felt between Jamaica and Trinidad and Tobago over the regional captaincy. Patriotic sentiment had been stirred by continued accusations that Lara was plotting and positioning for leadership, which rankled with Jamaicans because the incumbent skipper, Courtney Walsh, was a national icon.

'Why Jamaica getting on so, eh', asks Contender, to which he probably didn't need an answer.

When Lara finally acceded to the captaincy, Brother Marvin celebrated the fact in 'Bat On' by revelling in Lara's battle with the WICB. 'The kissing butt, I t'ink is what, Dey wanted you do, But you say nah, so it was pressure, Before Jamaica could say boo.' He finished by singing, 'Your stubbornness win, the Prince of Port of Spain has become the King.'

Rudder himself also wrote about Lara but in a more esoteric fashion.

'I wrote a song called "Legacy" but I didn't want to necessarily fall into the trap of writing about Brian,' he says. 'I wanted to write about the continuation that he embodied. Everyone was into Lara, Lara, Lara, and I just wanted to say well, OK, yes but hold on, what does he represent? So "Legacy" was based on this great lineage of cricketers that we have in the Caribbean and how Lara was the latest in that proud line.'

Raconteurs and racers

Lara had proved an inspiration not only for songwriters; his exploits were fuel for the written and spoken word as well.

Books soon followed his 1994 exploits, with Jack Bannister's *Story of a Record-breaking Year* being published in September of the same year. A year later Lara's autobiography, *Beating The Field*, was released, written with one of the most highly respected names in sports journalism, Brian Scovell. The prolific Scovell, the author of twenty-four books, celebrated over fifty years in Fleet Street in 2010.

Live performers also utilised Lara as material for their shows. Raconteur, storyteller, poet and author Paul Keens-Douglas is famed in the English-speaking Caribbean for his pithy observations of West Indian life, and a regular focus of his observational eye is cricket.

One Keens-Douglas poem, 'Lara Fans', describes blinkered Lara supporters who swan into games, plant their coolers down and then badger people for information on Lara alone, not caring about the team, other players or state of the game, only 'How much Lara make?'

It evokes the spirit of 'ole talk in the stands, with Lara fans lauding their hero and making excuses for any bad form or wrongdoing. As Keens-Douglas, who MC'd Lara's Trinidad and Tobago Cricket Board retirement evening in April 2008, puts it: 'Them don't care about weather, if it rain or if it snow, All them come to see is Lara on the go.'

Keens-Douglas's most famous and fondly regarded skit is 'Tanti At De Oval', which tells the story of an irascible Aunt (Tanti Merle) who the narrator is persuaded to take to a cricket match at the Queen's Park Oval, with lamentable consequences. He reprises Merle in a skit, 'Tanti An'

Lara', based on Lara's Test record-breaking innings of 375 in 1994. The story follows the events of the Antigua Test's third morning, when a diverse crowd, lured by the promise of curried goat and fuelled by some deadly babash (home-produced, illegal bush rum), gather at Tanti Merle's to witness the forty-six runs needed to break Sobers's record.

When somebody reaches a position of celebrity in their chosen field it is not uncommon for people to begin naming their offspring after them; witness the derivations of Barack Obama inflicted on newborns after 2009, the number of Jonnys in middle England after Jonny Wilkinson drop-goaled the nation to rugby World Cup glory in 2003, and even the abundant progeny named in honour of *Neighbours* actors Jason Donovan and Kylie Minogue (and their alter egos Scott and Charlene) in the late 1980s. In Trinidad and Tobago, this concept was given an interesting twist when a whole raft of animals began carrying Lara's brand, including a line of racehorses.

In the early 1990s one of Lara's biggest fans was racehorse owner Roger Hadeed. Hadeed had attended Fatima College with Lara, and Hadeed's father, Joe, is the most renowned figure in horseracing in the twin-island republic.

'I breed horses every year to sell but I always keep one back for Roger because he loves racing,' says Hadeed senior, who still breeds racehorses and is Chairman of the Trinidad and Tobago Racing Authority. 'I give him one horse each year to race and have a bit of fun with.'

In 1993 that horse was Lash Dem Lara. The name had been inspired by a local newspaper headline which ran after Lara's famed Sydney innings of 277, 'Lash Dem Lara!' By 1994, in keeping with its namesake, the horse was enjoying a fantastic year and trouncing all comers. In September, shortly after the conclusion of Lara's stupendous English domestic season, the connections of Lash Dem Lara were celebrating their own spectacular triumph when the horse won the most prestigious event on the local racing calendar, the 1994 Trinidad Derby.

'It was all over the papers here and someone told me Michael Holding had mentioned it during a cricket match he was commentating on: that a horse called Lash Dem Lara had won the Derby in Trinidad and it was named after Brian,' says the seventy-two-year-old, who has been involved in racing for over fifty-five years and at one time had more than seventy horses in training on the Queen's Park Savannah.

'Whenever I meet up with Brian we chat about it. He was really happy about the win, proud in a way, because he had that connection with Roger as well. They went to school together, and they're still very close friends today.'

Further to Lash Dem Lara, Roger Hadeed named other thoroughbreds after the batting hero, such as Captain Lara, Lara 501 and Lara Legend, but unfortunately without such successful results.

This racing nomenclature was not restricted to the equine world either. When Lara recaptured the world Test record with a knock of 400 against England in 2004, David Seetaram, of the Barataria Pigeon Club, was moved to name one of his feathered luminaries Lara 400 in honour of the Prince of Port of Spain.

10 Back down to earth

Lara's unparalleled run of form had gained him the recognition he sought as the world's best batsman but the attendant pressures that title would bring were unforeseen. His performances brought media attention unmatched in the life of any cricketer before him; everything Lara did was newsworthy and his own desire to benefit financially from his new status added to a frenzied schedule.

Lara had engaged in an uninterrupted run from January's Caribbean regional tournament into the England series and then, having rattled up a Test record 375, to a plane and Warwickshire for the four-and-a-half-month county season. By the latter half of that English season he had begun to take on a hunted and haunted mien and respite would not come with its conclusion: the West Indies were due to begin a two-month tour of India in early October.

The West Indies should have been high on confidence, having recorded successive wins over South Africa, Australia, Pakistan and England, but the India tour was to highlight their worrying lack of quality reserves. The side was without three mainstays in skipper Richie Richardson (acute fatigue syndrome), Desmond Haynes (dispute with the Board) and Curtly Ambrose (injured right shoulder) and it showed.

Delayed for a week, due to a pneumonic plague outbreak in India, the tour did not start well as Lara missed his flight from Trinidad and an unimpressed WICBC fined him US$1,000. Once in India, a geographically testing itinerary, suspicions of pitches prepared to assist the home team's spinners, and the huge crowds that had assembled largely to see Lara, took their toll.

'Every airport we went to we had the army with guns there keeping back thousands of people all come to see him,' says the star batsman's former Fatima coach Bryan Davis, who was in the subcontinent as a journalist reporting on the tour. 'I just used to jump in behind the team to get safe passage through those crowds. It was too much for Brian. He said, "Mr Davis, I don't think I can play this game longer than thirty, you know. I can't take this."'

On the field, Lara failed to spark, recording just two 50s in the drawn three-Test series, while the home side took the honours in the one-dayers. His one memorable moment came when he had the honour of captaining the West Indies for the first time, in Walsh's absence, in a one-day international, but that match had been lost.

Happier times lay ahead on a short tour of New Zealand in February 1995, where Lara, acting as vice-captain to Walsh, topped the ODI batting in a 3-0 West Indian whitewash and helped set up victory in the 2nd Test with a magnificent 147, to seal the series 1-0.

Champions dethroned

Rarely can one series have presaged such divergent fortunes for the two combatants as the 1995 Frank Worrell Trophy clash between Australia and the West Indies. The West Indians came in having not lost a series since 1980, the Aussies having not won a series against their Caribbean adversaries in two decades. During that long hiatus, the baggy greens had taken a lot of punishment from a succession of world-class pacemen but they were not going to be intimidated this time.

'Right at the start of the tour we said, "Stuff these guys. Their tailenders, their bowlers have bounced us for years, now let's get our own back,"' said Australian top-order batsman Mark Waugh. '"Don't worry about what might happen. They might get the shits and bowl quicker. Who knows? But one thing's for sure, and that is they're gonna bowl us bouncers and intimidate us, so let's get them before they get us.'"

With the Australians having enjoyed such a sustained period of cricketing domination in recent years, it is easy to forget there was a point in time when they were underdogs going into a Test series. They were in 1995, and compounded that tag by losing the one-day series 4-1 and frontline bowlers Craig McDermott and Damian Fleming to injury, prior to Barbados's 1st Test.

A lacklustre display at the Kensington Oval, though, displaying all the signs that the hosts had underestimated their opponents, tipped the early initiative back to Australia. A succession of cavalier shots, most notably from returning skipper Richie Richardson, left the West Indies three wickets down with only six runs on the board and requiring a rescue act from Lara and Hooper.

The pair restored some balance by adding 124 for the fourth wicket when, with the West Indian innings at 156, Lara leant back on a fierce cut shot and drilled the ball hard, but aerially, to a diving Steve Waugh at point. Waugh was unable to take the ball cleanly and juggled it as he fell to the ground, trapping it beneath him before his left hand emerged and he claimed the catch. Lara delayed for a second, feeling the ball may have been grounded, but was sent on his way by the umpire for 65.

Television pictures were unclear but West Indian fans were not. Waugh underwent a character assassination and was lambasted for cheating, to the point where veiled threats were made regarding his safety.

It was a contentious and decisive moment as the home side capitulated for a meagre first innings total of 195. It was advantage Australia and one they drove home, eventually taking the match by ten wickets inside three days. Though a diverting flashpoint, of which much would continue to be made, the Lara catch was just that, a distraction, and could not mask the lack of pride shown, particularly in a toothless second innings.

The Aussies were in no doubt as to the significance of the victory and maintained their lead with a keenly contested draw in Antigua's 2nd Test. Having bowled Australia out for a modest 216 in their first innings, the

West Indies and Lara were charging in reply when, out of the blue, a stunning David Boon catch dismissed the young batting star. Playing fluently and aggressively Lara had struck sixteen boundaries in his 88 runs, when he tried to whip a Steve Waugh delivery from outside off-stump into the leg-side. He found only the moustachioed Boon, who was positioned near the non-striker at short mid-on. The Tasmanian, who is more bulldog than whippet, looked shocked at his own athleticism as he leapt to take a one-handed catch wide to his left. It halted the West Indian charge in its tracks and the rain-interrupted game petered out into a draw.

As the series proceeded to Trinidad, one man began imposing his considerable personality on proceedings, and it wasn't the Prince of Port of Spain. The enduring image of the Queen's Park Oval's 3rd Test was that of Steve Waugh and Curtly Ambrose squaring up to one another in angry confrontation and the Antiguan delivering the infamous line 'don't cuss me'. Ambrose had just bowled a short delivery and followed through with an obligatory glare; Waugh offered him some strong-worded advice in return and a situation flared up which only ended when Richie Richardson pulled his fast bowler away.

Waugh had gained a reputation for being susceptible to short-pitched bowling. He had given up playing the hook shot for reasons of expediency – it got him out too much – but this had been interpreted as weakness not pragmatism.

'[Steve] showed he was prepared to put it all on the line, in the toughest conditions … against probably the best fast bowler of our time,' says Aussie opener Justin Langer. 'To stand up to him [Ambrose] and go toe-to-toe, it gave us a huge boost.'

Despite an unbeaten 63 though, nearly half of Australia's first innings total, Waugh could not prevent the West Indies from drawing level in a low-scoring game on a green, seaming track.

In Jamaica, at Sabina Park's decisive 4th Test, the home side's under-fire skipper Richardson hit a first innings century and was supported by 65 from Lara. It was an ultimately below-par first innings total of 265 but didn't look that way when Australia reached 73 for 3 in their reply. It was then that the two Waugh brothers, Steve and Mark, came together in a series-winning partnership, a magnificent stand of 231, and one for which the West Indies had no answer.

'Steve had made up his mind to bat and bat, to stay out there and anchor the proceedings,' says Australian bowler Paul Reiffel. 'In the process he copped a lot of blows on his arms, chest and ribs. When he came back to the dressing room at the end of Day Two, we could see the spots and bruises on his body, but as long as he was out there in the middle he just kept going at them.'

Waugh, who Reiffel described as being in 'a trance-like state', was last man out for an even 200, an innings which would define his career and cement his reputation as one of the game's toughest competitors. The innings both galvanised the Australians and demoralised the West Indians.

'Inspired by his innings and making good use of the conditions and the mental state of the West Indies top order, I grabbed three quick wickets late in the evening,' says Reiffel. 'After a day's rest we returned to complete the formalities and claimed the Frank Worrell Trophy.'

Waugh, with 429 runs at 107.25, was named Man of the Series and the Australians emerged victorious in the Caribbean for the first time since 1972/73.

The Caribbean went into shock and mourning. A dominant West Indies had been a cricketing truth for the best part of two decades, it wasn't any more. Although the evidence of the West Indian demise had been apparent long before this series, the manner in which they relinquished their crown was still a shock. Had it been a stirring final surrender, full of character and fight, it could have been stomached more easily, but the series had witnessed a string of lacklustre performances and a worrying air of disunity within the camp.

'It was a mix of emotions: anger, disappointment, confusion as to what had gone wrong,' says West Indies top-order batsman Jimmy Adams. 'And when you don't know the cause of something it's very difficult to start making a plan to go forward. That sense of confusion I think typified our cricket for some years afterwards.'

Walsh had been magnificent with the ball but it was clear Ambrose had yet to fully recover from his shoulder problems and there was little reliable support. Lara had topped the batting, with 308 runs at 44, but in truth all had underperformed. There were now inevitable question marks over Richardson's captaincy, a situation he exacerbated by bizarrely describing his opponents as the weakest Australian side I have played.

The 'weak' Australians would go on to establish their own cricketing dynasty; for the West Indies, the journey upon which they were embarking was a more unpalatable one.

England 1995

Discussions over the captaincy had raged following defeat to Australia, and the effects of that debate would dog the 1995 tour of England. Lara, whose stock had risen since his record-breaking feats the year before, was seen by many as heir apparent. He had never made a secret of his ultimate desire to lead the West Indies and was being vociferously backed but the WICBC opted for continuity, for now, and retained Richardson.

The tour, which began just ten days after the conclusion of the Australia series, would be a long one, nearly four months. For an already uncomfortable captain, there would be time for wounds to fester, factions to deepen and mistrust to surface.

For the West Indies, defeating England had become routine over the previous two decades, often by handsome margins, but this time round they were finding it difficult to establish dominance over a home side that was playing with dynamism and belief.

'We just couldn't play good cricket together for a long time; the psychologists might be better placed than me to explain it,' says Jimmy Adams. 'It really started to bug a lot of us that why was it, when we still had great players, that it just wasn't happening? There was a general feeling of discontent within the squad, which had begun before the England tour even started, and it reflected in the way we played.'

Many, including Lara, felt the reason was a lack of discipline and structure around the squad. The issue came to a fiery head in a team meeting after the 4th Test match at Old Trafford, which England had won, to draw level in the series at 2-2. Lara spoke his mind and accused Richardson of being complicit in the indiscipline affecting the team. The Antiguan responded by saying Lara had an agenda in criticising him, a thinly veiled insinuation that Lara coveted the captaincy.

'Brian went directly for Richie but I will speak for myself and say my issue wasn't particularly with Richie as it was with the management team and how they were doing things,' says Adams, who was present at the meeting in a Manchester hotel. 'The bigger issue was management and we had problems going back to, well, once they replaced Rohan Kanhai as coach and David Holford as manager coming back from New Zealand in early 1995.'

Legendary former West Indies batsman Kanhai had taken up the position of coach in 1992 and, alongside David Holford as manager, had been both popular and successful. The WICBC had replaced them with a team that consisted of manager Wes Hall, coach Andy Roberts and the captain, Richardson.

'Brian wasn't the only one, I think a number of us were a little confused as to how things were being run,' says Adams. 'One of the issues I had was consistency. I didn't see all members of the squad being treated equally and that was a day-in-day-out issue which just bugged the hell out of me.'

The confrontation between captain and star batsman led to an emotional outburst and exit from Lara.

'He got up in anger,' Richardson wrote later, 'and said a number of things including his life being destroyed, money did not mean anything to him and that he was resigning.'

If some thought Lara's threat to resign a fit of pique, team manager Hall was not amongst them. He told him to sleep on his decision but the next day Lara's mind was unmoved.

'I hugged him and wished him goodbye,' said Hall and with that the Trinidadian left the team for two days.

The walkout had, upon reflection, many root causes. Team discipline was certainly one, but the workload and focus placed on Lara since his multiple world-record-breaking feats the previous summer also played their part.

Gerry Gomez, a twenty-nine-Test veteran and later West Indian chairman of selectors, said he saw an indication of this when speaking to Lara during the 2nd Test at Lord's, after the batsman posted scores of 6 and 13.

'He was listless, his eyes dead. He did not seem very enthusiastic. He looked very tired. He hadn't scored that much to make him that tired. Here was a young man who was very unhappy.'

By the time the 4th Test came round at Old Trafford, Lara was at the end of his tether. He even called his family in Trinidad to ask as many of them as possible to be around him; sisters, brothers, nephews and his mother heeded the call and flew to the UK. One family member says Lara had had enough by this time and was telling those around him that this might well be his last tour.

After an emergency meeting with WICBC President Peter Short, though, Lara was finally persuaded back into the fold. Short ended the meeting saying that the whole matter would be dealt with by the manager and the tour committee. In the event it wasn't and the ramifications of that failure to act would be felt four months later.

Those simply watching the cricketing action would have been hard-pressed to know anything was awry in Lara's world, because from Old Trafford onwards he embarked on a blistering run of form. He hit big centuries in each of the last three Tests, including 179 in the final match at the Oval. As with many others throughout his career, it was a century he had predicted.

The night before his innings Lara had gone out for a meal with those family members now in the UK. The next morning he rang one of them to ask if they had left for the ground because he was going to make a hundred that day. They hadn't and Lara told them, tongue-in-cheek, that if they weren't in their reserved seats when he raised his bat, he would be putting them on the next plane back to Trinidad.

In a wonderfully vacillating if, for the West Indians, ultimately frustrating series, the tourists had twice held the lead and enjoyed positions in the 5th Test at Trent Bridge and the 6th at the Oval which many felt should have brought victories and consequently the series win.

Lara, who had scored over 300 runs more than the next best West Indian batsman, shared the Man of the Series award with England's Mike Atherton. But the 2-2 draw was an outcome that satisfied no one in the West Indian camp and there were calls for Richardson to be replaced.

'His [Richardson's] position has to be seriously discussed and looked at for the next tour,' said Lara's mentor Joey Carew, before offering up his views on a suitable successor. 'I don't feel that we should deny any longer that Brian Lara is the best man for the role.'

Lara drops out

The 'next tour' to which Carew referred was in late November to Australia and the Benson and Hedges World Series Cup; a tournament which would be used as preparation for the 1996 World Cup in India, Pakistan and Sri Lanka. Prior to departure, a WICBC meeting was held into the disciplinary matters on the England tour. The committee found four players – Curtly Ambrose, Kenny Benjamin, Carl Hooper and Brian Lara – guilty of misconduct and fined them 10 per cent of their tour fee.

Lara was incensed; having railed against the indiscipline of the tour he was now being grouped alongside some of those deemed responsible. What infuriated him further was that he felt the misconduct he was now being punished for had already been dealt with at the meeting with Short. The WICBC President seemingly agreed when he said that Lara might justifiably have felt it was the end of the matter.

Two days before the Australian tour was due to leave, Lara reacted by withdrawing from the party. It caused a furore and Lara faced stinging criticism. Many outsiders felt he was being petulant, the pampered child's reaction to being disciplined. It was something Lara would repeatedly deny, stating how at that point in time cricket was ruining his life.

One member of Lara's family agreed, saying that by the end of 1995 those closest to him were witnessing the game's impact on Brian's mental and physical state; they had begun to have serious concerns beyond cricket. Some within the family even felt his life was unfolding at such a pace that it seemed as though he might not live beyond a young age.

At the time of the crisis, Lara responded to the public backlash by broadening the argument and questioning the source of West Indian cricket's woes and then upping the ante by stating that he might never play international cricket again.

'It is more than a possibility that I may not be picked or decide not to go to the World Cup. The West Indies may never pick me again. It has happened to other players before.'

Close friend, international midfielder Russell Latapy, leapt to his defence declaring, in typically understated footballer terms, that he was '200 per cent' behind Lara, but this was not the case across the Caribbean. Clarvis Joseph, President of the Leeward Islands Cricket Association, stated that, 'The first thing I get when I walk in the streets [in Antigua] is, "I hope you guys aren't going to pick Brian Lara again."'

In the days following his announcement, Lara factored in fatigue as a major contributor to his state of mind.

'For the last 18 months ever since I made my world record against England I have felt pressure building upon me,' he said, before adding, 'I made my decision to take a rest and I just haven't been able to get any … I can't escape with all this going on … until I put my mind to rest, until this business is resolved, I just cannot consider the future.'

What was uncomfortably apparent to the WICBC, though, was that Lara was their future: the one man who could restore pre-eminence if anyone could. They could not control him as they would like, but they could not do without him either.

'Brian Lara is too great a talent to let him go like that, and we will find a way of bringing it together and coming out with dignity both for the WICBC and for Brian,' said WICBC President Short in a statement before a special meeting convened to discuss the matter.

That meeting took place at the Hilton in Barbados, where the face-saving measures were that the star batsman received a slapped wrist for dropping out of a tour whilst under contract and was put on notice about future behaviour, while Lara once again made himself available for World Cup selection.

World Cup 1996

That World Cup, in February 1996, would go down as one of the most memorable of all, with the fairy-tale victors being co-hosts Sri Lanka. However, 29 February 1996 is a date many Caribbean cricket fans would rather forget, marking as it does perhaps the most infamous West Indian defeat of all time, at the hands of African part-timers Kenya.

At the game's halfway stage there was little hint of what was to come, as the West Indies won the toss and bowled Kenya out for a modest 166. Even when the West Indians found themselves 22 for 2 the packed crowd at Pune's Nehru Stadium expected normal service to be resumed as Lara was welcomed to the crease with a huge ovation. He has always been enormously popular in India and spectators were anticipating fireworks when he got off the mark with a cracking cover drive for four.

'We went out there and made a mockery of West Indies cricket.' Lara walks off, to the delight of Kenyan wicketkeeper Tariq Iqbal and slip fielder Aasif Karim, as the West Indies head for a famous defeat in the 1996 World Cup.

That was as good as it got though, as Lara, displaying none of his famed concentration, unleashed a series of wild and ambitious strokes. Enter wicketkeeper Tariq Iqbal for the type of moment you feel sure, somewhere in a corner of Kenya, is still boring children and grandchildren to this day.

Bearded and portly, wearing a blue headband and large glasses, Iqbal was, without being unduly unkind, not the model of a top-level wicketkeeper. But as Lara aimed another expansive back-foot drive at a Rajab Ali delivery and succeeded only in snicking it, Iqbal's eyes widened. The keeper clapped his gloves together like a performing seal, with his legs soon following suit, and engulfed the ball as it buried itself in his midriff. With a look which married surprise, relief and euphoria, his hands emerged safely with the ball and he held it aloft in supreme triumph.

From there it was all downhill and, with a couple of confused run-outs thrown in for good measure, the West Indies were bowled out for 93, giving the Kenyans a remarkably comfortable seventy-three-run victory and driving another nail into Richardson's captaincy coffin.

'We went out there and made a mockery of West Indies cricket,' said Lara summing up the feelings of a region.

Within a week, Richardson issued a statement declaring his time at the West Indies helm was at an end and that he would relinquish the leadership after the World Cup.

For Lara there remained a sting in the tail of defeat, when reports began circulating of racist remarks made by him in the Kenyan dressing room post-match. A tape recorder had picked up Lara's comments, subsequently printed in India's *Outlook* magazine, saying that losing to the Kenyans wasn't as bad as losing to the South Africans because: 'You know, this white thing comes into the picture. We can't stand losing to them.'

Lara said his words had been taken out of context but then, with the West Indies subsequently squeezing through to the quarter-finals after a final group win over Australia, the sporting gods conceived an intriguing last-eight clash with who else but South Africa.

Whether spurred on by the adverse press or not, Lara returned to his sparkling best with an inspirational 111 that was the backbone of a compelling nineteen-run victory. It appeared as though the ignominy of Kenyan defeat could yet be turned into glorious ultimate triumph. That was until normal chaotic service was resumed in the semi-final against Australia, where the West Indies threw away an almost impossibly strong position.

With the West Indies at 165 for 2 chasing Australia's 207, they needed just forty-three runs from nine overs at a routine 4.78 runs per over. Somehow they contrived to lose eight wickets in fifty minutes in a panic-stricken display which saw none of the last seven batsmen scramble above three runs.

With Richardson stepping down, the focus was now thrown back onto his potential successor and there was widespread presumption that Lara would assume the mantle. But, just a few short months after he had dropped out of the Australia tour and with controversy continuing to dog him (Lara had a heated row with team physiotherapist Dennis Waight on the flight back from the World Cup), the idea of the man who had been groomed for the West Indies captaincy actually acceding to the position was still an unpalatable one for decision-makers.

Instead they opted for one of the region's stellar servants – and, incidentally, the favourite cricketer of Lara's mother, Pearl – Courtney Walsh. Walsh, who had debuted in 1984, served the West Indies with unwavering distinction and would go on to claim a world-record 519 Test wickets, sending down over 30,000 deliveries in the process, during a glittering seventeen-year international career.

The first series under the charismatic Walsh's new tenure was the visit of the New Zealanders and, far from being next in line to the throne, it now seemed Lara's stock had fallen further as the vice-captaincy was handed to Ian Bishop. He managed a best of 74 in the 1-0 Test series win, stating later that he was finding it harder to get pumped up for encounters with cricket's smaller nations.

'Playing against New Zealand with their sort of attack was not a great motivator,' he said, before adding: 'For the future, I feel I can look forward to great things because first of all the team situation motivates me more than anything else.

'I'm going out to Australia in October to regain the Frank Worrell Trophy, not to get 277 again or make sure I get three centuries. The first series in South Africa will be another big motivator [in 1998/99]. I don't think I'd be eager enough to set new records against not such good teams.'

Dealing with fame

With Lara not contracted to an English county for the 1996 season, it at last appeared he would get the break he so clearly needed. Instead of enjoying two years of glory since his record-breaking exploits of 1994, he had been ill at ease, a man harassed and harangued, his every move worthy of note, report and often criticism.

Lara's 375, 501, and the string of hundreds in between, had come in such a restricted timeframe – forty-nine days – that their impact was correspondingly pronounced. In terms of shock value, his explosion to superstardom was not dissimilar to that experienced by Olympic gold medallists who, after success on the global stage, have their lives catapulted into focus.

'It can be quite freaky – you're suddenly not sure where it will all start and stop, and what it means,' says four-time rowing gold medallist Sir Matthew Pinsent. 'You can end up feeling like you want time away from the sport, yet all you're asked to do is relive that one sporting moment – feeling torn between escaping and making the most of it. And you do want to make the most of it – in terms of fame, respect and money.'

Rhona Martin, who won curling gold at Salt Lake City in 2002, said the media intrusion is what she noticed most, while 1980 Olympic figure-skating champion Robin Cousins MBE said that for him it was other people's reactions. 'It's not so much how it changes your life as how it changes the way others perceive you.'

All sentiments familiar to Lara, and it was a situation one of his former Fatima College teachers, Barbara Jenkins, says she noted with sadness at the time.

'The enormous pressures associated with the way he shot to fame; there was nobody to guide him through that, he had no apparatus to deal with it. There was no balance in his life and it was inevitable something would have to give eventually.

'Here was a young man from a country village in Trinidad and I think he was quite naive when he left these shores. People began saying things about him, which amounted to little more than character assassination really, and so very soon he's wondering who he can trust,' says the Caribbean winner of the 2010 Commonwealth Foundation's Short Story Competition.

'There are plenty of players who have behaved far worse but did not get the same attention simply because they weren't as good as Brian. Anything he did was worthy of press attention; I think that broke him to some degree in the end. He loved the game from such a young age but a lot of that simple joy of playing was taken from him.'

Not that it was just media pressure that was suffocating Lara. Ironically, the adulation of his homeland was also an issue, says singer David Rudder.

'Every generation in Trinidad and Tobago needs someone to not just look up to but hold on to because it's a small society. When he became *the Brian Lara* I thought uh-oh they're going to grab on to him now. It's that extraordinary level of expectation and if you don't handle it right you can buckle.'

Others have suggested that the loss of his father, Bunty, meant he also lost the solid sounding board of advice and guidance which had been ever present before he was catapulted to fame. Those lucky enough to enjoy the type of father–son bond that Bunty and Brian had will acknowledge the residual strength and peace of mind that comes from knowing that your father is always there. Brian is a strong-minded man but it would have been natural to have turned to Bunty during some of his darker hours.

In a 1996 *Daily Telegraph* interview, Lara gave his own synopsis of his early career and the point he had reached emotionally and professionally by that time.

'Mentally, it's getting tougher. From the age of six to twenty-four, I was 100 per cent focused and there was a lot more wanting to be recognised.

I've moved out of that scenario – it's harder now to maintain [that focus] and live up to expectations.

'It all started after the Antigua Test [1994],' he added reflectively. 'When I remember someone telling me: "The headache has just begun" and I was wondering why? I was looking forward to becoming wealthy, and people were looking at me as a record-holder, and it was only after a while I realised what he was talking about – the pressure from the media and the public, the expectation from everybody.

'I found I didn't like the idea of being scrutinised. I'm normally a very outgoing person and now part of my life was being tampered with. I wasn't told I was going to be a record-holder – I didn't go to classes to study what to do … and you need some sort of guidance because you can be really naive. You can be used and abused pretty easily.'

You can't have it all ways though. At the time of the *Telegraph* interview, while many had assumed Lara (whose on-again-off-again negotiations with Warwickshire for a county contract that summer had ended in nothing) would be taking the break he had been craving, he was instead busy in England on a promotional tour launching his own range of cricket equipment, Lara International. Lara has always had an eye for making money and a lot of the extra pressure felt when shooting to fame came through the volume of sponsorship, advertising and appearance-related work he took on. It's a difficult balance of course, because quite naturally he wanted the rewards of what he had worked so hard to attain. He hadn't simply turned up on a cricket field in 1994 and broken records, he had been building towards it his entire life.

Unhappy Down Under

In November 1996, four years on from the 277 which put the world on notice of an extraordinary talent, a twenty-seven-year-old Lara was back Down Under for what would prove a tetchy, ill-tempered series.

Australia took the first two Tests at Brisbane and Sydney comfortably, and during the second an altercation between Lara, restored to the vice-captaincy, and Ian Healy soured relations and set the tone for the series.

Lara was certain that when he edged a Glenn McGrath delivery behind to Healy, the Australian wicketkeeper had not taken it cleanly, even though he said he had. Lara had to go but, incensed, later stormed into the Australian dressing room to tell them precisely what he thought of Healy. Tour manager Clive Lloyd later apologised for the confrontation, Lara did not.

Ambrose and Walsh bowled the West Indies to victory in Melbourne's 3rd Test to rekindle the series but hope was quickly and emphatically extinguished at the Adelaide Oval.

With Curtly Ambrose dropping out injured just before the start of the 4th Test, the West Indians' paucity of bowling reserves was again exposed and they were crushed by an innings and 183 runs. It gave Australia an unassailable 3-1 lead.

A consolation victory came in the 5th Test at Perth, aided by Lara's first and only meaningful contribution and Ambrose's restoration to the side. The Antiguan's five-wicket haul in the first innings and Lara's 132 set up the win but it was an ultimately disappointing series for the Trinidadian, with Chanderpaul usurping him as the West Indies top batsman. And the tour ended as it had begun – with antagonism and cross words – as Lara, acting as a runner for Courtney Walsh, mixed it with the Aussies to such a degree that both sides were warned about their conduct.

Returning to the Caribbean, a duel between two of modern cricket's great batsmen was predicted when the Indians came calling in March. Throughout the 1990s and into the twenty-first century, if the question was posited as to who was the premier batsman in the world, invariably it would result in a contest between Brian Lara and Sachin Tendulkar. Choosing a favourite often came down to stylistic preference, which batting characteristics you hold dearest.

For consistency, compact technical brilliance and longevity it is hard to look past Tendulkar; he is a batting machine. Lara himself said, 'If I had a son I would definitely like to see him bat like Sachin.'

Tendulkar is a supremely graceful batsman, a stylist out of the top drawer, but Lara fans counter the sheer exhilaration and flare of one of their hero's innings, and the fact that he so often converts them into huge knocks that change games puts him ahead. As with all sporting comparisons though, the debate is a pretty futile exercise, but that doesn't stop cricket lovers enjoying that exercise.

In March 1997 the duel between the Prince of Port of Spain and the Little Master did not produce the batting extravaganza everyone had hoped for. Neither Lara, who scored just one century, or Sachin Tendulkar, who scored none, could stamp their authority on a hard-fought five-Test series in which the home side ultimately prevailed 1-0.

Lara's behaviour since his record-breaking year of 1994 had received a lot of adverse press but an incident during the 2nd Test, at the Queen's Park Oval, was more reflective of the man behind the headlines, says former Trinidad and Tobago team manager Colin Borde.

'A very good Indian friend of mine, Mehul Shani, was here playing for my team at Queen's Park and he asked me if I could arrange for him to meet Brian because he was his hero.

'During the Oval Test match, West Indies were fielding and just before lunch Brian was near the boundary, so I asked him if it would be possible. He said yes, so after he went to get lunch quickly he came back out and I introduced him to Mehul, who was in a total mess. They had a really nice chat, with Brian asking him all about himself, where he's from, whether he speaks Gujarati … then Brian calls Sachin Tendulkar out from the other dressing room: "Sachin, come and meet my good friend." Well Mehul was nearly on the floor at this stage. And Sachin, thinking he really was Brian's good friend, approached him as such and spent a long time talking with him. Mehul took a load of pictures with both of them, got some autographs signed and everything.

'I saw Mehul later, when he'd had the pictures developed, and he just said: "Colin when I send these home I'm a god you know."

'Now Brian didn't have to do that, he didn't have to meet him in the first place, and when he did he could have just shook hands, said "hi, nice to meet you" and go. It was in the middle of a Test match don't forget.'

Lara had his own moment to remember during the series when he captained the West Indies for the first time, in the 3rd Test at Bridgetown, Barbados. With Walsh having withdrawn because of a strained hamstring, Lara oversaw the win which clinched the series. In so doing he became only the sixth West Indian to win his first Test as captain. Lara supporters saw the result as proof of his ability to inspire, and it certainly didn't help Walsh that he failed to achieve a positive result in the final two Tests of the series.

A 1-0 series win over Sri Lanka followed, but reports had surfaced of disharmony between Lara and Walsh which gathered momentum on the West Indies ill-fated tour of Pakistan. Prior to the trip, the West Indies selectors of Wes Hall, Joey Carew, Mike Findlay and Malcolm Marshall made their recommendation that Lara should be made captain but this decision was overturned by the Board and Walsh was retained. And an uncomfortable team atmosphere was assured when the Trinidad and Tobago Cricket Board stoked the fire by suggesting that Lara's rejection amounted to a calculated plot against him.

The series itself was an unmitigated disaster: the West Indies losing all its first-class matches and being blown away 3-0 in the Test series, with two innings defeats followed by a ten-wicket reversal. Not since the 1928 tour to England, sixty-nine years earlier, had the West Indies lost every match of a Test series. Lara's form deserted him – not that he was alone – and a top score of 37 and an average of 21.5 told its own story.

They made for chastening statistics and, added to the reports of disunity, led some Caribbean supporters to suggest Lara's lack of runs was part of a broader conspiracy to bring down Walsh and, further, that he would step down from the team if not made captain in the approaching home series with England.

Coach Malcolm Marshall, who would sadly pass away in 1999 from colon cancer aged just forty-one, denied the stories. West Indian cricket fans, though, are not known for letting a conspiracy theory pass lightly, especially when it carries with it the whiff of inter-island skulduggery.

'I don't think Brian's batting problems during the last few weeks have been technical,' said Marshall. 'The whole captaincy issue is affecting him and he has spoken to me about it a couple of times. When you know you are close to becoming captain I think it would affect anybody.

'He is very disappointed with his batting. But he loves to play for the West Indies and there is no way he would not play against England in the Test series if he was not made captain. He is not that sort of person.'

11 Captain of club and country

West Indies captain

'That was an aspiration from a young boy,' Lara once said of his desire to lead the West Indies. The fact that he had been routinely knocking heads with the WICB since he came to prominence was the reason he had so far failed to realise that aspiration. A distrustful Board seemed wary of what might happen were he given the power of the captaincy. They were having difficulty handling a strong-willed Lara as a player, what problems could surface with him as leader?

Yet by 1998 the support for Lara was growing ever louder and the WICB was running out of excuses not to make him captain.

'We now have to say, Brian Lara, this is your time, you come forward and lead the West Indies team,' said veteran West Indies cricket commentator Tony Cozier in a speech at the Queen's Park Cricket Club just before an announcement on the captaincy in January 1998. Cozier scorned Lara's passing over before the Pakistan tour (it had been revealed the decision was made via a series of telephone calls and not even a Board meeting) by rebranding the WICB, the West Indies Cricket Board of Crisis, Conflict, Controversy and Confusion.

'Selectors, experienced Test players, cricketers of knowledge, nominated an individual. And the Board, comprising a businessman, a racing pools operator, a bank manager, a school teacher and other sundry individuals who have never graced the Test cricket field, turn their recommendation down without a single explanation to the public.'

There was international support as well, even if slightly backhanded, as former England captain David Gower wrote in *Wisden Cricket Monthly* that now was Lara's time.

'Those who make the decisions in West Indies cricket have kept him down long enough,' he said. 'His response has hardly been that of the selfless team man, but now the West Indies must bite the bullet, make him captain and see if he has the ability to bring the team together in the same way as Clive Lloyd in the period of their greatest domination.'

Gower, who captained England thirty-two times, said the leadership would encourage Lara to 'prove to the Board, his colleagues, the West Indies supporters and all of us who watch intrigued from a distance just how wronged he has been ... The hardest to convince are likely to be his team-mates.'

With the selectors having met again and resubmitted their recommendation of Lara as captain for the England series the Board had little room for manoeuvre. The case for Lara had gathered such momentum that the fallout from a second successive rejection in such a short space of time would have been enormous. The WICB took the decision most were by now expecting and, just three weeks before the opening Test with England, Walsh was unceremoniously dropped from the captaincy and Lara installed.

The disastrous anomaly of the Pakistan tour notwithstanding, Walsh had registered series wins over New Zealand, India and Sri Lanka, plus, in an away series against the world's best side, Australia, a narrow 3-2 loss. In the context of the team he had under him it was a respectable record and Walsh felt understandably bitter at being removed. The great man was even contemplating retirement saying that whilst Lara would enjoy his full support, his own future would be discussed with friends and family in the coming days before a decision was reached.

It was hard for Lara to say the right thing at this point; he had always been ambitious and that ambition included the captaincy. There was nothing wrong in wanting to lead but he had to walk the tightrope of public opinion on whether that growing aspiration had affected both his cricket and that of his teammates.

As so often happens in sport, a delicious twist of fate threw up Walsh's home ground of Kingston's Sabina Park as venue for the first Test, and test, of Lara's tenure. Already unpopular in Jamaica for his apparent jostling for Walsh's position, he had received a poor reception from home fans when representing Trinidad and Tobago in the regional limited overs competition the previous October.

Lara reported how he had entered the field to a lot of loud and negative comments from the spectators, but said the late in-swinger from Franklyn Rose had had the bigger impact on him.

Having fallen first ball in a miserable total of 84 all out, the comments on the way back off the field can scarcely have been more complimentary.

An anti-Lara campaign was predicted on the first morning of the Sabina Park Test match and the new regional captain was aware he might undergo a lively baptism. He said all he could do was hope for the best, and trusted that good team performances would eventually win over all West Indians.

But Lara recognised other issues were already under regional discussion, such as his perceived lifestyle.

'I have to try as much as possible to make whatever minor changes – not major – that I have to make to ensure that I fit my role perfectly,' he said. 'Everybody seems to have an idea of how I live my life now. But of course as a West Indies captain compared to a normal West Indies player or an attractive batsman, or whatever, it's two different things. It's really leading the West Indian people, not just the cricket team.'

There was also a tacit admission that the team may not always have been his primary focus when it came to his batting.

'I've got to ensure that the team is benefitting from my batting now. In the past … you wanted to maintain yourself as the best batsman in the world or the most attractive batsman in the world.

'I think now that's gone through the window. I've got to focus more on the team. However attractive or unattractive I look now doesn't matter. At the end of the day the result is what is important.'

The fulfilment of a childhood dream. Lara becomes West Indies captain and shares a lighter moment with England skipper Michael Atherton before the ultimately abandoned 1998 Sabina Park Test match, in Kingston, Jamaica.

The intimidating Jamaican reception forecast did not materialise but that was due in no small part to Walsh, who not only played on but, showing tremendous magnanimity, threw his arms figuratively and physically around Lara. As the pair walked out onto the Sabina Park pitch for the 1st Test, the former captain diffused the potential for hostility from the stands by casting a fatherly arm around the shoulders of the much smaller Lara. Given the manner in which he had been replaced, it was a gesture which displayed enormous generosity of character. Even so, Lara was probably not hugely disappointed when, because of a dangerous pitch, the match was abandoned after just an hour. The England batsmen had been struck numerous times in those opening exchanges as a cracked and uneven wicket caused deliveries to rear alarmingly off a length, imperilling the players' safety beyond acceptable parameters.

If Lara had been worried about his reception at Sabina Park he had no such fears heading for a hastily organised replacement Test match at his home, Queen's Park Oval.

'The only criticism of Lara's captaincy that has ever been made in Trinidad is that his appointment did not come directly upon his admission to puberty,' wrote journalist B. C. Pires, who penned a hugely popular weekly column, 'Thank God It's Friday', in the Trinidadian press between 1988 and 2004 (reprised in 2010). 'Andy Caddick, the England fast bowler, said this week that Brian Lara is not God; Caddick clearly had not taken a straw poll at the Oval.'

Pires revealed the depth of the parochialism in a sequence of dropped catches.

The first, an ankle-high slip catch off England batsman Alec Stewart, was dropped by Lara. 'Total silence fell with it, but only for a second or two before a Rastaman on the cycle track under the scoreboard spoke. "Nobody coulda caught that," he declared, glaring round him, daring anyone to disagree. Intimidation was unnecessary.'

When Stewart had added just five more runs he was again dropped in the slips, this time by Carl Hooper diving across in front of Lara. '"Damned Guyanese," said the Rasta, smiling broadly. For the first time an Oval crowd was pleased to see a mistake made: it wasn't the hometown hero.'

The West Indies won the replacement Test by three wickets before that result was reversed just a week later, in the second Trinidadian Test, and the tourists tied the series up 1-1. Wins in the 4th and 6th Tests, in Guyana and Antigua respectively, re-established the home side's superiority, though, and ensured a successful start to Lara's captaincy as West Indies won 3-1. The home side followed this up with a 4-1 win in the five-match ODI series and Lara topped the batting in both formats. The results, and Lara's form, seemed vindication of the long-held assertion by his supporters that he could perform both as leader and principal batsman.

In the limited overs matches the star English batsman had been Nick Knight – the same young man so inspired by Lara's exploits in 1994 – who scored 295 runs at an average of 59. Lara and Knight would meet up again just nine days after the conclusion of the England tour, but this time as Warwickshire captain and vice-captain respectively for the start of the 1998 county season.

Channels had remained open between Lara and Warwickshire for a possible return, and he had stopped off in London on the homeward flight from West Indies' Pakistan tour, in December 1997, to sign a one-year contract to lead them.

Warwickshire 1998

Warwickshire's success had continued after Lara's departure in 1994: they won the County Championship again in 1995 as well as the C&G Trophy, and in 1997 had claimed the AXA Equity & Law (Sunday) League. Little surprise then that, with Lara returning, the Bears were installed as pre-season County Championship favourites.

Rejoining Warwickshire in 1998, Lara fell back under the microscope of the English press and was immediately reminded of his prior indiscretions; misdemeanours he attributed to the unforeseen demands of playing cricket up to six days a week.

'You can put aside what happened in 1994 and look forward to a much different Brian Lara this year,' he said. 'I believe we have a team that is capable of doing well in each and every competition, so it's not unrealistic to expect us to finish among the honours. It would be asking a lot to repeat the triumphs of 1994 but I'll be disappointed at the end of the day if I haven't helped Warwickshire win some trophies.'

Disappointed he would be, as the season proved to be a hugely frustrating one for all concerned.

'To be fair on him and everyone, none of us got any runs, it was a really difficult season,' says Knight, who having retired in 2006 now commentates on the game for Sky Sports.

'The pitches were not very good, generally damp, and they were pretty uneven at Edgbaston. There was a period where they became really quite hard to bat on and he struggled like all of us, which was quite pleasing for the rest of us in a way. Even the great man was having trouble,' he laughs, before sheepishly recalling an incident where he was complicit in his skipper's downfall.

'Halfway through the season, Brian still couldn't get any form going. Then came a match against Lancashire at Edgbaston and I was batting with him; he had got to 25 and started looking more comfortable, piercing the field like he did when he got going, and then,' Knight pauses before continuing through clenched teeth, 'I ran him out.'

The England opener clearly didn't relish the prospect of facing Lara straight away as he went on to compile a massive 192.

'I was petrified,' he says. 'I found him in the dressing room later and he was fuming. I didn't know where to look. There he was having a hard season, being written off in the press, people saying he didn't care and he must've felt like he was just starting to turn the corner and I ran him out.'

Things got worse for Lara in June when he was fined £2,000 by Warwickshire's disciplinary committee for missing a Sunday League match in Taunton, Somerset. Lara, who had been in Trinidad on business, missed the game when he failed to catch a return flight, pre-booked by the County, to the UK.

By late July, the Warwickshire crowd had begun turning on their star import and his team, booing and heckling them. One fan, following the Bears NatWest Trophy quarter-final defeat to Leicestershire, shouted at Lara: 'You are getting £200,000 a year and I have taken a day off work to watch this rubbish?'

Lara was feeling the pressure.

'I've failed Warwickshire this season but I want the supporters to realise that there is no team in the world that I've done better for than Warwickshire,' he said. 'That period in 1994 was the greatest of my life and I did it for Warwickshire, not for the West Indies, not for Trinidad and Tobago and not for my club side. I have played three more months of cricket for Warwickshire since then and now I seem to be one of the most hated people here.'

Part of the problem was one of perception, says Knight: the perception that Lara did not care about how he performed for Warwickshire.

'I knew batting with him just how much he cared. Maybe because of the relaxed exterior that wasn't always conveyed, but he has a lot of professional pride and when he was out there he wanted to do well.'

A week after being jeered and barracked at Leicester, Lara responded in typical fashion in what Knight says is his favourite Lara innings for Warwickshire, a blistering 226 against Middlesex.

'He had been really struggling and then, whack, out of nowhere he blasts this double hundred against Middlesex at Lord's. It was an incredibly pacey innings, such a quick tempo.'

Knight, who finished top of the 1998 Warwickshire batting with 1,057 runs at an average of 48.04, says batting with Lara in this mood was often intimidating.

'Batting with him is sometimes hard because it can be dangerous to try and tap into what he's doing, you have to accept that you may not have the capability to do the same. He made you feel completely inadequate at times. You're trying to fend one off, to survive and get through and he just steps out and whacks it through the covers for four. You realise then you're playing a different game.'

The Middlesex innings did not resurrect Lara's season, though, and with two championship matches remaining club and captain agreed to go their separate ways, with Knight taking over as skipper for the remaining fixtures. Lara's batting form had been sporadic. He had scored three centuries but could not inspire his charges to greater deeds through his captaincy. Warwickshire finished the season eighth in the County Championship and trophyless in all competitions. Given that he played in two less games, four less innings, than most of his contemporaries he still finished with over 1,000 runs for the season, the benchmark of a successful year for most. As always, 'failure' was a relative term with Lara.

'Some fans might look back and think maybe we could've got a bit more from Brian but I certainly wouldn't say that,' concludes Knight. 'I remember all the great things he brought to the club and to the sport, the attention, the performances, the inspiration. Looking back at my career I think how lucky I was, firstly to have played against him and then secondly to have played in the same side.'

Heathrow stand-off

With the 1998 English county season behind him, Lara was set to resume his duties at the West Indies helm. A home win against England had provided a happy coronation for the new captain but by the time the proposed tour of South Africa came round, in November 1998, a long-running dispute with the WICB over pay and conditions had dragged into an impasse. What followed was a stand-off that rocked West Indian cricket to its core.

The West Indies had just competed in the Wills International Cup in Dhaka, Bangladesh, losing to their upcoming hosts South Africa in the final. Seven players not in that team, but who formed part of the South African touring squad, flew from the Caribbean to London for their connection to Johannesburg. Lara and vice-captain Hooper flew to London from Dhaka to join them for a WIPA (West Indies Players' Association) meeting to discuss the ongoing issues with the WICB.

Following the meeting, the nine staged cricket's first strike, at Heathrow Airport's Excelsior Hotel on 4 November, refusing to go to South Africa until their contractual wranglings with the Board were settled. The players' stand covered a number of issues but the plain-talking Jimmy Adams says that much of it was simply down to being fed up with being messed around.

'There were issues that were not signed off but had been agreed on; the Board would say this will change by such and such a time and so on, and then you get a contract sent out which is exactly the same as when you started the whole process.

'You get angry, look at all the meetings, all the discussions, all the back and forth and then they send the same thing; so all along they were just taking you for a ride. You realise you're not being listened to and the six months prior to this were just a waste of time. So you ended up with a lot of angry players.'

The players would be criticised for the perception that this was a stand solely about money.

'The junior players found themselves dragged into a dispute in which the seniors were largely seeking a pay increase for themselves,' said Wisden.

Not true, says one of those junior players involved.

'There was a combination of issues but a lot of it boils down to the fact that there has always been a fundamental lack of respect for the players and what they do,' says Dinanath Ramnarine, a young leg-spinner just breaking into the West Indies side at the time.

'The Board has always used the big-stick mentality that you should be honoured to play for the West Indies and be prepared to play under any conditions. There was never any negotiation, you just had to take what you were given and this was the first instance where the players took a stand,' adds Ramnarine, who is now President of WIPA and as such has had his share of run-ins with the WICB. 'It was my first overseas tour and it was a nightmare to be honest but then again, I guess it prepared me for this job.'

WIPA was formed in 1973 by the then members of the West Indian team (including players such as Garry Sobers, Rohan Kanhai, Lance Gibbs and Deryck Murray). Murray says, from the outset, the Board did not see it as a welcome innovation and that he knew being involved would jeopardise his career. It was the same twenty-five years later.

'I accepted that what I was doing was probably going to be the end of my career but I really didn't care,' says Jimmy Adams. 'I was fed up and you have to take a stand at some point. At least this way we could get people to understand what we were dealing with on a daily basis.'

The Heathrow stand-off lasted a week, and began with the WICB inviting Lara and Hooper to attend a meeting in Antigua. The pair reciprocated with an invitation for WICB representatives to meet WIPA in London. Both parties declined the other's offers before the WICB escalated the conflict by sacking their captain and vice-captain, simultaneously dropping them from the tour squad.

What unfolded was an unholy mess, played out before the world's cameras, as agents, lawyers, sponsors, politicians, administrators and former players all got involved and the dispute dragged interminably on. South African Cricket Board's Managing Director Dr Ali Bacher even presented the nine rebels with a signed letter from South African President Nelson Mandela encouraging them to find a resolution.

Snippets of progress were swiftly followed by rebuttals and angry press releases before, finally, WICB President Pat Rousseau flew to Heathrow to meet the players. After nineteen hours of negotiations a deal was brokered which salvaged the tour, a deal with which, it seems, neither side was really happy. It included promises of comprehensive insurance, improved fee structures for players, more open accountability and assurances of a more professional attitude from the Board. Rousseau emerged saying the sacking of Lara and Hooper had been 'a misunderstanding', that they had been restored to their positions, and the tour was back on.

As captain, Lara had been a focal point of media attention during the affair but it was wrong to see him as the instigator, says Adams.

'All the senior players were in full agreement, Courtney [Walsh], Curtly [Ambrose], Carl [Hooper], me, Brian. All Brian had done was said that we should meet in England before, to decide on what we were going to do.'

Ramnarine adds that Lara actually played a key role in the team finally going to South Africa. 'He was very mature in the way he tried to bring some balance and perspective to the situation, something he has never been given credit for. There was a vote on whether to go or not and it came out even. Brian as captain had the casting vote and he said we should go. I think when he received the letter from Nelson Mandela that may well have tipped the balance.'

The cracks had been plastered over but nobody was kidding themselves that this was an end to the matter. Indeed, at the time of writing and under various guises, it still rumbles on. A decade after Heathrow, in July 2009, thirteen leading West Indies players, including skipper Chris Gayle, Shivnarine Chanderpaul, Ramnaresh Sarwan and Dwayne Bravo, similarly went on strike, refusing to play in a two-Test series against Bangladesh after a dispute with the Board over 'pay and contract issues'.

South Africa 1998/99

The historic 1998 trip to South Africa, the West Indies' first official tour of the nation, had political and social significance beyond sport; something which South African cricket supremo Dr Ali Bacher substantiated by urging the West Indies to 'provide role models … especially for the black youngsters who have begun to flood into the game in ever-increasing numbers'.

With the Heathrow stand-off and fallout it had not started well and Lara opened with an apology to the South African public for any offence caused. With more bearing on the series though was the fact that arriving ten days late meant missing vital preparation and acclimatisation time.

It was time they needed, if the performance in the 1st Test was anything to go by; where a second innings batting collapse saw the West Indies lose by four wickets at Johannesburg's New Wanderers Stadium. The tourists were as heavily dependent on Lara's contributions as ever and scores of 11 and 7 meant he had now gone nine Tests without a hundred. Going back further, he had averaged only 37 in his previous twenty-two Tests, dating back to 1996/97, well below his career average of 51.

It was a statistic which found old friend Sir Garry Sobers calling to offer assistance. He had noticed 'a little problem with his technique' which could explain the recent slump.

'He was following the ball in the air and not watching it off the wicket, in other words, playing too early,' and that too often the bat was angling 'from somewhere about second slip across the line of the ball' with consequential results for timing and fluidity. Sobers also suggested a reduction of back-lift in defence, reasoning 'the further the bat has to come, the more mistakes you're going to make.'

The advice did not yield the desired results in the 2nd Test, where the West Indies capitulated in dramatic fashion, losing by 178 runs in three days. So dramatic in fact that newspaper columnists and South African fans alike were already contemplating a possible whitewash. That possibility was given further credence when the 3rd Test was also lost, by nine wickets, and by now the West Indies were in freefall.

After losing the 4th Test in Cape Town the cliché of playing for pride was trotted out but it was evident from body language alone that pride had long since departed. The captain and coach blamed falling standards in Caribbean cricket, with Lara saying, 'We have a lot of guys here who dominate first-class cricket in the West Indies and don't seem to be up to Test class or international standards.'

Fast bowling great Malcolm Marshall bemoaned a general lack of application by players and shirking of the fundamental hard work necessary to make it as an international.

'I don't think a lot of players actually realise how important it is to play for the West Indies,' he said. 'I don't think they appreciate how much work was put in by those four heroes – Sir Frank Worrell, Sir Garry Sobers, Clive Lloyd and Sir Viv Richards – to get us where we are.'

The despair was evident in the words of all those who held West Indian cricket dear, but by then the losing momentum could not be halted and the West Indies lost the 5th Test emphatically, by 351 runs, to register its first-ever 5-0 whitewash. It followed up with a 6-1 loss in the one-day internationals before a dismal tour was mercifully at an end.

Professionalism, its presence in one side and not the other, was a regular theme of articles and editorials. The South Africans had been committed in their preparation and play, mentally strong and focussed, and above all had performed as a unit. In short, they were everything the West Indies were not.

Lara blamed disunities in the team, a lack of confidence exposing individual weakness, and even suggested some players might need psychological assistance.

'The unity needs to be much better,' he said. 'As a team I'd prefer to have guys tight [and] together off the field and things would work better on the field. Hopefully things will improve in those areas but you've got to remember we're all from different islands and slightly different backgrounds,' before adding, 'Maybe we need some sort of help outside of cricket that would make the guys more competitive upstairs.'

On his captaincy he said little except that he was on a 'learning' curve.

'I'm a learning captain in international cricket and this is my first overseas tour. As I told [South African captain] Hansie [Cronje], it's not been a pleasure, but a great learning experience coming to South Africa and I've learned a lot from him.'

The response from the media was damning. Lara, it was said, had looked disinterested and disenchanted throughout, unable to inspire or to unify. Barbadian cricket writer Tony Cozier was typical of those who took unerring aim and let fly with both barrels.

'For too long, he [Lara] has heard from sycophants and popularity seekers whose pandering has not properly prepared him for the responsibility of leadership.

'The South African experience has been a chastening experience for him. It was sad to hear him admit to disunity in his team, even sadder to witness only one of his players applaud after his mandatory interview at the on-field presentation ceremony at Centurion Park on Monday,' said the man who has become recognised as the voice of West Indies cricket.

'Lara is a unique talent who has, for some time, been in danger of self-destructing. We must make every effort to save that talent for the sake of our cricket and cricket in general. It is not too late.

'Above all, we need to save our cricket. Period. The passion of our people for it withers with each successive controversy and each new humbling defeat.'

The prospects of an imminent rebirth did not look good, with the mighty Australians due on Caribbean shores just twelve days after the final ODI capitulation in South Africa.

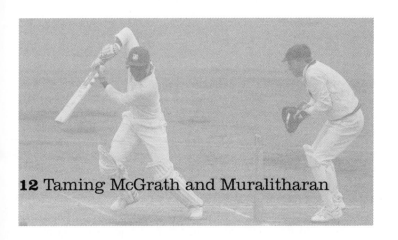

12 Taming McGrath and Muralitharan

On assuming the West Indies captaincy there is an acceptance that with it comes a place in the spotlight, the subjection to scrutiny, but Lara could not have contemplated the level of vitriol that greeted his return from South Africa.

The humiliating tour results were not all that provoked the reaction; a lot stemmed from the perception, as it had at Warwickshire, that Lara did not care enough. He hadn't helped himself with a body language which seemed to suggest the same, but his old teacher Harry Ramdass says this could not have been further from the truth.

'The boys who hang out with him couldn't find him around at all when he got back to Trinidad. He was locked away in a dark room watching video footage of his batting, analysing what the problem was, reel after reel of film. He was in there for hours and hours, rebuilding mentally and constructing ways to address the problem.'

A darkened room might have been where Lara would have preferred to stay but the Australians were looming and his captaincy was under question.

On 22 February, the same day that the Aussies got their Caribbean tour under way, the WICB met to discuss the leadership. Had there been an obvious captaincy alternative it likely would have been taken. There was not, and in a press conference broadcast live across the region, WICB

President Pat Rousseau emerged, with the air of a teacher on parents' night reporting the misdemeanours of an errant schoolchild, to explain the Board's decision.

'We have told Mr Lara that he needs to make significant improvements in his leadership skills. To this end he will be given specific performance targets by the chairman of selectors related to improvement in his relationship with his players, discipline and with an emphasis on punctuality, interaction with the coach and manager and nurturing and development of his team members.

'At the end of the 2nd Test, the selectors will assess Mr Lara's performances as captain against the targets set and decide on the appointment of the captain for the next two Tests.'

Publicly chastising and demeaning a man and then saying, good luck, you have two games, may seem a peculiar motivational strategy but that was the position. And those two Tests soon became one, after a disastrous opening encounter in Trinidad.

An Australian first innings of 269, with Walsh and Ambrose sharing six wickets, represented an encouraging performance from the West Indian bowlers at the Queen's Park Oval. At 149 for 3, the West Indies batsmen looked poised to convert it to something more tangible, but when Lara was run out for 62 a familiar scenario unfolded – the home side lost its last seven wickets for eighteen runs and were bundled out for 167.

That was bad enough, but when things seemingly couldn't get worse the West Indies proved they had reached the bottom only to start digging. A second innings 51 all out was their worst in seventy-one years of Test cricket, and handed Steve Waugh victory in his first Test as Australian captain.

Australia's arch destroyer Glenn McGrath had taken 10 for 78. Lara had not been among his victims but the New South Welshman already employed a successful tactic of bowling round the wicket to him, often resulting in the left-hander edging behind or being trapped LBW. Before the series began McGrath, keen to assert any psychological advantage he may have over the only man the Australians feared, issued his customary declaration of intent to target the opposition's best batsman.

Sabina Park 213

As the teams travelled to Jamaica's Sabina Park it is hard to imagine a player under more intense pressure. The 1st Test defeat, and its manner, seemed a predictable continuation of what had gone before in South Africa and calls had gone up for Lara's head, even before the two-Test probation had elapsed.

'When you're inside the camp, you know the pressure he was under following the whitewash in South Africa,' says Jimmy Adams. 'He hadn't scored any runs, there were issues with the Board and then he was basically given a team, which I didn't think was particularly strong, and told that is who you will captain or you won't captain at all. Then there was the two-match probation, which was such a bad management decision; I mean either the man's good enough to lead or he's not. That's pressure. But Brian's always done well under the sort of pressure that would break other players.'

The burden on the skipper's shoulders only got heavier after Day One with the Aussies scoring 256 and then reducing the home side to 37 for 4 by the close. Batting at No. 4 Lara may as well have been opening, as halfway through the fifth over the West Indies were 5 for 2 and he was already at the crease.

He emerged to restart his innings on the second morning alongside Jamaican left-hander Adams.

'We got there and the plan was to bat as long as possible but we decided we would do it over by over,' says Adams, his friend and long-time teammate from the days of junior representative cricket. 'So at the end of each over we would literally come together and say right we have 57 left for the day, or we have five overs to lunch. There were other plans in between but the basic premise was to chip away over by over, all the way down to the end.'

Lara began circumspectly, in full knowledge of the value of his wicket, taking 140 deliveries to record his 50. Nearly three deliveries for each run was a pace almost unheard of for Lara, but he was laying a foundation.

Aside from counting down overs, the only major tactic being employed was to limit the number of deliveries Lara faced from McGrath.

'He didn't overly like McGrath bowling too many balls at him, whereas he was always willing if you gave him the strike against the spinners,' says Adams. 'So it sort of worked out that we would take a single to give him a shot at Warne or MacGill or I would try to eat up some overs from McGrath. The success of the team was really going to be built around what sort of day he had so it was fair enough.'

The tactic worked, as early caution became replaced by fluent expression. Lara began dominating the spinners and went to 60 by launching Warne over long-on for six. The West Indian fans, laid low by recent results, climbed into the opportunity to celebrate.

Lara accelerated to his century, which, when reached, 'was like a pressure cooker just exploding', says Trinidadian writer Vaneisa Baksh. From then on the Caribbean sat back and revelled in the joy that is Lara in full flow.

'The emotional moments were many – back-to-back sixes against MacGill, four consecutive fours against Greg Blewett – but for me, the most inspiring came after he fell to a wicked Glenn McGrath snorter, that took him on the side of the head,' says Cricinfo contributor Baksh. 'It was numbing to all, but he rose. He rose from the blow and drove McGrath to cover for a four that resonated with the ring of steel.'

On that second morning, the West Indies batting frailties had looked primed for exposure but the scale of the turnaround engineered by Lara and the brilliantly unselfish Adams had reignited the series. The pair went undefeated throughout the entire day and when their stand was finally broken on the third morning it had realised 322 runs.

'It was my first match in the West Indies squad and what a match,' says former Trinidad and Tobago captain Daren Ganga, who was West Indies twelfth man at Sabina Park. 'Brian told me everything he wanted to do in that innings: how the only person who could get him out is Glenn McGrath, caught behind or LBW, what he was going to do to Shane Warne when he got the opportunity, everything.

'He believed a lot in that; he planned his innings, sized things up. He didn't believe so much in the practising and physical sessions, he said it's all up in the mind and how you prepare your mind will determine your success. And it worked. He came in the dressing room afterwards and just sat down and said, "You see what I told you."'

Pressure on and off the field had transferred to performance on it with a sublime double century which oozed character and strength. Of the duel between Lara and McGrath, McGrath did indeed get his man but not before he had made 213. Adams scored 94 and the partnership set up an imposing first innings total of 431. The demoralised Aussies could only manage 177 second time around and the West Indies polished off the formality of a ten-wicket victory with a day to spare.

Steve Waugh said that Lara's brilliant innings had 'torn the heart from our chest' and, in a measured post-match interview, the West Indian skipper acknowledged it could 'go down as the most important' of his career.

Thirteen years later, upon his induction to the ICC Hall of Fame, Lara would call this his greatest innings. He said the character and mental strength he had shown with everything on the line – the captaincy, the series, the respect and adoration of the fans – made it hard to measure any other knock above it.

In the euphoric post-match atmosphere it was nearly forgotten that the Board still had to announce whether Lara would retain the captaincy.

'There were criteria set out by the Board. I hope they were confidential,' said Lara, making playful reference to Rousseau's very public press conference. 'I'm just happy to be among the runs, happy to be in a winning team and happy to play that role. I'm looking forward to Barbados whatever the situation is.'

Kensington Oval 153*

To nobody's surprise Lara was still in charge as the series moved to Bridgetown, Barbados, for the 3rd Test.

The early Kensington Oval exchanges went the way of the Australians with a typically combative Steve Waugh hitting back-foot punches, drives and slog-sweeps on his way to 199 in a huge first innings of 490.

The West Indian reply was in trouble when their captain and talisman, Lara, was tucked up by a short delivery from Gillespie. The ball ballooned off his glove for a simple catch behind and the batsman walked without waiting for the umpire's decision. Only a stirring rearguard from Sherwin Campbell and Ridley Jacobs managed to lift the West Indies from 98 for 6 to 329 all out, leaving them 161 behind, but mercifully still in the game.

Trini Posse founder Nigel Camacho was in customary attendance at the Oval and is wide eyed and smiling as he recalls a key period of play during the Australians' all-important second innings.

'Ponting and Warne were putting together a stand which was taking the game away so we were thinking, come on, we need to do something to lift the boys. So we took this stuffed kangaroo and performed a ceremonial hanging in front of the whole crowd. They went crazy and a few minutes later Warne was dismissed; it was fantastic.'

The unfortunate national emblem was hoisted gleefully and frequently as the Australians went from a position of strength to collapse to 146 all out. Walsh had taken five wickets, and left the West Indies with the scent of a chance, however improbable, at 308 to win.

By close of play on the fourth day, though, the home side had already lost three wickets and Camacho remembers the Australians were in confident mood.

'We had got to know Justin Langer and were out at dinner with him that night. He said, "Well you guys can join me on the beach tomorrow about 2 pm; we'll be finished wiping out the West Indies by then because we have three plans. Plan A, to get Lara out, Plan B, to get Lara out and Plan C, to get Lara out and when we do that it's all over."

'We said, "Well what if Lara bats all day?" He just laughed and said, "That's not going to happen."'

Former Trinidad and Tobago team manager Colin Borde remembers watching Lara go about his pre-match routine the next morning.

'He didn't even go in the dressing room, he just got his gloves and bat and walked out into the middle and was shadow batting for forty-five minutes before the game on either side of the wicket, taking his guard, visualising what he was going to do.'

When play began on that fifth morning the West Indies soon slipped to 105 for 5, still over 200 runs short of victory, with only Lara, Adams and Jacobs remaining of the recognised batsmen.

If the West Indies were going to go down though, Lara would ensure they did so with a fight and he went to his 50 with a six off Warne, rocking back on a short delivery and pulling it high and handsome onto the roof of the Greenidge and Haynes Stand.

Soon after, he misjudged a delivery from McGrath and was struck on the helmet again. The delivery sat Lara on his backside but he got up and scampered through for the leg-bye. The single left him at McGrath's end and the two came head-to-head, remonstrating with one another at close quarters. Guyanese umpire Eddie Nicholls intervened before Adams guided his captain away, with Lara waving a dismissive glove at McGrath. The umpire might not have liked the confrontation but the crowd did, roaring its appreciation of the fight being shown.

Steve Waugh would later say that this was a method Lara employed to motivate himself: to sustain a confrontation rather than let it go, creating his own siege mentality. It seemed to work, as the next short delivery from McGrath was pulled ferociously into the boundary between midwicket and long-on for four.

Lara reached three figures in sumptuous fashion, advancing down the track to Warne and smashing him over the top for another four. It was a second hundred in successive Tests and Adams was still with him, sharing a crucial stand just as he had done in Jamaica.

With less than a hundred runs to win, and with Lara and Adams at the crease, the countdown to victory had long since begun in the stands. The tension was rising at the possibility of chasing down an imposing fourth-innings target against the world's best side. It was a tension, Adams said, that was not mirrored in the middle.

'There was more tension around the ground than in the middle. The atmosphere in the middle was no less or no more than any other Test innings you would play, because really you're just focussed on the ball at that moment in time. The state of the game and the crowd, players tend to block that out.

'It was the same thing as Sabina, counting overs the whole way down and trying to manipulate the situation as best he could. If he could get hold of some slow bowling for four or five overs he would really try to cash in. Just batsmanship, planning.'

Matters were going according to plan until McGrath snuck a beauty past Adams's defences, bowling him for 38 and ending a 133-run partnership. Caribbean hearts sank further as the willowy seam bowler then quickly removed Ridley Jacobs and Nehemiah Perry. Within minutes, 238 for 5 had become 248 for 8. The West Indians still had sixty runs to make and only two wickets remained.

Removed from the heat of battle, Adams was now amongst his teammates on the West Indies balcony and recalls moments of comedy amidst the growing anxiety.

'Everybody was sitting on the balcony and nobody was speaking. Clive Lloyd, the manager, wouldn't let anyone move from their seat. "As long as Brian's out there hold your positions," he kept saying, or he would just kinda look at us, yuh know.

'Man there were fellas bursting for the toilet but couldn't move. I don't remember much about the atmosphere, just big Clive eyeing people sayin "hold your positions" and man, guys dyin for a piss!' By now Adams is almost crying with laughter recalling his friends' discomfort. 'I know for sure Peddy [Pedro Collins] had been wanting to go for a lot of overs, just squirming in his seat.'

Out in the middle Lara went on the attack, marshalling the strike to keep the tail-enders away from danger. He skipped down the wicket and on-drove Warne for four; the bleached-blond leg-spinner tossed up a wide delivery and Lara hit a fierce cover drive for another boundary. This was cricket at its most visceral and gladiatorial.

One Curtly Ambrose shot demonstrated why Lara was trying so hard to keep the strike. McGrath dug in a short, wide ball to which Ambrose was offering a shot before a rethink left his bat half-heartedly dangling in mid-air. The ball flew off his blade towards the waiting slip cordon but perfectly bisected two close catchers and raced away for four. McGrath sank to his knees in frustration.

Thirteen to win.

Gillespie then produced a ball which was too close to cut and Lara, trying to guide it down to Third Man, got a thin top edge which flew through to wicketkeeper Healy. Diving to his left Healy went for a one-handed catch and the chance went down. Moments later Ambrose's good fortune ran out when he steered a ball straight to the safe hands of Matthew Elliott at third slip.

The West Indies last man was now at the crease. The towering figure of Walsh, who would register a Test-record forty-three ducks during his career, was greeted by Lara with words of advice, but the concern etched in the captain's face did not suggest confidence. Before entering the fray, the fast bowler had tried to escape the tension by watching the action on a dressing room television, away from his teammates. He was in the thick of it now.

Six to win.

First ball from Gillespie, Walsh went across as if to play and then flourished a comically extravagant leave which ended with the great paceman tucking the bat under his armpit and walking around the crease like a businessman with his morning newspaper. In the event it was a no-ball and six to win became five. Walsh saw out the over, prodding down in ungainly defence, each ball being met with roars of crowd approval.

Next over, McGrath came round the wicket to Lara, he got the edge and it flew towards the slip cordon. Warne dived full length at first slip but the ball tantalisingly evaded his grasp. Two more runs to Lara and he raised his eyes to the heavens as he trotted through to complete the second.

Three to win.

The pressure was unbearable by this stage and clearly got to the usually unflappable McGrath as he sent down a wide for another precious extra. Steve Waugh looked on ruefully.

Two to win.

Lara hooked the next down towards the boundary but it was fielded and he couldn't come back for the second. With the scores level, Walsh had one more ball in the over to survive. Lara watched helplessly from the non-striker's end but the former captain allowed the next delivery to pass, this time tucking the bat in exaggeratedly behind his pad.

The greatest run-chase ever? Lara is hoisted aloft as Barbados's Kensington Oval erupts, following a nerve-shredding 153 not out that sinks world champions Australia in 1999. No. 11 Courtney Walsh, souvenir stump in hand, is looking for an escape route.

Lara wasted no time in applying the *coup de grâce* and smashed the first ball of Gillespie's next over through the covers for four. As the crowd erupted, Lara ripped a memento stump out of the ground and charged towards his onrushing teammates.

'Peddy an mehself were the first two over the balcony,' recalls Adams.

With both arms raised in celebration, Lara was lifted off his feet as supporters poured onto the ground. Fans engulfed their hero and the red, white and black of a Trinidad and Tobago flag was draped across him.

Lara's good friend the racehorse owner Roger Hadeed was at the Kensington Oval that day.

'It was amazing. I was there with a couple of guys and we were saying afterwards that it is something you will tell generations to come, "I was there."

'That was what you call responsibility, he knew what he had to do and he did it, against the best team in the world – truly phenomenal. The atmosphere was electric, pins and needles; in fact it's pins and needles now just talking about it. It's only very special players like Brian that create an atmosphere like that.'

Lara had just completed what is widely regarded as the greatest chasing innings in Test match history. In terms of the series, his 153 not out meant the West Indies triumphed by one wicket to go 2-1 up with one to play. He had gone from pariah to hero in the space of two matches and those critics that wanted to see the back of him before Sabina Park were now lauding him to the rafters.

Lara would later reveal that the shadow batting he engaged in before play on that fifth day, and witnessed by Borde, had been inspired by an old schoolfriend. Nicholas Gomez had given him a book on basketball legend Michael Jordan in which Jordan described his technique of visualisation.

'He had an entire page on how he went about visualising what's going to happen in a game,' said Lara.

On the morning of his epic innings he called his former school pal and talked through plans for the match, running scenarios over in his mind.

'I remember calling Gomez at six o'clock in the morning, the last morning of the Test match, and we went about planning this innings against the best team in the world. It was amazing to see how it just came to fruition. You know, a partnership with someone – it happened to be Jimmy Adams – and the innings ultimately evolving into a match-winning one.'

The West Indian supporters took their shredded nerves to Antigua's Recreation Ground for the 4th and final Test match but, despite a blistering Lara century, the Aussies would not be denied and won to level the series. The eighty-four-ball hundred was more furious assault than the calculated knocks of Jamaica and Barbados but Lara could not find the support needed to mount a challenge to the Australians and the tourists wrapped up a 176-run victory, retaining the Frank Worrell Trophy in the process.

Two men, Lara and McGrath, had dominated the series headlines and the two paid fulsome praise to one another in its aftermath. McGrath's three dismissals of Lara had upped his personal tally against the Trinidadian in Tests to ten though Lara had taken 125 of his series 546 runs off the man nicknamed 'Pigeon'. McGrath had finished with thirty wickets in four Tests, the most by any touring bowler in the Caribbean.

'That to me will go down as the best series that I have ever played in,' Lara said in an interview with former England fast bowler Angus Fraser in 2007. 'I know a lot of people talk about my 153 in Barbados being my best innings, but the 213 I scored in the previous Test in Jamaica was better. The pressure I was under there – we had been bowled out for 51 in the first Test in Trinidad – was great and to produce that particular innings was to me the greatest show of character that I have ever shown.'

Resigning the captaincy

The West Indies lost the one-day series to Australia 3-2 and during the 1999 World Cup, which started in England just nineteen days later, it would be another defeat at the hands of the Antipodeans that would ultimately put pay to their campaign.

Three first-round wins and two losses, including the final group match with Australia, saw them miss out on qualification for the next stage on net run rate by the agonising fraction of 0.08 runs. New Zealand sneaked through ahead of them, in a tournament eventually won by Australia.

New Zealand would provide another sour note for Lara's West Indians as a tumultuous year ended with a tour in the land of the long white cloud. Two resounding Test defeats meant that, away from home, the West Indies had now lost ten Test matches in a row: Pakistan 3-0; South Africa 5-0; and New Zealand 2-0.

Jimmy Adams summed up his feelings and those of others in the team and set-up.

'We were on a rubbish tour getting our arses kicked by New Zealand playing bad cricket. A lot of us were going through a heap of emotions, anger, frustration; again you didn't have the feeling of a unit in New Zealand. It was just a collection of players that had come down to play cricket for six weeks; the performance reflected that. And at that time you were starting to lose some of the bankers, if you like. Ambrose wasn't on that tour, Hooper also, some of those guys were coming to the end.'

Defeat in the Tests was compounded by a 5-0 thrashing in the one-day internationals and a sorry tour was at an end. In mid-January, just over a month later, Lara decided he had had enough and announced his resignation from the captaincy.

'After two years the moderate success and devastating failure that have engulfed West Indies cricket have brought me to the realisation that there is a need for me to withdraw from my present leadership position,' said Lara, who had lost nine of his fifteen Test matches in charge.

In response, WICB President Pat Rousseau issued a statement.

'I would really like to thank Brian for his service as captain during a very difficult period in West Indies cricket. I know he has made a very hard decision and I appeal to the public to give him the total support that the WICB will be giving him, as he continues his career.'

But Brian wouldn't be continuing, at least not yet, for soon after his resignation he made the further announcement that he would not be available for the two upcoming series against Zimbabwe and Pakistan. He was taking an extended break from cricket.

Off the field Lara was concerned over the long-term health of his mother, Pearl; on it, he was mentally stale and left saying he needed 'to seek the assistance of appropriate professionals to rebuild all facets of my game'.

The results over the twelve months had proven, in vivid terms, just how the team's fortunes depended almost entirely on Lara's efforts. The fact that it was now taking ever more outstanding efforts to yield those results added to the weight on the thirty-year-old's shoulders. Even for someone as mentally strong as Lara, there is a breaking point, when the constant pressure to perform becomes too much.

England and Australia

After a four-month hiatus in which he spent time with friends and family, relaxed on the golf course and visited a New Jersey sports psychologist,

Lara returned to the team, under new captain Jimmy Adams, on the England tour of 2000.

Lara's final announcement that he was ready to return to the international fold came late, so late in fact that the sixteen-man squad for England had already been picked but space was made to accommodate him. Without Lara, Adams had enjoyed a successful start to his tenure as captain with wins over Zimbabwe, 2-0, and Pakistan, 1-0. The Pakistan victory in particular had pointed to hopes of a West Indian resurrection and, in light of this, some felt Lara's inclusion might disrupt rather than assist.

Concerns were also voiced over his lack of match practice as, in the five months between his last Busta Cup match for Trinidad and Tobago in February and the start of the England tour in June, he had reportedly netted just once at the Queen's Park Oval. Nevertheless, Adams was happy to have his friend back in the ranks.

'I'm very, very pleased to know that Brian is touring England,' he said, because 'of the positive contribution we know he will have on the team and the tour as a whole … not only as a batsman but as a senior player and as a person.'

Adams may have been pleased but Lara's presence was hailed with sarcasm by sections of the British press.

'Brian Lara has consented to join the West Indies tour of England this summer. Say "thank you" everybody,' wrote the *Telegraph*'s Michael Henderson.

'The staff at Heathrow airport can order a carpet of welcome this very day, and nobody should be in the least bit surprised if an angelic choir of customs officers rehearse a few thrilling choruses of "Lo! The Conquering Hero Comes".

'We should be honoured by Lara's presence. Zimbabwe are not grand enough for him, and neither are Pakistan.'

The thirty-one-year-old Lara revealed he was looking forward to playing a new role in the team, that of senior player passing on his experience to the new generation.

'I know what it's like coming to England for the first time and how tricky it can be for the new players and I hope that, being here, I can share my knowledge and experience with those here for the first time like Ramnaresh Sarwan, Wavell Hinds, Chris Gayle.

'When they lean on your shoulders, you should be able to provide the kind of knowledge and guidance that is expected, and that is what I am here for.'

But the tour would not go as planned for Lara or the West Indies. He hit 176 against Zimbabwe in a three-day game at Arundel Castle but, after a 1st Test victory at Edgbaston in which he added an even 50, the trajectory was downwards.

At Lord's the tourists were shot out for 54 in their second innings and lost by two wickets before managing to draw the 3rd Test after a sub-par first innings had left them in a precarious position. That they got out of that position was largely due to a second innings century from Lara. It was an innings watched with some fascination by England captain Michael Vaughan.

'The match, which ended in a draw, was also notable for the behaviour of Brian Lara, who had come in shortly before lunch on the third day,' said Vaughan. 'Rather than returning to the pavilion for lunch he went straight over to the nets, and we sat around in the dressing room watching the Channel 4 pictures of him practising. We thought it might mean trouble and it did, because he came out afterwards and proceeded to smack it everywhere until he was run out for 112.'

Yet it would not presage a change in West Indian fortunes as at Headingley, in the 4th Test, another second innings capitulation saw them dismissed for 61 and fall 2-1 behind. Allied to their 51 at Trinidad against the Australians in 1999, the Lord's 54 and Headingley 61 were three of the region's four lowest scores in seventy-two years of Test cricket. They had been registered in a little over seventeen months.

England had not beaten the West Indies in thirty-one painful – both physically and psychologically – years but their spirits were high heading for the final Test at the Oval. Their chances of ending that run had depended largely on their suppression of the threat posed by Lara. Nick Knight, who played in the first two Tests of the summer, said the tactics against him were simple.

'The England plans to combat Lara were to bowl full and straight early on, try to hit leg stump; maybe try the odd short ball with a man out but a lot of the time you ended up going back to top of off stump and hoping he nicks it.'

Full and straight at leg stump, a tactic devised by England coach Duncan Fletcher to exploit Lara's instinctive hop across the crease at the point of delivery, worked like a dream at the Oval as Craig White produced precisely that delivery, bowling him for his first golden duck in Test matches. The West Indies were chasing the game from then on and Lara's controversial dismissal in the second innings, adjudged LBW to Darren Gough for 47, all but ended their chances. England triumphed by 158 runs and took the series 3-1.

It had been a contest which captured the English public's imagination and for them it delivered the promise of brighter times but for the West Indies it was more of the same. There was also a sense of foreboding as the tourists watched their two world-class bowlers, Ambrose and Walsh, step onto the Oval pitch through guards of honour. For Ambrose, who debuted in 1988, it was his ninety-eighth and last Test; for Walsh, whose first game was even earlier, in 1984, his last hurrah would come against South Africa in less than nine months' time, after 132 Tests. The pair's performance in the series underscored the cavernous hole they would be leaving: they had secured two-thirds of all the West Indians' Test wickets, 51 of 76.

The day after the Oval Test match finished, 5 September, had brought sad news from the Caribbean when it was revealed that, almost a year on from the death of Malcolm Marshall from colon cancer, Lara's boyhood idol Roy Fredericks had died of throat cancer. He was fifty-seven.

Lara's return had not been a successful one, with a solitary century in the drawn 3rd Test, and the rumble of controversy continued to stalk him. Allegations, ultimately unfounded, surfaced from an unnamed South African businessman that Lara had gambled on matches during the 1993 tour there. It was the time of the Hansie Cronje match-fixing scandal and the claim had been made in an affidavit to the King Commission, which began in June 2000.

'Such is the mood of paranoia and distrust produced by the Hansie Cronje scandal that any high-profile international cricketer is now [as] at risk from unfounded accusations or bare-faced lies as they are from the individuals seeking to corrupt the game in the first place,' said Lara in his *Daily Mail* column.

By November, the West Indies were on the road again as they headed to Australia but the betting scandal followed them Down Under. Shortly before arrival, India's Central Bureau of Investigation published its report into match-fixing, a document which included the uncorroborated statements of numerous Indian bookmakers. Most prominent of these was Mukesh Kumar 'MK' Gupta who implicated a raft of top cricketers.

Lara was cited, with the report stating: 'MK discloses that [Manoj] Prabhakar introduced him to Brian Lara. Prabhakar has accepted this in his statement. According to MK, he paid a sum of US$40,000 to Brian Lara to underperform in two one-day matches when West Indies toured India in 1994.'

Lara denied the charges but it would take two years for his name to be fully cleared – which it was when a WICB investigation found no evidence to support the allegations.

In Australia, the under-siege West Indians had arrived to widespread derision. With the hosts needing just one more win to equal the Test record of eleven straight victories, set by the West Indies in 1984/85, most were predicting they would get another five.

'Our third team would beat them,' said former Australian captain Kim Hughes, 'The top 11 will murder them.'

Lara played through the series under the effects of a niggling hamstring injury picked up in England and could do little to combat the Aussies' predicted dominance. The home side's attack of McGrath, Gillespie, Lee and MacGill steamrollered the West Indies repeatedly.

They lost in Brisbane and Perth by an innings inside three days, and with it went the West Indian record for consecutive victories. The tourists took Adelaide's 3rd Test into its final day, mainly on the strength of Lara's 182, but ultimately lost by five wickets. The 4th and 5th Tests, at Melbourne and Sydney, followed in heavy defeats and the West Indies had been whitewashed 5-0 in an away series for the second time in two years.

Even Lara's renowned self-belief had taken a battering, as he revealed in an interview in 2007.

'There have been a few occasions when I have doubted myself,' he said. 'Mentally, I tried to stay as strong as possible when this happened, but there were occasions when I walked out to bat and I was not in the best frame of mind due to off-the-field factors. I remember in Australia in 2000 it happened when I went through a rut and doubted my ability to do things. I only got one good score.'

Lara's form had indeed been poor, just 321 runs from ten innings, but of all the reasons usually trotted out for substandard sporting performance the one proffered by the media was certainly original.

Lynssey Ward, an eighteen-year-old English lingerie model, had accompanied Lara to Australia. Despite other team members being permitted wives and girlfriends on tour, the former receptionist at Durham County Cricket Club was seen as a distraction and one of the reasons behind the left-hander's continued struggles.

With Ward's mother Claire being only two years Lara's senior, at thirty-three, and the fact the teenager had just been voted the *Daily Star*'s Millennium Babe, the nuances were too salacious for a slathering press to pass up. The international media got a second helping of the story when it was revealed in 2003 that the couple had made a sex tape – yes even cricket has them – and Ward had consulted her legal adviser about disclosure issues.

The Australian series had also claimed yet another captain, with the WICB sacking Jimmy Adams. The eminently likeable Adams had begun his captaincy stint well but his personal batting form had fallen away and the defeats to England and Australia persuaded the WICB it needed a new direction. It rolled the dice again, this time coming up with Carl Hooper.

That Hooper was chosen was symptomatic of the state of the Caribbean game. The casually brilliant but maddeningly erratic Guyanese batsman had retired from the game two years before after eighty Test matches. Having emigrated to Australia with his second wife and baby son, he returned to play for Guyana in the 2000/01 Busta Cup. It was the strength of those performances, scoring 798 runs at an average of 99.75, which encouraged the Board to offer the thirty-five-year-old the captaincy. They did so one week before the South Africans arrived in the Caribbean in March 2001.

A drawn 1st Test in Hooper's native Guyana stopped a run of seven straight defeats but was not the harbinger of better days as the series was lost 2-1. The 5th Test victory, when the series had already been lost, was the West Indies' first in fourteen Test matches and marked Courtney Walsh's final international appearance. He was the highest wicket-taker on either side and ended the series with twenty-five wickets, pushing his Test record to a final tally of 519. Lara was top scorer for the West Indies, narrowly ahead of Hooper, but his 400 runs at an average of 40 had not been enough to put pressure on a South African team for whom three men averaged over 50.

Yet if the start of 2001 had not been what Lara would have yearned for it would end with a series of vaulting brilliance.

Muralitharan and Sri Lanka

Contests between great bowlers and batsmen, whether during a protracted period or just a few overs, are part of cricket lore: Spofforth and Grace; Bradman and Larwood; Lindwall and Compton; Holding and Gavaskar; Donald and Atherton. Lara was engaged in a career-long duel with McGrath but by November 2001 another all-time great was awaiting his arrival in Sri Lanka.

Right-arm off-spinner Muttiah Muralitharan, nicknamed Murali, is the man with the most wickets in Test match history: 800 when he finally retired in 2010. The fizzing off-break, hurrying top-spinner or infamous 'doosra' all formed part of a magician's armoury that befuddled batsmen for eighteen years from his Test debut in 1992.

When the West Indians landed in Sri Lanka, Lara's protracted spell of indifferent form had seen his batting average fall from 60 to 48 in four years. For a batsman of Lara's class it was unacceptable and he was eager to push it back above 50 and return to the top of the international batting rankings. He would have to do so in the face of Muralitharan and Sri Lanka's other world-class bowler Chaminda Vaas, a master of reverse swing on the subcontinent's dry pitches.

Lara likes to impose himself on a match and the opposition bowling and it was he who forced the pace in his duel with Muralitharan. He took the spinner out of his comfort zone, asking him questions no other batsman had. The confusion imparted by Murali's jagging deliveries and controlled variations saw most batsmen fall back on defence, simply trying to survive, but Lara opted for scintillating attack and did so with a strategy in mind.

'There wasn't any sense going down the wicket when I was uncertain or going back when I was uncertain so I decided to sweep,' Lara had told his mentor Joey Carew. True to his word he swept the usually beaming Murali all over Sri Lanka.

'I have seen Murali turn the ball square across him [Lara], with no midwicket, enticing him to play against the turn, and I have seen Brian keep driving, flicking and sweeping into that one vacant spot,' said Sri Lanka's Kumar Sangakkara, a stylish left-handed batsman who had made his Test debut just four months before the 2000 West Indies tour. 'Doing it once or twice is comprehensible, but to watch him do it for an entire session, it made you raise your eyebrows in amazement and wonder.'

Lara racked up 337 runs in the first two Tests, but if those performances were good it was the 3rd where his dominance was fully and gloriously realised, as Wisden Cricinfo's Sri Lanka Editor Charlie Austin colourfully explains.

'It all came to a head during the third and final Test at the Sinhalese Sports Club in December 2001, where Lara scored 221 out of West Indies' first-innings total of 390, and then waltzed to 130 in the second innings just for good measure.

'Lara did not merely survive, he sang a song of supremacy. While others soft-stepped nervously, Lara mastered Muralitharan. It was not wild calypso, more calm reggae. While his team-mates floundered, Lara decoded every variation in Muralitharan's wide repertoire. Off-break, arm-ball, drifter, top-spinner – Lara picked them all from the wrist. He danced down the track, lofting imperiously down the ground. He swept clinically and cut quite viciously.'

Dinanath Ramnarine, who was the West Indies leading wicket-taker in the series, said the display also served as evidence to counter a charge often laid at Lara's door: that he is a selfish player.

'Amazingly Brian actually gave up runs in that series, protecting other players, and I don't just mean tail-enders. Plenty of top-line batsmen were uncomfortable against Murali so instead of maybe hitting a four-ball he would take a single to keep them away from the strike. And he was happy to do it. Many times he said to me he would give up the runs if we could just win a match.'

Even with Lara in this sort of form, though, the West Indies could still not win a match, and they lost the series 3-0. He had scored 688 runs at an average of 115 and, in the process, became only the sixth West Indian batsman to pass 7,000 Test runs. But another statistic, that he scored a remarkable 42 per cent of his side's runs in the series, explains why the goal of winning could not be achieved. One man, however great, cannot defeat another team alone over the course of a series.

Nevertheless, Lara's peerless display, his ability to read the ball from the bowler's hand, footwork, judgement of flight and length and shot placement, had cemented his place as one of the all-time great players of spin bowling.

'To my mind he is the only batsman to have effectively tamed the threat of Murali and dominated him and Shane Warne,' said Sri Lanka's wicketkeeper-batsman Sangakkara, adding '… what truly sets him apart and makes him such a fine player of spin, better than the rest, is that he is not content to react to the bowler.'

Warne has always said Brian Lara and Sachin Tendulkar are the two players that played him better than anyone else. Muralitharan, perhaps unsurprisingly, labelled the Trinidadian as the most dangerous batsman he ever bowled to, saying he felt he had three shots to every ball he bowled.

Prior to the tour, former Australian captain Bob Simpson, no stranger to inflammatory outbursts, had suggested Lara did not deserve to rank as a 'great' because he was too inconsistent. It was the sort of remark heaven sent for Lara, who utilises such fodder better than most, and he had proved himself with one of the most consistent series in living memory.

13 Cementing greatness

His brilliance against Muralitharan had demonstrated what a fit and focussed Brian Lara could achieve but, now in his thirties, one side of that equation was beginning to slip out of the star batsman's control.

Injuries are the bane of the ageing sportsman's life and the hamstring problem that plagued him through the series in Australia had forced his withdrawal from tours to Zimbabwe and Kenya. He had undergone various unsuccessful treatments, including acupuncture, and some now suggested it could be the beginning of the end. Sir Everton Weekes certainly thought so when, in October 2001, he said: 'We have seen the best of Lara and it's unfortunate to say that.'

At thirty-two another frustrating, and freak, injury would sideline him again. In a one-day match at the end of the Sri Lanka tour, Lara was attempting a quick single when he collided with Marvan Atapattu, positioned at the wicket to receive the fielder's throw, fracturing his elbow. Stretchered from the field in agony he was airlifted to a Colombo hospital where the extent of the injury was confirmed. It led to another four-month lay-off and Lara would miss the West Indies' January 2002 Pakistan tour, played in the United Arab Emirates and lost 2-0.

It was not a happy time for other reasons, as in late January he lost the second of the two great influences in his life, his mother, Pearl, when she passed away at her son Lyndon's home. The seventy-one-year-old family matriarch had been suffering from diabetes as well as lymphatic and breast cancer, undergoing two mastectomy operations in the course of treatment. Complications from the first of these had meant she eventually lost the use of her left hand. All of this Pearl had borne with the uncomplaining dignity which personified her life. Knowing the end was near she had enjoyed her final weeks touring locations, either old favourites or ones she had never seen, throughout Trinidad and Tobago.

At her funeral, in the Stanmore Avenue Seventh Day Adventist church, Lara was accompanied by his daughter Sydney and her mother Leasel Rovedas. On a day of heavy rain the champion batsman delivered a eulogy to his beloved mother loaded with cricketing analogy, saying, 'the player has gone back to the pavilion but her runs are on the board and the memories will be forever in our minds.'

For a humble woman the funeral was quite a send-off, attended as it was by government ministers, dignitaries, the entire Trinidad and Tobago cricket team, West Indies players past and present, former world 200-metre champion Ato Boldon, friends and family. She was laid to rest at the Santa Cruz Public Cemetery and left eleven children, thirty-one grandchildren and five great-grandchildren.

The day Pearl passed away Brian had been scheduled to host a function for a group of underprivileged children. His first and natural instinct was to cancel the event but, after discussion with family members, he decided his mum would not have wanted that and went ahead.

Throughout Pearl's illness Brian had experienced at first hand the high costs of cancer treatment, and her death prompted him, his sister Agnes and brother Richard, to explore avenues of assisting those less fortunate than themselves. On the evening of their mother's death, the three siblings met to discuss the options and agreed upon an organisation dedicated to the memory of their parents: the Pearl and Bunty Lara Foundation.

Originally planned to assist those afflicted with cancer or heart disease (from which Pearl and Bunty had respectively suffered) the scope has since broadened to encompass others in need of life-saving operations or treatment. In conducting such laudable work Lara said he wanted to honour the memory of his parents, in recognition of the love they had shown him down the years, by giving back to society.

The first people to be helped by the new society were the family of John and Leeba La Roche, following John's pancreatic cancer diagnosis on 18 January 2001, just six days after the birth of the couple's first child.

'Elena is John's only daughter,' says Leeba La Roche. 'He was so ecstatic because at that point in his life he was having his first child; he was in his forties and had never had children. There was so much to look forward to and then he got the news he had cancer. The doctor gave him six months to live.'

Leeba had three children from a previous marriage, who were in school and at university, and John had just opened up a shoe-importing business when he received the devastating news that he was terminally ill. Despite predictions, though, John made it through the year.

'It was very difficult,' says Leeba, who runs a nursery and is also a yoga instructor. 'The treatment took all our finances and by the end of that year we were barely getting by. I prayed a lot because things were so hard.'

Early in 2002 there seemed to be an answer to some of those prayers at least.

'A mutual friend told us Brian wanted to start working with cancer patients; this was soon after his mother had died. We got a phone number for his brother Richard and sister Agnes, made contact and they invited us up to Brian's mansion. Brian wasn't in the country at the time but his brother and sister were so kind and welcoming. Agnes gave me a grand tour of the house; showed me the pool, Brian's room and also the room where his mother had spent her last days. It looked so fresh and recent, all the wreaths, bouquets and cards from her funeral were still there, it was very touching.

'Richard and Agnes decided then and there they would fund whatever John required, prescription drugs, supplements, whatever he needed. It was wonderful news and when Brian came back we met with him and he spent a long time talking with John.

'I was captivated at how mild-mannered he was; he had a very gentle way about him. You look at him and for a man so pronounced in his career, a big man, I had expected him to be louder.'

Leeba says that the dignified way in which Lara interacted with them meant a huge amount.

'There was never any sense of "I'm giving you a handout". He knew the exorbitant cost of medication and what we were going through.'

John's condition was deteriorating rapidly and, beyond the financial assistance extended, Leeba says the fact a global sporting star was taking an interest had a profound impact on her husband.

'Entering his last days, the fact that his situation mattered to someone like Brian Lara, that realisation, gave him a great sense of pride and enabled him to pass with dignity.'

John La Roche died in July 2002 and in the four-month period since contact was first established, Richard and Agnes had made several trips to the La Roche home and John met with Brian at his house on a further two occasions. The assistance did not end there as the costs of the funeral, which Richard and Agnes attended, were also met.

'It is very hard to put into words the depth of gratitude you feel towards people who did not know you before this terrible thing happened in your life and who helped you so much throughout it.'

Leeba says the kindness shown to her husband and children by the Lara family is a testament to Pearl and Bunty. Brian need also have no fear of running out of resolute backers as long as Leeba and Elena La Roche are around.

'When people would be on at him for one thing or another I would always defend him. I feel a connection to him, a bond. I was never a cricket fan but the whole experience with Brian obviously made me more aware. I would have the cricket on and say to Elena, "Look, that's Uncle Brian." She was too young to know what was happening but I've always impressed on her how Uncle Brian really helped her dad.'

World Cup disappointment and a return to captaincy
By April 2002 India and Sachin Tendulkar were scheduled to arrive

in the Caribbean but Lara, still feeling the effects of his elbow injury, was short of match practice. How he went about getting that practice says much about his character, says former Trinidad and Tobago team manager Colin Borde.

'He came back here [Queen's Park Cricket Club] after four months without picking up a bat and asked permission to play with the 1st XI against a touring side from Surrey, England.

'The guy who was captaining the team was a youngster, about nineteen or so, and was in complete awe of Brian. He asked him where he wanted him to field but Brian, gauging the young fella was feeling a bit of pressure, said: "No, you're the captain, you say, if you want me to go fine-leg, I'll go fine-leg." And that's where he went. He understood he was just another player. A lot of people assume he's the sort of character to grandstand but he's not like that.

'When he batted he scored 71 and then had two days in the nets before scoring 190-odd in another practice game.'

Unfortunately Lara couldn't carry this form into the Test series. The elbow injury had necessitated some technical restructuring of his batting and he was well below par, averaging just 29. He explained the issues the injury had caused during the 2nd Test at the Queen's Park Oval.

'I got out caught behind twice – at slip and by the wicketkeeper – because of the lack of strength in my hands because of the injury. I tried to use the pace of the ball behind the wicket instead of playing up in front.'

The West Indies had nevertheless won the series 2-1, largely due to fantastic performances from the rejuvenated skipper Carl Hooper and left-hander Shivnarine Chanderpaul, who both scored over 550 runs in five Tests.

A deflating 1-0 home loss to New Zealand followed in June 2002 and, just as Lara's elbow was nearly fully recovered, he was struck down by suspected hepatitis at the ICC Champions Trophy in Sri Lanka in September. Another protracted lay-off followed, with Lara missing the India and Bangladesh tours.

He courted controversy, though, when, just before the Bangladesh trip, he had deemed himself fit enough to participate in the Barbados

Open golf tournament. Frustration brewed amongst certain sectors upon the belief Lara was picking and choosing his tours. Calls were made for the selectors to take a stand by leaving him out of the World Cup squad travelling to South Africa in 2003. It was never a likely scenario and when his health was cleared by a London specialist in late December, Lara was one of fifteen names announced.

He was short of cricket practice again when the tournament began in February but it didn't seem to matter as he hit the ground running against hosts South Africa in the opening match. His 116 was the basis for a thrilling three-run victory; an innings 'that immediately re-established his place among the greats of the modern game', wrote Tony Cozier, adding that, 'to watch a master craftsman at work, such as Lara was over three hours and 134 balls, is always worth any money.'

Unfortunately it proved another false dawn and the West Indians failed to progress beyond the first round for a second successive World Cup, in a campaign that would cost Carl Hooper his job as West Indies captain.

Hooper's renowned inconsistency had seemingly been remedied by the responsibility of captaincy with his twenty-two matches in charge yielding 1,609 runs at an average of 46. Yet just four wins in those twenty-two games and complaints of overly defensive tactics were compounded by World Cup disappointment, and the WICB was once more casting its eyes about for alternative leaders.

The move was not without controversy, especially after chairman of selectors Sir Viv Richards had publicly backed Hooper's reappointment. WICB President Wes Hall did not see it that way and rumbles of the Guyanese batsman's impending sacking began while the team was still at the World Cup in South Africa.

West Indies Players Association (WIPA) President Dinanath Ramnarine, an international leg-spinner who had been marginalised since an on-field disagreement with Hooper one year before, was privy to the fact that the WICB were coming to Lara's door to offer the leadership for a second time.

'I called Brian in South Africa and ending up having a two-hour discussion about taking on the captaincy. I promised to send him the bill for that but never did,' jokes Ramnarine. 'He was reluctant. The thing was convincing him to take the captaincy based on the discussion I had had with the then President of the WICB [Wes Hall]. He wanted to make sure he was going to get the full support from the Board and not go through what he did the first time again.'

Hooper, though deemed surplus to requirements from a captaincy perspective, was still amongst the region's best players and was named in the squad of fourteen for the opening Test against the touring Australians in April 2003. Reports surfaced that the veteran of 102 Test matches would have played under any player bar Lara, but Lara it was who was chosen as skipper and four days before the 1st Test the thirty-six-year-old Hooper retired from international cricket, for the second and last time.

Ironically, just as in his first stint as regional captain, the opening game of Lara's reign would be at the embittered home ground of his deposed predecessor. Lara had to face a baying crowd at Georgetown's Bourda but turned his detractors around in typical fashion with a scintillating second innings century. He was accompanied all the way by Daren Ganga, who was registering his first Test match hundred.

'He met me at the crease on 40-odd and raced past me and scored his hundred before me,' smiles the former Trinidad and Tobago captain. 'Batting with Brian sometimes made things easier that way because a lot of the focus would be on him.'

The Trinidadians' twin centuries, and a 185-run partnership, could not undo the damage of a low first innings total, though, and prevent the West Indies going 1-0 down.

As the teams headed for the Queen's Park Oval, Lara was heading for another defining contest with a bowler at the height of his powers.

Throughout most of the first decade of the twenty-first century Brett Lee vied with Pakistan's Shoaib Akhtar for the title of world's quickest bowler. Lee's fastest recorded delivery was 99.9 mph (160.8 kph) and those that saw his spell against Lara on the fifth day at the Queen's Park Oval say he touched those heights in that session. The quickest bowling he had seen in the Caribbean was how former West Indies paceman – and now eloquent commentator – Ian Bishop rated it.

Lara had never scored a Test match century at his home ground and narrowly missed out in the first innings of the game with 91, bowled round his legs by Brad Hogg. Now in the second innings he had been joined by Ramnaresh Sarwan and was attempting to stave off defeat.

Deryck Murray described the blond-haired Lee's spell with the second new ball as being 'as fine a spell of fast bowling as you could want to see … There was pace, hostility, swing, control from a fast bowler and that was a storm Brian had to weather, to get through, and transform a good innings of a 50 or 60 into his first century on his home ground.

'What that's showing is the technique and ability at the start, the flair as he started dominating the bowling but then coming back to the grit, the concentration, the determination, the discipline needed to go through that difficult period until he could get back and exert his authority on the game again, and go to his century with the flourish that we know is a Brian Lara innings.'

Lara finished with 122 and, years later in a speech before the Queen's Park Cricket Club, recalled the hostility of Lee's bowling that day and its effect on his batting partner.

Sarwan had been having some trouble playing leg-spinner Stuart MacGill and disclosed as much to his captain between overs. Lara, who loved playing spinners, offered to swap ends and take MacGill for a while whilst the Guyanese batsman took on Lee. Sarwan swiftly concluded his problems with spin were not as bad as first thought and declined the offer.

Lara's overcoming of Lee aside, there had been little for home supporters to cheer in the series and by the time the teams arrived at Antigua's 4th Test the Aussies were 3-0 up with one to play.

What happened at the Antigua Recreation Ground, though, set Caribbean pulses racing and provided what Lara described as 'the greatest cricketing experience of my life'. He had long stated that what he desired more than anything before he retired was for the seeds of a West Indies resurgence to be sown. In Antigua, with a side containing six players under twenty-four, that process appeared to have begun against a hitherto overwhelmingly dominant Australia.

Pace like fire. Lara overcomes a brutal spell from Australian fast bowler Brett Lee to score 122, his first century at his home ground, Trinidad's Queen's Park Oval, 23 April 2003.

The match, in which the West Indies were battling to avoid the dishonour of a first home series whitewash, had been even until Australia's second innings when they posted a mammoth 417. That performance left the West Indies requiring 418 for victory. No team in history had ever scored more than 406 – India's total against the West Indies, in Trinidad, in 1976.

One world record had already been established in the game – the Australian openers Matthew Hayden and Justin Langer recorded their fifth opening partnership of 200 or more – but it was the one established on the final day that would garner the headlines.

Fourth-day centuries from Ramnaresh Sarwan and Shivnarine Chanderpaul were the backbone of the West Indian run chase but there were vital partnerships all the way through. It would need another on the final day to secure victory. Rejoining battle on the fifth morning the home side was 371 for 6, still requiring forty-seven to win, but Caribbean nerves began to jangle as Chanderpaul perished early. It was left to twenty-year-old Leeward Islands all-rounder Omari Banks, the first Test match player from the tiny island of Anguilla, and thirty-three-year-old fast bowling veteran Vasbert Drakes to guide the West Indians home with a resolute forty-six-run partnership.

The fight and talent was there for all to see: the highest ever last innings total to win a Test, set against the world's best side and achieved by a combined team effort, not on the back of a big Lara innings – he scored 60.

The series had seen a return to form for Lara, against his favourite opponents, with 533 runs at 67, yet, Antigua notwithstanding, his efforts had once again failed to avert a crushing series loss.

The visit of the Sri Lankans in June brought with it a morale-boosting 1-0 win, and Lara's fifth Test double hundred, but four months later came the news that one of his world records had fallen.

On 10 October 2003, Australia's Matthew Hayden had obliterated a mediocre Zimbabwean attack in Perth to register 380 and break Lara's Test record score of 375. Whilst on the surface Lara was magnanimous about his nine-year mark being bettered by the burly Queenslander, those closer to him revealed a different story.

'Brian phoned Hayden from Jamaica to congratulate him and Hayden was still in the dressing room celebrating at the time,' says former West Indies opener Bryan Davis. 'Brian told him who it was and that he wanted to congratulate him, that it must've been tough and so on and Hayden just said, "Yeah, thanks but I can't talk to you now," and pretty much hung up the phone.

'Well that got Brian stinking mad because he didn't think Hayden had been very courteous and Brian is a man who was brought up to be well-mannered. And he turned around to my son Gregory, who he was with at the time, and said, "I'm going to break that record, he's not keeping that."

'It motivated him, got him angry because he felt he had been slighted. But it's one thing to say you're going to do something in the heat of the moment, it's quite another to go out and do it.'

Lara would have to wait for his opportunity to reclaim the record, though, as, following a frustrating and laboured 1-0 victory away to Zimbabwe, the West Indians travelled on to South Africa and the scene of their 5-0 drubbing in 1998. That a whitewash was not repeated was thanks largely to Lara's blade and statistically only by a drawn 3rd Test; the four-match series was lost 3-0. In the six Tests in Zimbabwe and South Africa Lara had again led the way by a distance, averaging 63 with an aggregate of 753 runs.

His lone hand was most in evidence in the 1st Test at Johannesburg's New Wanderers Stadium, when a first innings 202 accounted for nearly half the team's total but the West Indies still lost by 189 runs. His double century did include one extraordinary passage of play, though late on the third day; one which, as with so many Lara innings, will live long in the memory.

South African skipper Graeme Smith brought on left-arm orthodox spinner Robin Peterson for the penultimate over of the day's play with a plan in mind. He brought the field in trying to tempt Lara, who was 150 not out, to hit over the top and force a mistake in the process. It worked, to a degree, Lara did hit over the top, quite venomously in fact, but there was no mistake.

To Peterson's first delivery Lara stepped back and cut hard through point for four; next he skipped down the track and launched the spinner mightily over long-on for six; the third ball was dispatched in the same imperious fashion for another maximum; the fourth went straight back over Peterson's head for four; the fifth was similarly smashed over the bowler and into the long-off boundary; and the sixth was used to display 'the full range of his greatness', as commentator Ian Bishop described it at the time.

As Peterson approached the wicket for that final ball he was simply trying to avoid being hit for another boundary; he bowled it flat and hard outside off-stump but Lara, having dummied as if to move forward, now leaned back and late cut him sumptuously behind square for another four. Two sixes and four fours and the over had gone for 28, the most ever in a Test match. Another world record – the way it was achieved, pure Lara.

Despite these efforts there was no hiding the fact that the West Indians had lost heavily again and the optimism stoked by the record-breaking victory over Australia in Antigua now seemed a distant memory. Less than a year into his second stint as skipper and Lara's position was already under threat amidst renewed talk of player disunity and an inability to inspire.

As the West Indies returned home they welcomed a resurgent English side that arrived a stronger unit than in previous years. To show how the cycle of cricket had shifted it was England, not the West Indies, who now held the fast bowling aces, furnished as it was with the four pacemen that would wrest the Ashes from the Australians' grasp just over a year later. Andrew Flintoff, Steve Harmison, Matthew Hoggard and Simon Jones would all have an impact on the series but it was Harmison who was the standout performer, and he announced himself in the second innings of the 1st Test at Jamaica's Sabina Park.

Unusually for a fast bowler, Harmison is a man of gentle and even temperament. He is not fond of touring, revelling in the familiarity of home surroundings, but he found the Caribbean very much to his liking. The match had been evenly poised after the first innings with both teams posting totals in excess of 300 but then the West Indies collapsed spectacularly. They succumbed to a devastating Harmison spell: the 6ft 4in Durham man taking 7 for 12 in 12.3 overs to lead the rout of the home side, dismissing them for 47. It was the West Indians' lowest Test score of all time.

The record-breaking capitulation meant losing was assured but the way in which some went about accepting that defeat raised eyebrows.

'Soon after the game had finished, though, some of the West Indies players were the ones dancing giddily in the stands, partying with their supporters as though ten-wicket defeats by England were all in a day's work,' noted the Wisden Almanack report.

The event fuelled the fire surrounding Lara's leadership and the lack of application being displayed by his players.

'The West Indies squad assembled in Jamaica five days prior to the 1st Test. In that time, they had only one practice session,' wrote Tony Cozier, sounding like a man pulling out his hair. 'Much of the time was spent in psychological sessions, ironically some watching motivational videos of the American basketball legend Michael Jordan stressing the importance of practice, which is precisely what they were not doing.'

The 2nd Test in Port of Spain was lost by seven wickets, the 3rd, in Bridgetown, by eight wickets. The team had been thrown into further disarray in Trinidad, when the frustrated team manager, Ricky Skerritt, resigned saying: 'I regret that, despite my best efforts, I have been unable to instil in the entire team the fullest understanding of their obligations on and off the field to the people of the West Indies.' Skerritt said his decision had been made after the 'partying-in-the-stands' incident in Jamaica.

At 3-0 down in a four-match series the home side was once again staring down the barrel of a first home whitewash and the vultures were circling for Lara, whose bat had been conspicuously silent.

World record reclaimed

When Antigua's 4th Test arrived Lara was in familiar territory: under immense pressure and being roundly criticised by a large section of both media and public, the focal point for the region's woes. His response was equally familiar.

Almost ten years before, to the day, against the same opponents and on the same pitch, Lara had scored 375 to claim Garry Sobers's Test match record. In the decade which followed that first record, Lara's batting had matured and from the outset his innings in Antigua had a more calculated feel. Certainly those commentating on the West Indies first innings had a sense of what was coming by the time he reached 150.

'That's 150 for Brian Lara, he's off and running in one of those marathon innings once again,' said Ian Bishop.

Not many batsmen could be said to have just got going when they're 150 not out but Bishop, a fellow Trinidadian who had played a lot of cricket with Lara, knew what was in the offing. And he was right; there was hardly a flicker as Lara raised his bat for 100, 150, 200 and 250, just acknowledgement of applause. At 300 there was more exuberance as he leapt and punched the air; the smile was back as he removed his helmet and kissed the West Indies badge.

Just as there had been a tense overnight wait to endure a decade before, though, so it was in 2004. One of those waiting was a man who delights in the nickname 'West Indies No. 1 Fan'.

'Overnight he was 313 not out and I was like a schoolboy, pacing up and down,' says Peter Matthews, who is a familiar and flamboyant sight at West Indies matches around the world, with his tall, colourful top hats and multifarious flags. The West Indies have been blessed with some legendary supporters down the years and Matthews, a garrulous and friendly man, is the latest in a celebrated line of characters.

'This was one of the greatest batsmen trying to break the biggest record there is. I was staying by Curtly Ambrose, who, incidentally, used to call me Peter Green because he couldn't remember my name,' adds the man who carries Lara's career statistics around with him 'in case of healthy debate'. 'I was sleepless that whole night before Brian broke the record. The next day Ambrose went fishing, he couldn't take the tension.

'Oh gosh, boy, the stress that morning; real pressure. I remember doing a radio interview live as Brian's getting closer and closer to the record and I had to be real careful with my words you know,' he says raising his eyebrows.

Throughout the innings Lara was a man in supreme control. On a pitch which allowed him to express himself with certainty he skipped down the wicket to spinners Gareth Batty and Michael Vaughan and dispatched them nonchalantly; to the previously unplayable pace quartet, he had all the time in the world and marched inexorably towards Hayden's 380.

'There was no doubt in my mind that he was taking the mickey when it came to the way he milked Gareth Batty,' wrote England captain Vaughan in his autobiography *Time to Declare*. 'Whenever I moved a fielder for Batts he would deliberately hit the ball there, in fact whatever I did he would try and make me look stupid. He was brilliant.'

At 374, with Caribbean hearts in mouths, Lara launched a nerveless lofted straight drive off Batty into the Sir Vivian Richards Pavilion for six. It took him level with Hayden on 380. At a time when most players would be thinking of taking singles, restricting the risky shots and making sure of the record, it seemed an extraordinary shot to take on. That Lara thought nothing of it displayed his approach to the game in the starkest of terms.

On an evening out with friends and family a couple of years later in Port of Spain, the subject of the most audacious cricket shot ever played came up. Some suggestions were made before this record-equalling six off Batty was proffered. Lara dismissed it, saying matter-of-factly that he had expected the ball which was bowled and, as he was seeing it like a breadfruit, already knew what shot he was going to play to it.

Daren Ganga, who was in the West Indian team that day and watching from the dressing room, says the manner in which Lara equalled the record was no great surprise. As a young player in the Trinidad and Tobago and West Indian teams, Ganga had been the recipient of much advice from the great batsman.

'Brian would always say when you go into bat it's about believing in yourself, it's about being confident in your ability to play your shots. No matter if a ball is bowled on sand or water a half-volley is a half-volley and should be put away, a long hop outside off-stump should be put away. You should be confident enough to do it, whether it's the first ball of the innings or the last, whatever the stage of the game.'

Lara levels Matthew Hayden's Test record score of 380 with an audacious six off England's Gareth Batty. Obscured is wicketkeeper Geraint Jones, while Andrew Flintoff, at slip, watches the ball disappearing.

It was a credo that Lara lived up to throughout his career but most memorably in this moment. He didn't waste any time surpassing Hayden's record either, as a misdirected delivery from Batty was swept for four past a tired-looking Graham Thorpe – the only Englishman who had also been on the field ten years previously for Lara's 375.

He kissed the pitch as he had done a decade before but that times had changed was evidenced by the reaction to his achievement. The travails of the intervening decade, the state of the series and of West Indian cricket, and the fact that a good proportion of the watching crowd was English, meant the celebrations were altogether more subdued. There was delight naturally but no pitch invasion, save a lone fan who was shepherded away by police before he could reach his hero.

'There was a great joy in the country but I don't think it could ever match the 375 because there was a freshness about that, an innocence almost, which could never be revisited,' says calypsonian, and Antigua Recreation Ground regular, David Rudder.

In any event Lara still had another milestone in his sights, the first quadruple century in Test match history, and he had support from some unexpected quarters.

'It seems a little strange, but a few of us, when 400 came into Lara's sights, were actually willing him to do it,' said English skipper Vaughan. 'The sheer majesty of it all had been a marvel to witness … When Lara is in that kind of mood, the only thing capable of getting him out is a missile.'

Another sweep off Batty, this time for a single, ensured that he would achieve the milestone. Lara was now the only first-class cricketer to register single, double, triple, quadruple and quintuple hundreds. It was another landmark in an incredible career. Ten years may have separated Lara's records but he had produced a near identical thirteen-hour masterpiece, facing 582 deliveries and hitting forty-three fours and four sixes in an innings of supreme will to reclaim the cherished mark.

His powers of concentration were well known by this stage but a cricketer that played alongside him as a teenager in league cricket says he noted another attribute which proved essential in big innings such as this.

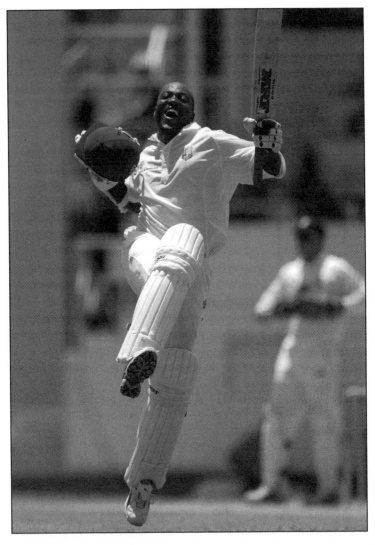

What it feels like to take back the biggest batting record of the lot. Leaping for joy as Lara reclaims the Test highest score, finishing on 400 not out.

'He conserved his energy well,' says Tony Dharson, an attacking left-handed opening batsman who played National League cricket with a nineteen-year-old Lara.

'The first time we played and batted together was against Crompton, on the Queen's Park Savannah. Every time I drove the ball I would race down the other end and be ready to get back but Brian would just amble down. This happened a few times, I would be racing and Brian just ambling. After a few of these I was beginning to get mad, there didn't seem to be any urgency. I said to him: "What happenin, you not runnin today or what?" He just said: "I runnin, but you don't expect me to run so fast when I know it's only one."

'In hindsight it's then you look at the 375 and the 400 in a different way and you see how he can do that; ambling up and ambling back, judging the runs and conserving energy. Often when he made these huge scores he didn't actually look that tired.'

Lara had been suffering with a dislocated finger on his left hand coming into the series but refused to use that as an excuse for his poor returns up to Antigua. Now, after losing the record, he had taken just nineteen innings to become the first man to retake it. And, in so doing, it seems even international players were not impervious to a little Laramania.

'We all became fans for the moment as he signed our tickets, bats, shirts, and anything else we could get our hands on,' said Vaughan.

Lara gave his own assessment of the innings when interviewed by Mark Nicholas for the *Daily Telegraph*.

'My game is mental. If you are fit you should not run out of steam physically but you can lose concentration. For me it is fun to find ways to make big scores. When I was younger my play was based on flair and flamboyance but now I have matured and am more prepared to accumulate.

'In the Antigua Test we had to avoid a whitewash and on a flat pitch I decided to focus on resisting the new ball, which meant overs 1–15; 81–95; 160–170. In between times the field was set back and it was easier to pick off runs. This is "my time", the new ball is "their time".'

The 400 meant that in his last sixteen Tests, Lara had scored 2,000 runs.

The reaction from most was to laud an extraordinary achievement but some were not so charitable, saying Lara had put personal ambition first, in the ultimately drawn game, and cost his team a chance of victory.

'Their whole first innings might have been geared around one individual performance, and they could have let a Test match slip because of it,' said Australia's Ricky Ponting who was far from alone. 'They ran out of time in the game. That's not the way the Australian team plays.'

Lara's fans raced to his defence saying the avoidance of a whitewash had been paramount; whether that desired outcome came by way of a draw or a victory mattered little. His innings had put the England win out of the equation and simultaneously reclaimed the biggest record in Test cricket, one the Caribbean had come to view as its own.

If celebrations had been relatively subdued in Antigua, that was never likely to be the case in Trinidad and Tobago.

Lara was welcomed at Piarco Airport by family members and a host of dignitaries, including Prime Minister Patrick Manning, before emerging through a guard of honour to a clamouring public. Tassa drums thundered, Austin 'SuperBlue' Lyons performed 'Signal to Lara' and a group of dancing Moko Jumbies guided Lara to his first public function in the airport car park.

Manning, who would later name Lara the country's Ambassador for Sport, set down an early contender for most over-the-top tribute when claiming, if there was cricket playing on Mars or Pluto, Lara would be the greatest cricketer of the universe!

Lara was whisked onto a motorcade which travelled from Piarco to Port of Spain's Brian Lara Promenade, making numerous stops along the way. Tens of thousands of people lined the streets en route to his final destination. Lara mingled with his fans but on one occasion with painful results: the champion batsman wincing as the dislocated finger on his left hand was grabbed a little too enthusiastically by one well-wisher.

The following day he was off again, shaking hands, cuddling babies, being feted and lauded by all and sundry in the south of the island. The

Trinidad Guardian devoted eight pages of coverage to the returning hero, TTPost released a limited-edition set of Lara 400 stamps, and it was 1994 all over again, as the nation indulged in heady celebration.

One-day winners

After a 1-0 home triumph over Bangladesh, which was more problematic than might have been anticipated, Lara led his troops to England for a four-Test series and the ICC Champions Trophy. His world record could not deflect from the pressure he had been under as captain and Lara, who had sought assurances on a number of issues before taking up the reins a second time, clearly felt he was still not receiving full support.

'The word is trust,' he said. 'People such as Sir Viv [Richards, chairman of selectors] and I are put in positions without the full backing, the full support of the people who put us there [the WICB]. It is all about trust, if they trust us we can do something, if not, well, then …'

He was sanguine about the possibility of losing the captaincy.

'I would play on and restructure myself while doing so. I am a servant of West Indies cricket, of my people here and of myself. Of course it can be taken away from me but that is out of my control, my reaction to it is not.'

What happened in the Test series did not enhance Lara's position, as his side was thumped 4-0 and his own form fell away as he failed to register a century. A ten-wicket defeat at the Oval in the final Test led straight into the ICC Champions Trophy, where the West Indies were more keenly fancied for early elimination than ultimate triumph. Yet during the near-decade-long slump since 1995's loss to Australia, the West Indies had always proved more competitive in the shortened format. Now, in a competition second only in status to the World Cup, they would prove so again.

Lara's young side defeated Bangladesh and South Africa in the group stages and Pakistan in the semi-final to set up a showdown with hosts England on 25 September.

England had been the West Indies' chief tormentors for the majority of the preceding six months and were expected to apply a *coup de grâce* in the final. The West Indians had not read the script, though, and chased down England's 217 with seven balls remaining for a famous two-wicket victory, with two Barbadians – wicketkeeper Courtney Browne, 35 not out, and left-arm fast-medium bowler Ian Bradshaw, 34 not out – coolly bringing the West Indies home in the Oval's gathering gloom. It was Lara's first major honour at international level.

Having watched every West Indies game throughout the competition, it was a match their greatest fan, Peter Matthews, had to miss due to work commitments back home in Trinidad. He vividly recollects a phone call from a jubilant skipper on the Lord's balcony as the West Indies closed in on victory.

'When the game was almost won Brian called me and said: "So, where are you on the ground, man? Come out on the pitch and have a good time. Where you at?"

Lara's only major international trophy. Jubilation at winning the ICC Champions Trophy against host England at the Kennington Oval in September 2004.

"'I'm in Trinidad."

"'What the **** you doin there?'"

Lara was overjoyed with the win, saying it had been special in terms of what his side had gone through in the previous months.

'There have been many personal highs in my career – the one-run win in Adelaide, the win over South Africa in 1992,' he said. 'But in terms of the battering we have received from everyone in the past few months and then doing it against England, who smashed us in seven of the eight Tests, is pretty special.'

It was the West Indians' first victory in the final of an international competition in twenty-five years and Lara could be forgiven for reading some of the press reaction with a wry smile. He had been mercilessly castigated for failing to inspire his men over the previous year but now many were hailing his motivational qualities as being the key component to success.

'Lara was inspirational … a man transformed,' wrote Vic Marks in the *Observer*.

Thoughts also turned to those at home for, while the West Indies team had been in England, the 2004 hurricane season had proved a devastating one in the Caribbean. Hurricanes Ivan, the tenth most intense Atlantic hurricane ever recorded, and Jeanne, the deadliest storm of the season, ravaged wide areas but hit Grenada and Haiti respectively with most shocking effect. Grenada would take years to get back on its feet after Ivan whilst Jeanne was responsible for over 3,000 deaths in Haiti.

'We all lay in our beds very comfortably while our people in the Caribbean were fending for their lives,' said Lara. 'It was the catalyst for this very young team for what they achieved in England over the past three weeks.'

14 World Cup and retirement

Old foes lock horns

Following the 4th Test match in England in 2004, it had been odds-on Lara would soon be asked to step aside as West Indies captain. Now, after Champions Trophy success, his future in charge looked rosily secure. But Lara, a man for whom the term rollercoaster appeared invented, was about to enter turbulent waters once more as he squared up alongside other WIPA members against their old foes the WICB.

Like a couple of warring neighbours continually casting suspicious glances across each other's backyards, peace would often be publicly declared between the two but undercurrents of suspicion remained. It had ever been so, but the world of modern sport had thrown up a new area of dispute and one not easily resolved: that of players' image rights and their relationship to the Board's principal sponsors.

The subtext to the affair was the pitiful state of the governing Board's coffers. Between 1999 and 2005 the WICB had not turned a profit and a cumulative deficit of US$14 million was predicted by 30 September 2005. Against this background, big business and the fight for control of the Caribbean telecommunications market entered the fray. The newest player on the telecoms block was Digicel and, though only established in April 2001, its owner and founder, Irish entrepreneur Denis O'Brien, had expansionist ambitions. He now looked to promote those ambitions by linking his brand with the region's highest-profile sporting team.

Sponsorship negotiations between Digicel and the WICB were undertaken and progressed to the point in July 2004, at a London meeting attended by Lara and WICB President Teddy Griffiths, where an agreement to sponsor the West Indies Test and one-day teams was signed. The deal, worth US$23 million over five years, would begin with the January 2005 tour of Australia.

Cable and Wireless (C&W), who had been sponsors of the West Indies team for eighteen years, reacted angrily to the news they were being replaced and increasingly vitriolic accusations flew back and forth between C&W and the WICB. It was only the start of the Board's problems, for as part of the Digicel deal they had also sold on the players' individual image rights. The issue there was that seven players, Brian Lara, Dwayne Bravo, Fidel Edwards, Chris Gayle, Ravi Rampaul, Ramnaresh Sarwan and Devon Smith, had entered into personal sponsorship deals with C&W. The timing of when those deals were signed would become key; Lara's agreement had predated the change of sponsors but those of the remaining six players had not.

The issue surfaced before Digicel's first tour as sponsor when WIPA stepped in, stating the Board's contracts with Digicel infringed its members' rights. An acrimonious dispute erupted, threatening the likelihood of some of the side's best players undertaking the Australian tour. The matter went to arbitration, temporarily patching over the problem and enabling a full-strength team to be sent.

Though the Australia tour proceeded, the West Indies fared poorly, winning just one of six matches in a tournament eventually won by the hosts. The cricketing performances were not the most damning part of the month-long trip, though. On the team's return a report, by Digicel Group Sponsorship Manager Richard Nowell to Chief Executive Denis O'Brien, was leaked to the *Trinidad Guardian*.

The *Guardian* reported that in the account, Nowell bemoaned the lack of cooperation of the players contracted to C&W, slammed WIPA and questioned the return Digicel was getting on its investment.

'With no relationship, access or support from the highest-profiled players who should be at the forefront of the sponsorship, combined with a terrorist players' association, our current rights have negligible value, if any.'

He was equally damning of the players' professionalism, with particular reference to the amount of female company enjoyed on tour. Nowell was said to have overheard doors banging and female voices along the players' hotel corridor well after 1 am on the eve of the match against Australia in Brisbane.

'Perhaps more astounding was, following the team's defeat against Pakistan, the player rooming next to me had company 20 minutes after returning from a crushing defeat … Even in Perth, the most crucial time of the tour, one player had flown in a girl from Adelaide.'

On return from Australia, and with the visit of South Africa looming, the issue of personal image rights flared again and this time the Board opted for a hard line approach by banning the C&W sponsored players: Bravo, Edwards, Gayle, Rampaul, Sarwan and Smith. Lara, having escaped censure because of his C&W agreement being a pre-existing one, nevertheless stood in solidarity with his teammates and removed himself from selection for the series. It was a stand which automatically brought with it the end of his second term as captain.

It was a distressing period for West Indian fans who, having witnessed a decade-long decline of a once proud team, looked on from the sidelines at a rancorous dispute which sapped the energies of both players and administrators. Supporters cared little for the rights and wrongs of such disagreements, looking only for the seeds of revival. There appeared little hope of that in such an environment of enmity; West Indies cricket was distinguishing itself only with a capacity for self-implosion.

With Lara's second tenure at an end, Shivnarine Chanderpaul was appointed captain for the 1st Test in Guyana, and he began with a bang, becoming only the second player (after New Zealand's Graham Dowling) to register a double century in his first game leading his country. However, a Jacques Kallis century ensured South Africa held out for the draw.

Chanderpaul's stunning double hundred would afford him but a brief time in the limelight, though, as the teams headed for Trinidad's 2nd Test. C&W had temporarily softened its position, releasing the players at the centre of the image rights furore from their contractual requirements for the remainder of the series and the seven were available again. After such a spirited performance in the 1st Test, not everyone was convinced the banned players should come straight back into the fold. It was never likely that Lara would be omitted, though, and he returned at the Queen's Park Oval with Chanderpaul retained as captain.

He announced himself with a vintage performance, showing no ring rustiness in his first Test innings in eight months. Clearly in the mood for something special, he tamed a tricky pitch and marched commandingly to a century. A short-arm pull off the pacey but raw Monde Zondeki brought up his twenty-seventh Test hundred, a West Indian record, usurping Sir Garfield Sobers, and moved him to third on the all-time list of Test run-scorers. Only the Australians Steve Waugh and Allan Border now stood before him.

He went to 159 overnight and looked a certainty for his first double hundred on home soil the next day. However, the irrepressibly madcap fast bowler Andre Nel changed his angle of attack in the morning and, coming round the wicket with Lara on 196, produced a ball which angled in and then nipped away, clipping the off-stump. It silenced the Oval crowd and ended the West Indian innings on 347. Nobody else had scored above 35.

That night Lara went out with his friend, former Trinidad and Tobago team manager, Colin Borde.

'He asked me a couple of questions about people he had seen in the crowd that day,' said Borde. 'I said, "What are you talking about people in the crowd, you were in the middle of a war." He said: "Yeah, but I only concentrate for five seconds at a time." So between balls he was relaxing and looking about. That's really something you have to learn to do, to switch on and off like that. He said, "I'm only human you know, the average man cannot concentrate for ten hours straight."'

Despite Lara's innings the West Indies, under new Australian coach Bennett King, the first foreigner to take charge of the side, lost the 2nd

Test by eight wickets. Another imperious exhibition during Barbados's 3rd Test, when Lara brought out the full repertoire and blitzed 176 from a total of 296, could not prevent an even heavier defeat, this time by an innings and 86 runs.

The pattern for Lara was familiar, off-field wrangling with the Board followed by virtuoso performances on it, but ones which, frustratingly, were not sufficient to stave off repeated defeat.

Lara's batting approach had matured and evolved over the years and he was now reaping the benefits of this refined methodology. At an age when many would be winding down their international careers Lara appeared to at last be gaining the consistency which he had always craved. He had built a reputation as a flamboyant player taking scintillating risks, and it was what the crowd loved him for, but he had long known that the team's dependence on him to score the bulk of its runs meant his natural all-out attacking style had to be tempered.

'Now I'm trying to cut down on those risks,' he said. 'You know that if you spend 40–50 minutes and you're still on five or ten, that you're going to build it into a major innings. Before, you think that you need to set the tone for the innings immediately, and in doing so, you risk your shots. I'm thinking less that way now.'

With the 4th Test against South Africa drawn and the series lost 2-0, Lara followed up his terrific form by scoring 331 runs, including two centuries, against the touring Pakistanis in a two-Test series tied 1-1.

Contractual issues and the bitterness they were provoking would not go away, though, and attention turned to them once more as the touring party for Sri Lanka was assembled. Agreement was not reached on the issue of sponsorship guarantee fees and a number of leading players, including Lara, Ramnaresh Sarwan and Chris Gayle, consequently bowed out of the tour. The squad was shored up with eight 'A' team players already in Sri Lanka but, devoid of three of its principal run-makers, posting big scores looked the likeliest problem, and so it proved. An under-strength batting line-up was bowled out for less than 150 in three out of their four innings and the series lost 2-0.

Another world record

By late 2005, the thirty-six-year-old Lara was moving into the autumn of his playing days, a time when more attritional records come into view. It had been fifteen years since his Test debut in Pakistan, thirteen since he announced himself to the world with his 277 in Sydney, and that longevity had seen Allan Border's world record for most Test match runs edge onto the horizon. With his customary sense of timing, Lara would make his bid for that landmark in the country of the record-holder, and one which had so shaped his Test career, Australia.

The West Indies three-Test tour Down Under was always going to be daunting, against a rampant Australian side, and began badly with a 379-run reversal in Brisbane's 1st Test. For a team now accustomed to heavy defeat it was a performance their captain Chanderpaul described as 'probably the worst we have had so far'.

Chanderpaul himself was not having a happy time of it and his batting was suffering with the added burden of captaincy. A quiet and reserved man, he seemed an unlikely character to motivate in a crisis; his post-match interviews were becoming tortured and, additionally, it seemed to many as though Lara was still responsible for much of the decision-making.

Hobart's nine-wicket 2nd Test loss did not improve Chanderpaul's mood, where he again failed to score heavily, but he was not the only experienced player struggling for runs. Lara's bat had been quiet and the consistency of the previous year, when he struck four hundreds in five Tests against South Africa and Pakistan, seemed to have deserted him. Poor umpiring had played its part, though, fuelling the argument of those who believe Lara has had more than his share of bad decisions on Australian soil.

'For the third time in four innings he was on the wrong side of a contentious decision, Rudi Koertzen this time misinterpreting a caught-behind appeal off Shane Warne,' wrote Peter English, Cricinfo's Australasian Editor, of Lara's second innings dismissal in Hobart. 'He suffered an awful lbw dismissal to Brett Lee in Brisbane and was given out the same way to a desperately close call in the first innings. The master is

36, his wrinkles are showing and his skin must loosen further with each incorrect decision.'

The West Indies were in familiar territory by the time the teams arrived at the Adelaide Oval for the final Test – attempting to avoid a series whitewash. Batting first, they had been reduced to 19 for 2 when Lara came to the crease. From the outset, he had the demeanour of a man who had decided today was his day. The quality of his footwork and placement were back. He swept Warne hard to leg and drove him equally fluently through the covers against the spin; there were deft deflections off the hip and a flurry of back-foot cut shots, square drives and pulls off Lee. His century, his ninth against Australia, came up with one such pull off the home side's premier fastest bowler.

Once Lara hit full stride an air of resignation encompassed the fielders; boundary chases became more laboured, dives less full-blooded, throws to the wicketkeeper more routine. Australia were waiting for Lara to make a mistake and they would have to wait a long time. He registered his double century with a fierce pull off Lee; remarkably his third such double against the world's best side.

By now he was closing in on Allan Border's Test record 11,174 runs. He had needed 213 runs when he walked out to bat, now he required just one. Stepping across his stumps, he paddled another of McGrath's suffocating off-stump deliveries around the corner and down to fine-leg for the single. It was a stroke of great unorthodoxy but made to look the most natural in the world.

Border's record had stood for twelve years and nine months and the nuggety Queenslander had taken 156 matches in making his runs. On 26 November 2005, Lara had passed it in just 121 games and become the sixteenth player to hold the record. (When Sachin Tendulkar subsequently passed Lara's record, in October 2008, it took him twenty-one more matches than the Trinidadian.) Lara now held the three most prized individual batting records: highest Test score, most Test runs and highest first-class score. He remains the only man to ever hold all three simultaneously.

His reaction when he was finally bowled by McGrath, trying to hit the legendary seamer over the top, was typical. He was annoyed – for Lara,

226 was not enough; he had treated the watching crowd to something special but, in his Australian swansong, he wanted it to be something spectacular.

At each stadium on the tour, Lara had bid farewell to the Australian crowds as he exited the arena but this departure, to a standing ovation, had the ring of finality to it. As he neared the boundary he turned and walked a few steps backwards, taking in the scene and applause, raising his bat and waving in acknowledgement.

As so often before it would not be enough to carry his team to victory and the tourists succumbed to a seven-wicket defeat and a 3-0 series loss. Defeat, though, took little off the gloss of the post-match presentations which, understandably, focussed on Lara. Veteran Australian commentator Richie Benaud spoke glowingly, the former Australian captain saying he classified players by whether he would pay money to watch them and Lara was one he undoubtedly would. He said the Trinidadian was, in a word, entertainment.

In responding, Lara, a man for whom charm and the right words come easily, ensured warm applause when calling the Adelaide Oval the most beautiful cricket ground in the world, referring to Border as an icon and then thanking Australia for providing many of the defining moments of his career.

There was more to celebrate for Lara on his return to the Caribbean, when he helped Trinidad and Tobago secure its first regional title for twenty-one years. Needing to defeat regional powerhouse Barbados away from home to take the title they did just that, with a 264-run victory.

'To beat Barbados in Barbados, to literally take the cup off their shelf is an amazing feeling,' said Lara.

'On the international circuit, playing Australia and beating Australia is real cricket to me. On the regional scene, playing Barbados in Barbados and beating them is what it is all about.

'You've got to understand I'm now aged thirty-six, and any sort of success on the playing field would be greeted with uncontrollable emotions because I am not sure to experience it again.'

Less fulfilling times were on the horizon as the West Indies headed back Down Under for their tour of New Zealand, a team Lara had famously said he found it hard to get motivated for. Whether it was lack of motivation or good bowling from the Black Caps, Lara failed to fire in the first two games of the three-Test series, registering just seven runs in two defeats. An 83 in Napier's 3rd Test would prove irrelevant on two counts, the series was already lost and the game was washed out by rain with no result.

But, just as with Lara in February 2000, the New Zealand tour would prove the last straw for a West Indies captain as Chanderpaul stepped down. In truth, he had never looked comfortable at the helm and was far more valuable to the team as a batsman than as a leader. In fourteen Tests he had won just once with ten defeats and three draws. He resigned to concentrate on re-establishing that batting form, and the merry-go-round of the West Indian captaincy was on the move once more.

With just a year to run until the West Indies was scheduled to host the 2007 Cricket World Cup, other issues entered the debate over who would be offered the job this time round. A number of names were thrown into the ring, including Ramnaresh Sarwan, Chris Gayle, Wavell Hinds, Daren Ganga, Sylvester Joseph and Denesh Ramdin, but there was a new President of the WICB, Trinidadian politician and businessman Ken Gordon, whose influence would win out.

Gordon brought with him great anticipation of a resolution to the contract disputes which had so dogged player–Board relations in recent times. He also saw Lara as the best option for the immediate future in West Indian cricket and, as a businessman, could scarcely have neglected Lara's power as a drawcard and symbol for the impending World Cup.

Lara was quickly seen as the standout candidate: the man to mould and nurture a young side on the pathway to a global tournament in its own backyard, to groom the team's next long-term leader, and the only one with sufficient standing and experience to help bridge the divide between players and Board. Yet he needed persuasion.

'Now Brian loves to lead and he's a natural leader but he was still very cautious,' explains WIPA President Dinanath Ramnarine. 'He was again in a position where he was reluctant. There was a discussion between myself and Ken Gordon to ask Brian to rethink and he finally agreed. I went to the press conference really because Brian said, "You put me in this thing you need to accompany me."'

At that press conference Gordon told reporters: 'It is logical to go back to Lara … Of the players available, they each had varying strengths but there were also varying weaknesses. The best [option] is to go with Lara, whose experience and knowledge is unquestioned.'

Lara said Chanderpaul had done 'a wonderful job under the circumstances', before adding, not without nuance, that he was confident he had the necessary support to move West Indies cricket forward this time.

Pitches and protests

A 5-0 one-day series win over a spirited but outgunned Zimbabwean team was Lara's first cricketing action of his third term as West Indies captain, itself another record, but sterner examinations would come with the visiting Indians.

India are notoriously bad travellers and despite the West Indians' demise had still not won in the Caribbean for thirty-five years when they arrived in May 2006. It all began encouragingly for the home side – especially in view of the 2007 World Cup – with a 4-1 win in the one-dayers, but Test match cricket is a very different game. Deficiencies within a team can be masked in the shortened formats, they are much harder to cover up over five days.

From the start it was evident that West Indian supremacy in the fifty-over game would not be transferred to the Test arena. Only a tense last wicket stand at the Antigua Recreation Ground had prevented defeat in a controversial 1st Test. Once again it was Lara at the centre of the flare-up when Mahendra Singh Dhoni was seemingly caught on the boundary by a back-pedalling Daren Ganga. Confusion reigned as it was debated whether Ganga had touched the rope in completing the catch. Dhoni stood his ground and as Lara remonstrated with both him and Pakistani umpire Asaud Rauf it was clear he was getting progressively angrier. Ganga said he had taken the ball cleanly and the West Indian skipper was finding it hard to understand why this would be questioned in the absence of conclusive television footage. When it looked as though Dhoni would be allowed to bat on, Lara huffily snatched the ball from Rauf. A potentially ugly aftermath was only avoided when Dhoni finally walked and Indian captain Dravid declared the tourists' innings.

Had it been a simple loss of temper in the heat of battle or were other issues resurfacing?

What had become clear was that what had at first appeared such a rosy new relationship between Board and captain just months before was now showing signs of familiar strain. As always with West Indian cricket there was as much action and intrigue off the field as there was on it. Lara, who had often sung the song of positivity and kept his counsel, had by this stage clearly had enough.

As the hard-fought series progressed Lara complained of repeatedly being denied the players he wanted, bemoaning the lack of fast bowlers in his team.

As the sides arrived in Jamaica for the 4th and final Test still all-square at 0-0, Lara's dissatisfaction boiled over. The focus this time was the pitch and the feeling it was undeserving of such a crucial match. The facts that the game was over inside three days and the track was roundly described as a minefield would suggest he had a case, but the way he went about presenting it was questionable.

When a Harbajan Singh off-break turned past his outside edge on the third and final morning, with the West Indies chasing an improbable 269 to win in a low-scoring game, he aimed a sarcastic round of applause at head groundsman Charlie Joseph. It was a defeatist gesture, unbecoming and uncharacteristic.

At the post-match press conference, after the West Indies had lost by forty-nine runs and with it the series 1-0, the captain laid bare his grievances. Amidst them was the startling revelation that, after weeks of agitatedly and unsuccessfully requesting players, he had received a letter, dated 28 May, on the eve of the final Test match, 29 June, informing him that he had actually been appointed as one of the selectors for the series.

'It's unfortunate that I have been a selector since the series started,' he said. 'It's painful what has gone on for the last couple of months … But the natural fact is that I was never given the team I wanted. I feel let down. I must tell you there is a meeting coming up in a couple of weeks, depending on the selectors, I would definitely revisit my decision to captain the West Indies team.'

The pitch came in for repeated focus with an eyebrow-raising accusation: 'It seems that this one was prepared for the Indians.'

Cricket pundits blasted Lara, saying his comments tarnished the regional game, and that his threat to resign the captaincy was aimed only at ensuring his ongoing increase in influence.

Trinidadian journalist Fazeer Mohammed said Lara needed no lessons on tact or diplomacy from anyone, as he was too well schooled in the ways of the cricketing world to be accused of hot-headed naiveté.

'They might have deflected attention away from his own tactical deficiencies on the field but, more critically, they acted as a distraction from the task at hand,' wrote Tony Cozier.

Yet a month later, it seemed Lara did indeed regret his actions as he penned a formal apology to the WICB. In the fax, he wrote: 'I recognise that I broke the confidence placed in me as West Indies captain by my overreaction during and after the 4th Test against India and I apologise to all concerned.'

Pakistan 2006

In November 2006 Brian Charles Lara was engaged in his final Test match series, though he did not know it at the time. He had voiced his intention to tour England again in the summer of 2007 and had previously stated a desire to continue playing Test cricket until the age of forty. He was thirty-seven years old and was still clearly the best batsman in the Caribbean, something he would demonstrate again beyond question in Pakistan.

Had Lara known this was his final hurrah in the longest form of the game he could not have performed better. In the land where his Test career had begun in December 1990, sixteen years later he would deliver another batting exhibition and finish with 448 runs in three Tests at an average of nearly 90. He played with finesse and elan throughout, perfectly balanced, he was a master on top of his game. The resoundingly contemptuous thwack of a perfectly timed ball rang out time and again in Lahore, Multan and Karachi as he dominated the bowling. Leg-spinner Danish Kaneria, Pakistan's highest wicket-taking spinner, endured a torrid time; one over during Multan's 2nd Test was especially brutal.

Lara simply decided to go on the attack. He began with a lofted straight drive back over Kaneria's head for four; none were scored off the second delivery but he made up for that with three successive sixes, one smacked mercilessly over wide midwicket followed by two more towering straight hits; a four flicked hard through wide long-on wrapped up an over which had disappeared for twenty-six runs. It was the equal third highest in Test match history, stirring memories of the onslaught launched upon the unfortunate Robin Peterson in South Africa three years before.

'Kaneria didn't bowl poorly; he troubled Daren Ganga; got the ball to do funny things, made it to drift, to land on the spot. But to Lara, it became a football, tossed up by a child,' wrote Cricinfo's Osman Samiuddin. 'The turf then became a dance floor, Lara its Travolta … Sixty Lara runs from 29 Kaneria deliveries in that period was murder, nothing short.'

Kaneria was not alone, the quicker bowlers suffered as well. The trademark cover drive was in abundant evidence but so was Lara's ability to manipulate the ball into the gaps. Time and again well-placed deliveries on off-stump, the kind routinely defended by batsmen, would be sent to the boundary. With maddening regularity, for the bowler at least, he allowed the ball to come into him before angling the face at the point of contact, using the bowler's pace to guide it away into the vacant areas. Abdul Razzaq, attempting McGrath's successful tactic of bowling around the wicket, suffered repeatedly in this fashion as Lara skipped to his fourth hundred against Pakistan in four Tests. This would also be his last Test century and fittingly it would be a double, a magnificent 216. Fittingly, because only Bradman has scored more Test match double hundreds, twelve to Lara's nine. Yet still the West Indies would lose the series 2-0.

West Indies World Cup 2007

Despite the Pakistan series loss there remained belief in the Caribbean that the West Indians' one-day form – they reached the final of both the Malaysian Tri-Series DLF Cup and the ICC Champions Trophy in India in late 2006 – added to home advantage, could be transferred into a World Cup winning performance. At the very least it was anticipated Lara's team was capable of securing a semi-final berth, and from there anything was possible.

It began to script, with a convincing win over Pakistan in the tournament opener, and three wins out of three saw them top their first-round group. That, though, was as good as it got for as soon as the home side hit the Super 8 stage the wheels came off in spectacular style, with defeats to Australia, New Zealand, Sri Lanka and South Africa putting pay to any realistic chances of reaching the last four.

Following the South African defeat, Lara announced his retirement from one-day internationals, saying it was time for younger players to take up the fight. That move had been largely anticipated – the end of a home World Cup campaign was a natural cut-off point and top players often retire from ODIs to extend their Test careers – what came next was not. Just days later, on 19 April, Lara announced he would in fact be retiring from all international cricket.

'On Saturday I'll be bidding farewell to international cricket as a player,' he told a news conference. 'I've already spoken to the Board and my players.'

The timing and the fact that Lara had consistently made reference to playing in England that summer after the World Cup sent up the whiff of intrigue. Rumours circulated he had been informed he would not be captain in England and, furthermore, would not even be required as a player. For such a proud man the prospect of being dropped seemed more than he was prepared to stand.

'He was forced out, there's no question about it,' says WIPA President Dinanath Ramnarine. 'I got a call from him, I was in England, he called to tell me he was doing it and it was very sad. It was emotional for me, listening to him talk. I wouldn't divulge the discussion but in my view the whole thing was very unfortunate.'

Many felt the position Lara had taken over the preceding months, as an ever more vocal critic of the administration, had hastened his demise. His response to continued questions over players' perceived lackadaisical attitude to fitness, fundamental professionalism and charges of indiscipline had been increasingly to divert attention to what he felt was the root cause.

'I don't think you'd see an indisciplined team if you have a disciplined Board,' he had said in a November 2006 Cricinfo interview. 'You need to see the whole spiral, where it starts from.'

Ramnarine says that Lara's demise was an unhappily familiar one.

'It's sad but at the end of the day Brian is no different to any other player in terms of being forced out. It has happened to so many over the years. Most players who leave, they've given their whole career, their whole life to West Indies cricket and it never ends the way it should: Viv Richards, Desmond Haynes, Brian Lara, the list goes on. How can you expect people to be loyal to you when you use that as your example?'

Former West Indies wicketkeeper Deryck Murray says player jealousy and infighting also played its part.

'There were a group of players who weren't too unhappy to see him go, which is so sad; that clash of personalities and egos, some felt he was too demanding of them. The West Indies team was doing so badly but here was a shining light and so the spotlight was on him, so obviously you're going to have jealousy.'

Tinged with bitterness though Lara's announcement may have been, its timing, coming two days ahead of the West Indians' final Super 8 match against England, at least ensured he would get a send-off befitting the man.

Lara's final game, before a capacity 22,500 crowd at Barbados's Kensington Oval, was appropriately a nail-biting run feast with over 600 runs scored and England winning by one wicket with a solitary ball to spare. Yet Lara had not been part of the glut, run out for 18 when Marlon Samuels sent him belatedly back to the non-striker's end. Even in this final innings Lara could not escape rumour and hearsay, with the story circulating later that Jamaican Samuels, unhappy with how his captain

Saying goodbye. A bittersweet moment as the old champion undertakes a lap of honour around Barbados's Kensington Oval following his farewell appearance against England on 21 April 2007.

had treated him, opted for the ultimate payback and purposely ran him out.

Whatever the truth of that, what was certain was it brought down the curtain on one of cricket's most controversial and brilliant international careers. His ODI record stood at 299 games, 10,405 runs at 40.48, with a highest score of 169. He hit nineteen centuries and sixty-three half-centuries and is one of only eight players, at the time of writing, to score more than 10,000 runs in one-dayers. But it was his Test match career for which he will be most fondly remembered and the bare bones of his record in that arena read 11,953 runs in 131 matches at an average of 52.88. He hit 1,559 fours and 88 sixes, took 164 catches, and his highest score was the world record 400 not out.

Speaking to former England captain Michael Atherton post-match, Lara said he was unconcerned as to the outcome of his final ODI innings, preferring to concentrate on the occasion. He recounted great series, matches and achievements during his career but admitted regret that he had not seen a revival in the team's fortunes. He went on to thank people for their support throughout his career and to mention old schoolfriends who were present for his final day.

'I've enjoyed every single minute of it.'

He broke off to ask the assembled masses a question.

'All I want to ask is did I entertain?' he said, sounding like a cricketing version of Russell Crowe's Gladiator. Not satisfied with the initial response he asked again. A resounding roar suggested that he had.

15 Themes and reflections: the man beside the name

Character

'He is charming, vulnerable, endearing, moody and impossible to work out at times, and endlessly fascinating,' so wrote former Australian captain Steve Waugh of Brian Lara in his autobiography *Out of my Comfort Zone*.

Ask people to describe Lara's character and the responses are many and varied: charismatic, affable, polite, strong-willed, quick-witted, loyal, generous and caring will say some; whilst others will offer arrogant, controlling, stubborn, complex, aloof, prickly, selfish and unpredictable, even schizophrenic.

Selfishness – that Lara is a self-seeking individualist – is a proposition given repeated airing. It was such a stubbornly held belief that writer Morgan Coulthurst suggested, in a brilliantly tongue-in-cheek article in the *Trinidad Guardian* in May 2005, that it even gave rise to a separate sub-section of West Indies cricket follower: the Anti-Lara Fan (ALF).

For the ALF two basic principles hold firm: firstly, all runs scored by Lara are for himself not the West Indies; secondly, runs are made when it suits Lara, failures resulting from indifference or a calculated effort to undermine the incumbent captain. Any facts seemingly to the contrary are flat-batted with a series of improbable, but passionately delivered, hypotheses. There is an answer for every scenario: Lara's 213 and 153 against Australia in 1999 were him trying to cement the captaincy; playing through injury is not dedication but pursuit of personal glory; and so it goes on. The underperformance of teammates can even be explained: Lara simply makes fellow batsmen feel inferior, affects bowlers and fielders with his negative body language and 'at the same time he inspires the opposition to play better'. The inevitable conclusion of course is that Lara is bad for West Indies cricket.

'Lara should realise that his over-achievement is frowned on by the growing population of ALFs among us,' concludes Coulthurst.

It may seem far-fetched but anyone who has spent an extended period of time in the Caribbean can attest to how these views, especially of Lara's selfishness, are cherished by many. They are attitudes given short shrift by two who played with him.

'Inherent in performance at an elite level there has to be a huge level of focus on yourself as an individual, not only in the game but in preparation,' says former West Indies captain Jimmy Adams.

'Honestly, how could you say Brian Lara was selfish?' adds Tony Gray. 'A lot of the time his batting partner was not good enough to face the bowling coming down, him rotating the strike so that he faces is not selfish, that's common sense.'

Former Trinidad and Tobago team manager Colin Borde, who has been friends with Lara for many years, says criticisms such as this are often proffered by those looking on from the outside.

'People say a lot of things about Brian and it's mostly people who don't know him. He's selfish, he's pompous, he's arrogant, he's this, he's that, but Brian is just a regular guy, he's a cool fella.

'Brian is an exceptional player on the field but off the field he's just another cricketer, it's hard for people to see that unless they've shared a dressing room with him. He doesn't impose himself or need to be the centre of attention; he does that in the middle.'

Another of the commonly held beliefs about Lara is that he is aloof, something which Borde says is a product of him being treated as public property.

'Everyone needs their own space but people want a piece of Brian the whole time. They may mean well but people come over continuously at parties asking the same questions as everyone before them. It goes on all night. So when people say he's aloof a lot of that comes as a defence mechanism to keep people at arm's length at times.

'When he's in his own crowd he's an extremely talkative guy, that's something you would never see. That's really the way he is, a very quiet man in public but once he gets to know you he's a chatterbox.'

The gruff-voiced Borde gives an example of the situations Lara routinely faces.

'We were having a night out and a guy just walked up and started abusing Brian. This was no short thing, he was there for five minutes telling him what a terrible cricketer he was and how West Indies didn't need him, you name it. Brian stood there cool as you like and let the guy finish. Then he asked him his name, fella's name was Jeffrey, and he said, "Jeffrey, let me buy you a beer." And he chatted with this Jeffrey for ten minutes or so, after which Brian was the best cricketer in the world again.

'I asked Brian how he put up with that and he said: "There's nothing else I can do, it happens all the time. If some idiot tells me something and I say leave me alone, he goes off and tells a hundred people how much of an arse I am. You can never win." That's true; you meet Brian in a bad mood that will be your only impression of him.

'Of course I'm not saying we should be crying for Brian, fame brings a lot of things, you get the girls, the attention, the ego-stroking, money and all that but the other side is the false accusations, false perceptions, the abuse, the unrealistically high expectations.'

Lara's years in the spotlight have left him reserved and cautious about people's motivations, says Borde. 'He doesn't make friends easily, and that's understandable, but he's also extremely loyal and trusting to those he does count as true friends.'

Like any man, of course, Lara has his difficult side and another long-time friend and colleague says he can be temperamental.

'He can be a moody sort of character,' says Trinidad and Tobago batsman Daren Ganga. 'Sometimes when he's under pressure he can be very erratic in the way he deals with you but a lot of that's just the nature of the stress he's feeling. If you've been around him a lot you can read and predict him. He's a much more relaxed man since his retirement though; he's very peaceful now.

'Brian is a strong character, someone that knows what he wants, spends a lot of time thinking about things and plans his moves. He doesn't act on impulse or in a haphazard fashion, he would sit and work something through.

'He has a very paternal side to him as well, that fatherliness when it concerns his players and friends. He's also very respectful of players' parents and very appreciative of the support that a young player needs and that is something I admire about him.'

Despite being very different people, long-time West Indies teammate Jimmy Adams says he has always found Lara an easy man to get along with and feels he has received a lot of unfairly negative press.

'He loves clubs, I love church; he's into golf, I hate golf. I know his ways and he knows mine and we're comfortable with that. When the war starts I'm happy to know I have him behind me and he's happy to know I'm there for him.

'Brian's no angel, but then neither am I, neither is [Nehemiah] Perry or whoever. We went back a generation and discussed the so-called great team that never lost, there's enough stuff there to fill three books. In an era where media intrusion reached unprecedented levels, Brian's status as a world icon meant he was always going to be on the receiving end.

'Everything is magnified ten times over so I don't get carried away with a lot of what you read. You tend to hear more about the negatives than the positives with Brian and that's unfortunate, because it's important to know the other side. He does a lot of great work for charity, mostly behind the scenes, and at the end of the day he's a top-class individual; that often gets overlooked.'

Of course nobody is better placed than Leeba La Roche, whose husband John was the first cancer sufferer to be helped by the Pearl and Bunty Lara Foundation, to substantiate the authenticity of this charitable side of the star batsman's character.

'I would like more people to know about that part of Brian; everyone sees the great cricketer but they don't know about that side of him, the man beside the name. He is special.'

Dry runs and absences

Lara enjoyed unprecedented success as a batsman but there were also tremendous troughs in form, compounded by extended layoffs from the game: several due to injury; others following conflicts with the Board; and some seemingly by design.

'The dry runs and absences from cricket, for someone as demonstrably talented as Brian, are hard to fathom. Was it mental, he was so tired and he needed a break, or was it technical? I suspect it was a bit of both,' says Lara's former Warwickshire teammate Nick Knight.

'He was always under enormous pressure, and he put himself under enormous pressure as well.

'He also achieved so much so early in his career, that the motivation to keep going out there time after time may have become a factor. As you get older you realise there are other things out there and that cricket is not necessarily the be-all and end-all in life.

'From a technical standpoint, he does move a long way across his crease and with all that movement it's not hard to get out of position.'

Lara's unconventional technique is a theme taken up by Sri Lankan wicketkeeper-batsman Kumar Sangakkara in a 2008 article.

'Brian's technique and style are not orthodox. Though he starts with a beautifully balanced stance, he progresses into a flamboyant and outrageously high back-lift that would be a coaching book no-no.

'His initial movement seems to be a split step-jump that flings his body into the position required to play his shots ... Many are the times when, though his feet are nowhere near the required position they should be in to play a shot, the correctness of his balance and head position frees his hands and allows them to catch up with the ball at the exact right moment.'

Lara himself had admitted that 'in many ways I have an unstable technique, which, from time to time, needs unravelling'.

Such a 'natural' game is more exposed to the vagaries of form, with greater scope for things to go awry, especially early in an innings. Many players fall back on solid techniques to weather periods of poor form but Lara was never like other players. 'Flamboyant', 'extravagant' and 'high bat speed' are words which often describe his batting; they are not words that generally help negotiate a bad run. Lara's game at its best was based on flair, aggression and rhythm; it made the highs incredibly high but also rendered him more susceptible to the lows.

His form was clearly not just a technical matter; what was happening off the field always had an influence on what happened on it. Lara stressed the mental aspect of batting and for him to perform at his peak he often needed stimulus.

'Brian needs a challenge,' says Lara's former Fatima College teacher and sports coach Harry Ramdass. 'I recognised that from his schooldays, as soon as there was a challenge then you see him up the antenna.'

Another former coach, and now Cricket Administrator/Technical Director at QPCC, Bryan Davis agrees, describing Lara as 'a mood player'. It is a characteristic borne out by the marked regularity with which periods of intense criticism and pressure would prove the inspiration for sublime performance. Unwittingly, this inspiration would sometimes be provided by the opposition, as Ricky Ponting discovered when he sledged Lara for batting too slowly at Adelaide in 2001.

'From that moment on he just smashed us,' said Ponting. 'After the game he came into our dressing rooms and said to me, "Thanks very much."'

Lara recognised the character trait and, if not provided externally, often factored it into his own game plan: inviting challenges, pursuing confrontations, engineering a siege mentality. It was something not lost on Australia's Steve Waugh.

'Lara is a good player against average bowling sides and a great one against formidable attacks, but when harassed into a corner by his own brinkmanship or if he's targeted he elevates himself into a genius.'

Fast bowling

'Only one reason prevents this observer from placing Lara at the apex of modern West Indian batsmen. Against extreme pace he got hit too often, and he could seem extraordinarily jumpy at the crease,' wrote former England captain Michael Atherton in April 2008.

While Atherton was using his observations to distinguish between the very best – and for him that meant Viv Richards – others took the argument a stage further, suggesting Lara being struck occasionally meant he was in fact weak against fast bowling.

Objectively speaking, though a batsman being hit by a short-pitched, high-octane delivery is a powerful image, in cricketing terms two things matter most: whether he is dismissed by it and how he responds. More often than not Lara's response was to be galvanised by the challenge, particularly if he had worn a couple, and he rarely came off second best in the final analysis.

Among numerous incidents of him standing strong in the face of the fastest bowling is his famous duel with Australia's Brett Lee at the Queen's Park Oval. Gladstone Small recalls another, in 1994, when Lara was hit by England fast bowler Devon Malcolm, as Warwickshire faced Derbyshire at Chesterfield.

'That year people bowling against Brian went up a notch; a player like Brian brings out that competitive instinct. Devon Malcolm bowled a really quick spell at Chesterfield and actually hit him on the helmet quite early in the piece. It wasn't a glancing blow either. It was one of those moments where you think, OK, this is going to be a test of the little maestro.

'The wicket was spicy and you also had Dominic Cork who wasn't afraid to test out the middle of the pitch. Well Brian just stepped up a gear and absolutely slapped it, cut the bowling to ribbons, he got 142.'

That same year Lara was given a working over, and was again struck, by Curtly Ambrose at Northampton but went on to register 197.

'The dramatic nature of his [Lara's] movement at the crease may have moved him into the line of some of that [short bowling] at times,' says Nick Knight, Lara's former Warwickshire teammate and a fellow left-hander. 'As a left-hander it can tend to follow you a bit because you're actually on the move, which then makes it difficult to get out of the way.

'Maybe that's one of the difficulties or downsides to the method he employed. But he didn't get out to it a lot. I mean every top order batsman is going to come up against some really fast deliveries that are going to cause them trouble; it's just part of the game. I wouldn't look back at his career and say he was overly susceptible to the short ball though.'

Of all the bowlers Lara faced, the one he had most problems with was Glenn McGrath and that wasn't because of pace, it was due to metronomic accuracy and movement of the ball.

'I don't hook like I used to because most teams put two men back on the boundary straightaway,' Lara told commentator and journalist Mark Nicholas in 2004. 'And I have never really ducked. Swaying is a problem when the ball follows you and occasionally I've got out fending it off. Fast bowlers have always hunted me, of course they have, and sometimes I have been unsettled but, you know, just look at the record. I am the fastest batsman to 9,000 [Test] runs, what else can I say!'

Captaincy

One issue hotly debated throughout the career of Brian Charles Lara, and a stick with which he was regularly beaten, was that of the captaincy. The kernel of much debate centred upon a seemingly simple question, was he any good? As with most matters Lara, standpoint was key, with one man's unorthodox and attacking tactics being another's proof of schoolboy naivety.

That he had the tools for the job was evident as a youngster: a sharp analytical mind; an all-consuming passion for the game; and the knowledge gained from a nurturing environment at the home of former West Indies player Joey Carew.

There was considerable early promise shown at school and regional youth level, both for Trinidad and Tobago and West Indies U19s. But many felt this progress cut short when a twenty-year-old Lara was made senior Trinidad and Tobago captain. Too much too soon was the cry, with players and pundits alike saying Lara should have been afforded time to develop.

'He was very good on his knowledge of cricket but that is not the whole package,' says Tony Gray, a man who played under Lara's captaincy that year. 'Brian's captaincy is tactically based, it's not man-management based which is why he should have been allowed a grace period to learn how to manage players, by being a follower before being a leader.'

By the time Lara ascended to the West Indian captaincy in 1998, three years after their defining loss to Australia, the team was in decline and disarray. It was a pivotal period in regional fortunes and one which would require more than tactical knowledge alone. The unique dynamic of the West Indian side, made up as it is of individuals from a range of nations and backgrounds, renders a man-management capability of heightened importance. Many felt, at this point in its history, it needed a unifier in the mould of their first great captain Sir Frank Worrell.

'Worrell had an awareness of the differing needs of the various islands; people from different places and backgrounds,' says Deryck Murray, who was just twenty years old in 1963 when he was selected for the West Indies tour of England. 'Traditionally the West Indies had been eleven individual players just brought together. So this process of unifying the team had to be built in and Worrell recognised that.'

Worrell initiated a rooming system that integrated the team by mixing players by age, experience, nation and aptitude (separating bowlers and batsmen). Such practices were out of favour by 1998.

'So much of what Frank Worrell did almost as a matter of course is out of the window now,' says Murray, 'and then you wonder why there is insularity and disunity.'

If a side is winning of course differences can be plastered over, just as the spat between Lara and Reeve at Warwickshire did not ultimately prevent the team from enjoying its most successful season ever. But in a losing side those differences become more pronounced and players gravitate towards who and what they know. The Caribbean can be a parochial place and just because cricketers are professional sportsmen does not mean they are immune. Lara spoke to this geographical disparity as a mitigating factor after the 5-0 drubbing in South Africa in 1998/99. Tony Cozier, though, reporting on that ill-fated tour, felt Lara could have done more, saying, 'he was seldom seen in the company of his players away from the cricket grounds,' and calling him 'an individualist … not a natural leader of men'.

Murray feels this perceived inability to engage and manage his team was an upshot of Lara's extraordinary talent.

'It's very difficult for an exceptional player to be a nurturing captain because they adapt to conditions and match situations instinctively. So to explain to a younger "mortal" player how they needed to build an innings or combat a certain defensive strategy was not part of their make-up.'

It is a point supported by Nick Knight, vice-captain to Lara at Warwickshire in 1998.

'He found it difficult to understand why we were so average and we couldn't attain his levels, so we couldn't quite meet in the middle. He had plans, very good tactical plans, but if your players haven't got the skills to implement them unfortunately they sometimes don't mean much.'

It was a situation that leads former West Indies captain Jimmy Adams to an unhappy conclusion.

'I'm not sure if at any point in his career as West Indies captain Brian was ever in charge of a *team*. My gut feeling is that, even on the best of days, it was a group of players rather than a team.'

Yet in trying to analyse the cause of a cricket team's failings the obvious should not be ignored: player capability. From the mid-1970s and throughout the 1980s the West Indian conveyor belt of precocious batsmen and thoroughbred fast bowlers seemed unending, but nothing in sport is unending. The lack of investment in nurturing the region's next generation of world-beaters meant that, by the time Lara was rising to prominence, West Indian pre-eminence was on the wane. A lot of the players led by Lara from 1998 onwards were simply not as good as their predecessors.

Clive Lloyd had overseen the transformation to world powerhouse up until early 1985. Lloyd was undoubtedly a wonderful captain, but the building blocks of a great side were there when he took over. In Lloyd's first series as skipper in India and Pakistan in 1974/75 his top six read: Roy Fredericks, Gordon Greenidge, Alvin Kallicharan, Viv Richards, Clive Lloyd, Deryck Murray. Desmond Haynes would soon join Greenidge at the top of the order to establish one of the greatest opening partnerships in history, and in the bowling department, Lance Gibbs and Andy Roberts were already in the side. Within a year Michael Holding would make his Test debut and soon after would be joined by Colin Croft, Joel Garner and Malcolm Marshall. A great captain, yes, but he had great players to captain.

In contrast, when Lara assumed control there were only Courtney Walsh and Curtly Ambrose who could realistically be classified as West Indian 'greats' and they were nearing the end of impressive careers.

Would Australia's Ricky Ponting be the most successful captain of all time, as he is now in terms of aggregate wins, if he had led the West Indies from 1998? Extremely doubtful. If Lara had been in charge of Australia instead of the West Indies throughout the same period, would his win ratio be better? Certainly.

The captain is not powerless of course, but ultimately he is there to lead the best of what the national system has produced. Furthermore, he needs the support of that national system while in office.

'My own approach to a lot of these matters is to start at the level above. The answers lay at Board level,' says Jimmy Adams, who became West Indies captain from 2000 to 2001, following Lara's resignation. 'The players tend to mirror a lot of what is going on behind the scenes. A lot of those issues are decided, planned and executed by the management structure with the team or by the Board itself without any player involvement.

'I found that to be the biggest challenge for me because the vision I had of where the team should be and how a team should operate was not echoed by the structure that was in place. It made anything you were trying to get across to the players useless. At the time it was very frustrating. Brian, Courtney [Walsh], Carl [Hooper], myself, we all faced it.'

Michael Vaughan empathised after witnessing the state of Caribbean cricket when he captained England's 2004 tour, saying that much of what Lara was criticised for was outside his control.

'It's tough in the West Indies because they don't play much first-class cricket, so they are basically learning the art of the game in the Test arena – and that's not easy.

'I'm sure Lara got very frustrated at having to teach people in the Test matches – and I'm talking about the real basics such as running between the wickets.'

Once on the field, Lara's tactics also came under frequent fire. Ask fellow professionals to sum up his approach and you will hear words like 'risk-taker', 'aggressive', 'attacking', 'gambler', and 'unorthodox'. He said as much himself once when being criticised for excessive tactical experimentation, replying that he wouldn't have to experiment to such a degree if he were captaining Australia.

What is clear is that Lara's captaincy got better as he got older, with Adams saying, 'In his second stint as captain, from 2003 to 2006, he had more realistic expectations as leader, given a better understanding of some of the core issues that were affecting our cricket in the Caribbean.'

Whatever people's ultimate positions on Lara's leadership capabilities, though, former Trinidad and Tobago manager Colin Borde says detractors should look elsewhere to find a scapegoat for the region's continued woes.

'He took the captaincy on three occasions and it didn't work out for him. It hadn't worked out for anyone for a long time before that and hasn't worked out for anyone else for a lot longer since.'

16 Life after cricket

As Lara jogged a lap of honour around Barbados's Kensington Oval following his final West Indies game, shaking and slapping hands with fans bent over the railings, there was a mood unlike that of other high-profile retirements. This really was the end of an era.

Yet it was not the last time Lara would be seen on a cricket field. Though the creaking body may have told a different story, in many ways he was still at the peak of his powers.

'He became the model of consistency right up until his retirement,' says Jimmy Adams.

He played on in inter-island cricket and in his next match, against Guyana at the Queen's Park Oval in January 2008, I witnessed one of the most effortless hundreds you are ever likely to see.

It was a Saturday, the second day of a four-day game, and a small group of us settled down to take in the action. The Oval was not full, it never is for regional cricket these days, but the numbers on the gate were higher with Lara's participation.

Soon after he strolled to the crease, a friend of mine, purportedly engaged in project work in Port of Spain, strolled up to our party. He was welcomed with the customary raucous Caribbean mix of delight and disbelief, as if greeting a long-lost family member rather than someone you met up with the previous night. He was asked how long he was staying before heading back to work.

'What, yuh can't see ah wokin, ah have meh jacket 'n' tie, ah have meh phone!?'

Having subsequently admitted he should only stay for an hour, a tortuous dance with responsibility commenced.

An hour having passed: 'Ah will just see Lara make he 50,' rapidly turned into, 'well ah nex five overs,' and with tie now scrunched in pocket, jacket on chair and shirt sleeves rolled up, 'ah nex beer, then ah goin fuh sure.'

The phone rang, often, but at a glance, was studiously ignored. Lara, beer, food and friends was proving too much temptation for the already weak-willed. Finally, with evening approaching, and Lara approaching three figures, it seemed the matter had been taken out of his hands.

'Ah have to see de man make he hundred nah,' he exclaimed with a resigned shrug of the shoulders.

The productivity decline in the stands had not been mirrored by Lara in the middle who had been serving up a consummate batting demonstration. If there was exertion it hadn't shown, he never hurried a stroke. His presence had proved an inspiration for his younger teammates, with whom he shared several telling stands, as players raised their games, eager to prove their skills and worth to the great man. Trinidad and Tobago has one of the best youth systems in the Caribbean and players such as Adrian Barath, Lendl Simmons, Darren Bravo and Kieron Pollard could only benefit from spending time at the crease with a batsman who has seen it all.

As Lara brought up his century, a rotund man left the stands below us, navigating the advertising hoardings before embarking on a spirited if protracted and wobbly journey to the wicket to congratulate his hero. On arrival he collapsed to his knees in adulation, and presumably exhaustion, bowing and praying at Lara's feet. It had been another memorable innings and day. My recalcitrant friend ended up staying to the end, by which time he was royally inebriated, and Lara was 115 not out.

The second innings of the match saw Lara in even more emphatic form as he blitzed his way to 53 not out from just twenty-seven deliveries, carrying Trinidad and Tobago home to a nine-wicket win. It was a performance which, for some, displayed the mark of intent.

'I genuinely believe he was thinking of making a comeback to Test cricket, and then to leave on his terms,' says former Trinidad and Tobago team manager Colin Borde. 'I know his intention was to score as many regional hundreds as possible; he would've forced his way back into Test cricket which is where you really want to retire. He may say no publicly but I know there's that tinge of unfinished business for him.'

If it was the plan then it was cut cruelly short in Trinidad and Tobago's next match, when Lara's forearm was broken by Leeward Islands pace bowler Lionel Baker, ruling him out for the rest of the season.

The Trinidad and Tobago Cricket Board honoured Lara in April 2008 with an evening dedicated to his international career. A host of former stars of the game, including Sir Garfield Sobers, Sir Clive Lloyd, Joey Carew and Deryck Murray, were present to pay homage, as well as family, former coaches, teachers, old schoolfriends, current players, entertainers and dignitaries.

No such similar gesture was forthcoming from the WICB, a fact that Barbadian broadcaster Tony Cozier feels deprived the batsman of 'the fanfare and acknowledgment he fully deserved'.

There have been rumours of, and flirtations with, a return to cricket ever since. Most of these have focussed on the less physically demanding and more showbiz-oriented arena of Twenty20, with Lara having captained the Mumbai Champs in the inaugural 2007 season of the now defunct ICL (Indian Cricket League).

In what was widely perceived as a stepping stone towards an IPL (Indian Premier League) contract, and a gesture of advertising his preparedness for it, Lara was reportedly paid a staggering US$30,000 to make three appearances in a week-long Twenty20 tournament in Zimbabwe in November 2010. He has always been hugely popular in India – the majority of his fan mail still originates from there – and it was felt he would prove a huge drawcard. But there would be disappointment in

January 2011 when, in the glitzy two-day player auction which precedes every IPL season, Lara's reserve price tag of US$400,000 was deemed too much and he did not receive a bid from any of the ten franchises.

That frustration was put firmly in perspective, though, when on 8 January 2011, Lara's mentor and 'second father' Michael Conrad 'Joey' Carew passed away at his Woodbrook home. The seventy-three-year-old had been suffering with blood circulatory problems and had been discharged from a Port of Spain hospital on the day of his death. A week later, Lara delivered a heartfelt eulogy at the St Theresa's Roman Catholic church funeral service calling him, 'the best captain the West Indies never had'.

With each passing year it becomes less likely that Lara will renew his interest in the IPL but his current removal from the game is no bad thing, says Deryck Murray.

'When you leave the game in the way he did there must be bitterness. It's better for him to be away for a while rather than let that rub off on others and perhaps affect his decisions. I would hope though that a Brian Lara could find a way to help West Indies cricket get back to a position of strength sometime in the future. You don't want his experience to be lost to the next generation.'

This need for catharsis is a notion upheld by Tony Gray, who says, 'There must be a disintegration of the pains and the hurts' before progress can be achieved.

'It's not easy but you have to get back into bed with the administrators if you want to change anything. He must come with an open mind and they must accept him with an open mind. Brian has a great contribution to make but in what role is an important factor.'

The future role best suited to Lara is one with little consensus of opinion. Many former players progress to coaching after retiring but one family member says this is too mundane and predictable a path for Brian. There might be other issues as well, says former teammate Nick Knight.

'I'm not sure he would make a great coach because he operates at such a different level with what he was capable of doing that I think it would be difficult for him to almost come down to the level of those he was trying to instruct.'

If conventional coaching, taking charge of a team for an extended period of time, is a seemingly unnatural fit, Lara's vast knowledge and experience might be better tapped in the manner it currently is at the University of Trinidad and Tobago's (UTT) High Performance Centre.

'Brian is here as a Sports Consultant to give motivational speeches, conduct masterclasses with our cricketers and that sort of thing,' says Tony Gray, who works alongside Lara at UTT. 'He's great at that but where he's even more valuable is the quality of people he can bring in, the amount of contacts he has and who will come just because of who he is.'

Lara has always been more than simply a cricketer, though, and his standing has led to speculation that his ultimate future may lie away from the sporting arena. As he moved towards the end of his career, Lara progressively took on more statesmanlike roles and bearing. He was appointed Ambassador of Sports for Trinidad and Tobago by Prime Minister Patrick Manning, affording him a diplomatic passport to represent the nation abroad. As the global face of his nation, he was charmingly at ease as an international ambassador. In April 2009, at the Fifth Summit of the Americas, held in Trinidad, he spent time with US President Barack Obama, who reportedly greeted him with the words: 'I always wanted to meet the Michael Jordan of cricket.'

Later that year, on 29 November, and on another continent, he was honoured by Australian Prime Minister Kevin Rudd with the insignia of the Order of Australia, having already received the highest honours his country and region – respectively the Trinity Cross (TC) and the Order of the Caribbean Community (OCC) – could grant. The OCC is presented to those 'Caribbean nationals whose legacy in the economic, political, social and cultural metamorphoses of Caribbean society is phenomenal'.

While he may continue to rub shoulders with the world's top politicians, representing his country at home and abroad, those closest to him feel a full-time life in the political realm is an unlikely scenario.

Down the years there have been many honours bestowed from a grateful homeland but the largest of these threatens to turn into a poisoned chalice. The Brian Lara Stadium, at Tarouba in southern Trinidad, is a sprawling cricket stadium and academy complex, on 180 acres of former agricultural land, which has promised many things since work began in June 2005. Not least of these was that it would be finished in time to stage warm-up games for the 2007 Cricket World Cup. As 2012 dawned it was still not finished and the cost had ballooned from TT$275 million to estimates as high as TT$1 billion, amidst allegations of corruption and use of substandard materials. It was launched as a flagship venture and it can only be hoped that it eventually blossoms into a facility commensurate with the man whose name it carries.

Trinidad and Tobago is not a nation without its problems. That the patriotic Lara wants to help is unquestioned, showing, as he does, genuine concern for the soaring rates of murder and gang crime which inhibit the everyday lives of Trinbagonians.

'Brian cares deeply about what is happening in the belly of society,' says entertainer David Rudder. 'And anything we can do, through people like him, to change the perception of the youths about life is worth trying. A lot of them are not looking to pass thirty-five. If there's someone around, a respected figure, that could say, listen, these were some of the best years of my life. Don't throw them away. We need young people to understand and believe they have alternatives. Brian could be such a figure.'

Lara is already using his profile for good through his charitable work, something I witnessed first hand in August 2009 at the WIPA-organised Balls of Fire charity event at the Queen's Park Oval.

The event is a double-header of Twenty20 cricket and football, both between a West Indies XI and Trinidad and Tobago, and as well as Lara, has attracted high-profile participants such as Chris Gayle, Russell Latapy and Dwight Yorke. But there is only one man the crowd has come to see and, more than two years after retirement, his crowd-pulling power remains undiminished.

Regional cricket matches might not sell out the Oval any more but the combination of Lara, high tempo floodlit sport and the chance of an evening lime [social] has. A buzzing throng surrounds the stadium as we approach and I am amongst hundreds who have arrived ticketless. Two fruitless circuits of the ground later I am forced into the inevitability of a ticket tout trade.

'Yes, 150, 150,' he barks and shoves the tickets into my left hand whilst removing the cash from my right. He departs a little rapidly for my liking and I am left eyeing what look suspiciously like photocopies run off in an office. Remarkably, they gain me entry and I learn later that some paid as much as five times the cover price of TT$60.

The Oval's official capacity is 25,000 but there looks like more tonight as people clog gangways, squeeze into vacant areas behind back-row seats or sit with knees under chins on the boundary-edge grass.

I comment on the remarkable turnout to a neighbouring fan sporting a T-shirt emblazoned with Lara's image and the words 'His Excellency Brian Charles Lara'.

'If Lara come to bat at sixty he fillin de Oval,' he replies emphatically.

It is a sentiment reinforced when Lara marches to the wicket to a thunderous standing ovation. The atmosphere is akin to a rock concert as Mexican waves peel around the stadium. The Trini Posse Stand's rhythm section is in fine form, and the Carib Girls shake their flags and backsides in time to the beat as dry ice and confetti plume into the air. In the middle Lara is displaying the deft touches of old, the late cuts, glances and sweeps. Every shot in anger is applauded vigorously.

'Lara! Lara!' ring out the chants.

Yet just as the noise and mood build to a climax his innings is over when he chips down the wicket and launches a strike towards the long-off boundary. The clamour quietens momentarily as the ball sails into the night sky and the fielder moves in off the fence. He is caught, to a collective groan of disappointment, and the catcher is left in no doubt as to his mistake. An intimidatingly large and evidently angered lady pivots her considerable girth on the restraining barrier at the front of the stand. All flailing arms and dancing hair she launches a tirade at the offending fieldsman, while Lara acknowledges another ovation walking back to the pavilion that now bears his name.

A number of Trinbagonian stars, in various fields, have moved away from the twin-island republic once international success has been achieved but Lara has so far resisted that temptation. He is part of the fabric of this society and continues to do what he can to help it. He has given his name and support to the Brian Lara Cancer Treatment Centre of Trinidad and Tobago, launched in 2007, and looks to expand the operations of his flagship Pearl and Bunty Lara Foundation (PBLF), with his sister Agnes being employed full-time in running its affairs.

The foundation is funded by a now well-established and hugely popular annual fete held at his Lady Chancellor Hill mansion on Carnival Sunday. People pay around TT$1,000 for the privilege of rubbing shoulders with the great man at his home and it's a hot ticket for Port of Spain's movers and shakers. More funds come from another annual party Lara holds at his luxurious Ebworth Plantation property in St Peter, Barbados, during the island's Crop Over celebrations (the Barbadian equivalent of the Trinidad and Tobago Carnival), as well as one-off events such as Balls of Fire.

In addition to charity, business has always been uppermost in Lara's life and he owns and operates two: LAY (Lara and Yorke) Management, a sports management and sponsorship company which was established with his great friend Dwight Yorke; and Brian Lara Design, a sports facility design and project management company, currently overseeing the Brian Lara Ground renovation in Cantaro.

'There is a gap that you bridge between school cricket, school soccer or any other discipline, until you get to international level,' said Lara of LAY Management. 'During that period of time there is no major management company that actually focuses on any young sportsman and that is if you get to the international level.

'So we formed this company and at present we are reaching out to corporate Caribbean to ensure that these young sportsmen and sportswomen have what it takes – the support financially, the academic background and the social support to make it to the top.'

LAY Management already has young cricketing talents such as Adrian Barath and Lara's fellow Cantaro native and distant relative, Darren Bravo, on its books and is looking to assist young golfers as well.

Barath is short and compact, an energetic rubber-wristed batsman with a fantastic eye. He was scoring regional hundreds for Trinidad and Tobago as a sixteen-year-old schoolboy and had caught Lara's eye long before that. As a nineteen-year-old, Barath fulfilled expectations when he was elevated to the West Indian side in November 2009 against Australia at Brisbane. His debut century, a second innings 104 with his side following on, meant he had become the youngest ever West Indian Test centurion, usurping the great George Headley. Lara's doppelganger Bravo has similarly made an encouraging start at international level with some mature performances and looks set for a long career as a mainstay of the West Indian batting.

'Adrian and Darren have started really well and have learned a lot from Brian not only on the field but off it as well, how they should conduct themselves, how you look after contracts, it's important,' says Borde. 'There's nobody better to give advice on that, Brian understands the business of cricket and is trying to guide the young guys wherever he can.'

LAY Management was also responsible for Lara's fortieth birthday celebrations, and these were given an entrepreneurial twist with an all-inclusive event at the Santa Rosa Park horse racing track. Big screens and marquees, representing top Trinidadian businesses, surrounded the course in an Ascot-themed event to a backdrop of continuous live entertainment. The day of racing and celebration was rounded off with an evening party featuring more live music. The consummate host, Lara remained to the last to ensure everyone enjoyed their day and got away safely.

As well as his own two companies, Lara still actively promotes a number of others – something which is apparent to anyone driving around Trinidad and Tobago, as his face beams down at you from ubiquitous billboards advertising his first employers Angostura and telecommunications company Bmobile.

This blend of business, ambassadorial duties, charity and sport (Lara worked as a batting consultant with Zimbabwe during the 2011 World Cup) is adding up to an agreeable life mix and, since retirement, many have pointed to a more contented and relaxed man, one happy to be taking time away from the spotlight and being afforded the freedom to pursue his own interests at his own pace and without distraction.

'I'm playing cricket again which is good; I'm practising which is great,' said Lara in late 2010. 'I'm still playing my golf; I'm still doing my business. At my age you just do everything at a good pace and see where you get to,' adding, 'I'm enjoying my life. I can still do a few things because I'm feeling fit and capable of doing it.'

His passion for golf remains undimmed and he plays as often as possible, especially when Dwight Yorke is also in the country. Unsurprisingly, the two are competitively matched, with Lara a six-handicapper and Yorke playing off four, and are often seen battling out a friendly rivalry on Trinidad's Moka or Millennium Lakes courses.

Lara's enjoyment of life was taken to another level in May 2010 when former model Leasel Rovedas, mother of his first child Sydney, gave birth to a second daughter. Coming from a large family, Lara has always expressed his desire to have children and is relishing being a father again to Tyla Chayil Lara, who weighed in at a mere 5 lb when born.

Contented though he may be, Lara is not a man to slip quietly into the shadows, and since retirement there has been a sense he is merely taking a break, regrouping for the next chapter. Whether in business or sport, or a combination of the two, Lara will do as he has always done: bring a competitive focus and attention to detail in pursuing whatever path he ultimately chooses.

'I think it's important at this transition stage in Brian's life to find that calling and to be comfortable with it,' says Lara's great friend Jimmy Adams. 'He has no need to rush into anything. Once he's sorted out his time, his resources, his direction and settled on whatever Chapter Two is, he will always be a success.'

17 Conclusion

When assessing the impact of a sportsman there are great players and then there are those whose achievements and personalities transcend their sport. Brian Lara is such a man. Driven from childhood to carve his name into the lineage of West Indian cricket greats, his ability and attitude separated him from the pack on the road from gifted child to sporting icon. Ambition, belief and a limitless desire to acquire knowledge were the framework to his formative years and, as his talent blossomed, he strode through the ranks from school to national and international cricket.

He demonstrated command of the mental aspects of batsmanship, visualising and predicting his innings. Deeply thoughtful and competitive, he created plans to combat opponents but had the flexibility and skills to adapt them under pressure. Though his technique was not of the coaching manual the elemental hallmarks of batting greatness ran deep: an unerring judgement of line and length; reading the ball from the hand; speed of thought and footwork. The dexterity with which he created angles at the point of impact between ball and bat ensured his shots counted, piercing the field with exasperating regularity for opposition captains.

His stamina and ability to concentrate for extended periods was unmatched in modern cricket; indeed few have matched it down the ages save the possible exceptions of Hanif Mohammed and Sir Donald Bradman. This insatiable hunger for marathon occupations of the crease combined with a high batting tempo led to him rattling up nine Test double hundreds, all against the top nations. When you look deeper into the numbers, his penchant for the big hundred is even more apparent. In nineteen of his thirty-four Test hundreds he scored over 150 (56 per cent of the time) and only registered under 130 on nine occasions.

What the numbers also highlight is that there has never been another batsman, besides Bradman, who has hurt opponents more once he gets in. He finished with the enormous figure of 5,889 runs being yielded from his centuries alone in Test cricket, virtually half of his final aggregate tally of 11,953. Lara revelled in these mammoth knocks, never tiring of dominating the opposition bowling once he was on top.

Big players play big innings and Lara's best are so celebrated they are recalled merely as numbers: 277, 375, 400, 153, 213, 501. That what are generally considered his top three – the 277, 153 and 213 – do not include any of his world records is symptomatic of the man; no other batsman could have three world best scores and not one of them rank amongst his finest performances.

His best innings displayed his versatility and brought different qualities to the fore. For the purist, Sydney's 277 was the closest to batting perfection; for nerve and skilful manipulation of the tail, the 153 against Australia in Barbados; for a prolonged and sustained onslaught unique in the history of the game, his world record 501 against Durham; for overcoming an opponent at the peak of his powers, the dismantling of Muttiah Muralitharan in Colombo in 2001/02; for mastery of batting craft and becoming the only cricketer to recapture the Test highest score, his 400 not out in 2004; and for a young man showing the maturity and courage to break a thirty-six-year-old record, there is the 375 in Antigua.

Lara made these huge scores always as the principal focus of the opposition attack. Many point to Viv Richards as the greatest West Indian batsman of all time and the Master Blaster was an awesome player. He bludgeoned and intimidated bowling, never taking a backward step, all bristling machismo, but throughout his career he enjoyed something Lara never did, sustained and consistent support. Openers Gordon Greenidge and Desmond Haynes blunted the initial fire of attacks, and then followed the class of players like Alvin Kallicharan, Lawrence Rowe, Clive Lloyd, Larry Gomes, Richie Richardson and Jeffrey Dujon. What a relaxed Lara might have done coming in with a regular, solid base on which to build is speculation but it is speculation often referenced by his fans.

There were times of failure, as in all sporting careers, but Lara distinguished himself by the number of game-changing innings he played for club and country.

'His ability to turn matches was phenomenal,' says Nick Knight. 'I know playing with and against him how threatening he was to opponents. The whole attitude towards setting a target changed. The opposition under-standably said to themselves, "Well, if we set them 450 and Brian gets 280 then we've lost the game." It has a dramatic effect on thought processes.'

Instances of these game-changing innings are legion but his most famous were two epics, the 153 and 213 against Australia in 1999, when his batting inspired a weak and demoralised West Indian side to two victories and ultimately a share in a series in which few had given them hope. Yet moments of team triumph were fleeting, for Lara was to endure near continuous disappointment in his long Test career, rendering so many of his runs of statistical value only.

'I'd have loved to have experienced a better ride during my career, but to each his own,' said Lara prior to his last Test series in Pakistan in November 2006. 'For me to be part of it still means that I'm part of history. Just the fact that I've played for West Indies for so long is, to me, a lifelong dream come true.'

The historical element was important for Lara, it always had been, and with knowledge of the past players came pride, for – just as genealogists enjoy a greater sense of familial self – Lara recognised kinship with the legends of yesteryear. In May 2006, following a rained-off ODI against Zimbabwe in Guyana, an 'Evening of Nostalgia' was held at a Georgetown hotel, in which two of the legendary three W's, Sir Everton Weekes and Sir Clyde Walcott, were heading up a cricketing discussion. All the West Indian players were invited, only three turned up, and Lara was alone in staying throughout. This link to the past still mattered to him, even if it didn't to anyone else.

Lara has often seemed a player who bestrode two ages, a relic of the past whose lot it was to play in the present, the last in a line that began with Learie Constantine and 'the black Bradman' George Headley. His single-minded pursuit of excellence, vaunted concentration, stamina and lonely vigil as chief run-scorer mirror uncannily the experience of Headley. The region's first great batsman, the Jamaican was nicknamed 'Atlas' because of the manner in which he carried the West Indian team through its early Test-playing years. Lara would do the same for the better part of fifteen years between 1992 and 2007 and the pair currently stand as bookends to the greats of West Indian batting.

But his journey to such a position would not be as envisaged as a youngster growing up in the streets of Cantaro. His record-breaking feats in 1994 catapulted him to the status of public property, placing his game and character under intense scrutiny. He was cricket's first global superstar in a mass media age and did not always react well to the attention.

Few players have provoked the range of emotions and opinions he has, with admiration of his undoubted genius often countered by accusations of self-seeking ambition. It is a point reflected in the assessments written at his retirement. There were eulogies as you would expect but, alongside, a conspicuous number of less-flattering appraisals. Some of these were even pursued to the conclusion that it was Lara who carried responsibility for the decline of West Indies cricket.

It seems an extraordinary accusation. That one man can be so omnipotent that he is wholly and solely to blame for the failure of an entire regional sporting structure; a structure he did not head up. For that to be true he would have to have rendered all those around him, players and administrators, coaches and managers, selectors and Board members, utterly impotent, incapable of action, devoid of all responsibility. If that is a slight on Lara it seems equally a slight on others.

It also tends to ignore some awkward truths: the great West Indian side of the 1980s had plateaued and was already teetering over its first downhill steps by the time Lara became a regular team member; he single-handedly propped up the batting for most of his career; and results have not improved since he retired.

Of course Lara is not blameless, he has admitted as much, and that he used his position as premier player to garner influence is indisputable. But it seems too convenient a leap from that to labelling him lone assassin of West Indian cricket, its issues are too widespread and profound. The murky machinations of Caribbean cricket administration are beyond the remit of this book but one thing is clear: Lara achieved what he did despite the system and not because of it.

'The Caribbean can be a strange place, even our heroes are never quite good enough and we love, as a people, to criticise,' says Tony Gray. 'Every man is human and will fail at times but it's how he reacts to that failure. More often than not, Brian came back strong and, under intense pressure, would answer those critics.'

That he did continuously bounce back was imperative for the region, as the gems Lara served up on a seasonal basis provided solace and inspiration for a generation of West Indian cricket fans. Without them the depressing years, which began with Australian defeat in 1995, would have been even harder to navigate.

'What he has meant to Caribbean people at a time when things have not been going so well on the field, you cannot quantify it,' says former West Indian middle-order batsman Jimmy Adams.

You still get a sense of the pride felt by many in Trinidad and Tobago today when, more often than not, cricket fans don't talk of 'Brian Lara' but rather 'Brian … Charles … Lara', with an announcer's emphasis and regal flourish, or simply 'Lara boy', whilst raising reverential eyebrows to the heavens.

'Brian will be remembered as a legend of the game; the impact he has had on West Indian cricket, the joy and value he has added to the game is immeasurable, it's hard to put a value on that,' says former West Indies captain Daren Ganga. 'It will be very hard for somebody to come and equate with what he has done.'

Going forward, his charitable work will ensure he continues to have an impact in other ways.

'He has made his parents proud before they departed this world but they would be even prouder to see the man he has become,' says Tony Gray. 'There are plenty of famous sportsmen but relatively few use their name and presence for good after they retire. Brian has done that, continues to do that and should be applauded.'

Whatever Lara's next chapter, it is as a beguiling compiler of colossal scores that he will be best remembered, cricket's ultimate entertainer. Just as an entertaining story never follows an even course, so Lara's career and life became part of the performance. Once at the wicket, though, distractions were forgotten and the show began: the all-action technique, telescopic back-lift, blurring bat speed and flamboyant follow-through. Shots as instinctive as the smiles they raised, consummately carefree, maddening for bowlers, joyous for fans. The sheer theatre of it all translated to an electricity only special players can generate. There are batsmen you can take your eyes off, Lara was never one of them.

'Flawed brilliance' is how some choose to sum him up but watching from the stands it is brilliance alone. There have been statistically superior batsmen but none have surpassed the aesthetic grandeur of his strokeplay. The game needs heroes and he was that to millions.

'There is so much that has been said about Brian Lara, this great player, great in the true context of greatness, not just a word that is used and that is so often misused. I think when you speak of Brian Lara as "a great", "a genius" … you're speaking of him in the truest context,' says cricket's ultimate all-rounder Sir Garfield Sobers.

When people are asked, years from now, to encapsulate what Lara meant to them they will not open with talk of Board disputes or an indifferent captaincy record, but rather of audacious shots recalled, remarkable feats achieved in the face of overwhelming odds, days spent in the presence of an unfathomable talent and the joy and pride it gave a region. A man of style, substance and success, Brian Charles Lara TC, OCC, AM, is one of the greatest batsmen to grace the game of cricket and he remains a great West Indian.

Brian Lara: a statistical review

Compiled by Andrew Hignell (Secretary of the Association of Cricket Statisticians), with grateful thanks to http://cricketarchive.com

Full name: Brian Charles Lara
Born: 2 May 1969, Cantaro, Santa Cruz, Trinidad
Batting: Left-hand batsman
Bowling: Leg-break and googly
Major teams: West Indies, ICC World XI, Marylebone Cricket
                Club, Mumbai Champs, Northern Transvaal,
                Southern Rocks, Trinidad & Tobago, Warwickshire

Test batting and fielding by opponent

Opponent	Matches	Inns	Not Out	Runs	HS	Av	100	50	Ct
Australia	31	58	2	2856	277	51.00	9	11	34
Bangladesh	2	2	0	173	120	86.50	1	1	2
England	30	51	3	2983	400*	62.14	7	11	45
India	17	29	0	1002	120	34.55	2	6	22
New Zealand	11	17	0	704	147	41.41	1	5	13
Pakistan	12	22	0	1173	216	53.31	4	3	11
South Africa	18	35	0	1715	202	49.00	4	9	20
Sri Lanka	8	14	1	1125	221	86.53	5	2	14
Zimbabwe	2	4	0	222	191	55.50	1	0	3

First-class batting and fielding by team

Team	Matches	Inns	Not Out	Runs	HS	Av	100	50	Ct
ICC World XI	1	2	0	41	36	20.50	0	0	0
Trinidad and Tobago	46	78	3	3847	206	51.29	11	18	73
Warwickshire	30	51	2	3099	501*	63.24	12	6	26
West Indians	44	65	2	2569	231	40.77	5	15	46
West Indies	130	230	6	11912	400*	53.17	34	48	164
West Indies Board President's XI	2	4	0	184	134	46.00	1	0	1
West Indies Board XI	2	2	0	92	56	46.00	0	1	0
West Indies Under-23s	3	5	0	225	182	45.00	1	0	5
Young West Indies	3	3	0	187	145	62.33	1	0	5

Career batting and fielding

	Matches	Inns	NO	Runs	HS	Av	SR	100	50	Ct
Tests	131	232	6	11953	400*	52.88	60.51	34	48	164
ODIs	299	289	32	10405	169	40.48	79.51	19	63	120
First-class	261	440	13	22156	501*	51.88	-	65	88	320
List A	429	411	43	14602	169	39.67	-	27	86	177
Twenty20	3	3	0	99	65	33.00	115.1	0	1	0

Career bowling

	Matches	Inns	Balls	Runs	Wkts	BB	Av	Econ	SR
Tests	131	4	60	28	0	-	-	2.8	-
ODIs	299	5	49	61	4	2/5	15.25	7.46	12.2
First-class	261	-	514	416	4	1/1	104.00	4.85	128.5
List A	429	-	130	149	5	2/5	29.80	6.87	26.0
Twenty20	3	-	-	-	-	-	-	-	-

Index